To Bob

We are changing the world !!

God Bless You

TransMontana

A MEMOIR OF TRANSFORMATION
IN BODY, MIND & SPIRIT

BY

ROBERTA R. ZENKER

www.KCLighthouse.org
The LIKE ME Lighthouse
3909 Main
Kansas City, MO 64111

For Kynni, Peggy, Mom, Terry & Kath, Dede,
Judy & My Wise Women, Monique,
Barb and the 4th Day girls, Bernie and
all the women who have made me

First we need to find this soul of our own. We must wake up, journey, name, challenge, shed, reclaim, ground, and heal. We need to follow our Big Wisdom, the thread that spins out of our feminine core. And then, then we find the means – the authority, the solidarity, the internal coagulation — that allows us to voice this soul.[1]

⸙

Ultimately our experience needs to become a force for compassion and justice in the world. We must bear witness to what we have experienced.[2]

~ Sue Monk-Kidd.

FOREWORD

If Loving You is Wrong, (I Don't Want to be Right)

Gregory Hinton

Reading about Montana hunter and county attorney Robert Zenker's 'crash' in *TransMontana*, when Peggy, his loving wife and best friend comes home early and catches him with women's clothes strewn about the room and scrubbing makeup off his face, I was reminded of Millie Jackson's hit 1975 single, *If Loving You is Wrong, (I don't Want to Right)*; about a lonely woman desperately in love with a married man.

If she can't see him when she wants, the song professes; she'll see him when she can.

Roberta Zenker could have written this song – a love song to herself—to Robert Zenker, the married man and father of two whose body she inhabited for nearly fifty years before her transition from man to woman in 2007; when she finally got tired of dressing up in the dark and proclaimed to the world how much she loved herself. Throughout her book, Bobbie utilizes favorite song titles as frontispieces to each chapter. Her choices are telling.

Thirty-five years ago, as a student of the University of Colorado, I co-wrote an article called "Telling it like it is at a Denver Drag Show" for my college newspaper, *The Colorado Daily*. My friends and I drove weekly from Boulder to Denver to a dive bar called The Back Door, where performers Nina, Stephanie, and Scotti Carlyse – "I've got my mother's features but my father's fixtures"— used to mime Vickie Carr, Diana Ross, Cher, and my favorite, Millie Jackson.

I wrote a gushy, effusive first draft. Yet, when the edited article came out in print it was snarky and condescending. I felt like I had betrayed them and didn't go back to The Back Door.

Before she was Chaz, Chastity Bono graced the cover of a 1998 October issue of *The Advocate* as the *enfant terrible* daughter of Sonny and Cher. I was deep inside the now famous issue, included in an article about 'Queer Filmmakers to Watch,' which described me as 'proudly HIV Positive', discussing my future book and movie plans.

I met Chastity Bono briefly in Palm Springs several years later. We were both reading and signing our new books in the Author's Village at Palm Springs Pride. She didn't seem happy to be there. Her beautiful grandmother, Georgia—Cher's mom—hovered protectively nearby. When she spoke, her anger felt palpable.

So when Chaz Bono recently competed on "Dancing with the Stars" vulnerability, not anger, was the palpable emotion. There had been public backlash at the idea of the first transgender celebrity participant on the wildly successful reality TV show. If Chaz felt awkward to us in the spotlight, he seemed comfortable in his skin and well—very nice. (For my mother, 'nice' was as high as you could go.)

So too was Roberta Zenker, who I met at an afternoon get-together in Bozeman, Montana. I noticed Bobbie immediately, watching her circulating in the crowd but didn't read her as transgender.

"Read' is a new term in my vernacular, taught to me by this book. To be 'read' means to be recognized as transgender, or as gay, or mixed-race or as 'the other' by a stranger—sometimes a stranger with power. Reading *TransMontana*, I better understood the complex, courageous and sometimes dangerous journey of the transgender man and woman.

I never had a transgender friend before Bobbie; and to define her first and only as 'transgender' limits her. Roberta Zenker is many things including a warm human being, a beautiful woman, a caring advocate for the rights of others and a dear new friend. Bobbie is also the beloved daughter of her caring mother, supportive friend to her ex-wife, but sadly, at this writing, the disowned father of her two adult children.

Her unusual perspective about the sexes fascinates. Women passing, for instance. (When women pass each other on the street they note each other and smile. Not so when she was a man.) A very important gift Bobbie has given me with *TransMontana* is the reminder to be patient, that we must allow others time to get accustomed to our rarity when they read us — for whatever differences we all present as walking-around, unique individuals.

Juxtaposed against the sparing, darkly beautiful, and plainspoken Montana landscape, Roberta Zenker's *TransMontana* is a powerfully wise, emotionally savory "must-read" memoir about spiritual growth and physical transformation.

Author's Note

Gregory Hinton is the creator and producer of *Out West at the Autry,* which he first developed with the Autry National Center in Los Angeles in 2009. Out West is a historic program series of lectures, films, plays and gallery exhibitions designed to illuminate the contributions of the Lesbian, Gay, Bisexual, and Transgender (LGBT) community to the history and culture of the American West. Hinton partners with museums, libraries, and universities and presents Out West programming all over the U.S.

The son of a country newspaper editor, Gregory Hinton is an author, filmmaker, and independent curator. Hinton was born on the Fort Peck Reservation in Wolf Point, Montana, raised in Cody, Wyoming and Denver. After graduating from the University of Colorado at Boulder, Hinton moved to California to pursue a writing and film career.

Hinton has published four critically acclaimed novels, including *Cathedral City, Desperate Hearts, The Way Things Ought to Be,* and *Santa Monica Canyon.* His films include *Getting it Right, Circuit* and *It's My Party,* which premiered at Sundance. For its diverse cultural themes, *Cathedral City* is taught at the university level and collected in libraries all over the world. His play, *Beyond Brokeback,* is performed in community theaters throughout the West.

Gregory Hinton holds a 2009 Residency at Ucross Foundation in Wyoming and is a 2011-2012 Resident Fellow at the Buffalo Bill Historical Center in Cody.

ACKNOWLEDGMENTS

Peggy is a remarkable woman. I was far too fragile and fearful to have even begun transition, let alone complete it. Her selfless love and support made it possible. And yet, she relived it all time and again as she reviewed this manuscript both for content and accuracy. Patty told me when I started that I should write a book. Kynni said it again three years later. You really do have to tell me twice. Ken Spencer gave a workshop about telling our stories and persuaded me that perhaps I do have a voice. I started writing as soon as I got home. Claudia and Judy read it both the sake of content and for the sake of our beloved and honored traditions. Franci and Marilyn read it too, and made good suggestions that I incorporated. Bernie allowed me the time and space to work, and provided me with valuable feedback and encouragement as she read and re-read each of the edited iterations. Heidi and Rhonda gave me a place to stay beside the sound, gave me sound where I stayed, and fed me ice cream too. Catherine Ockey copy-edited it for publication. Kayrn Cheatham formatted it for electronic publication. I wish to thank Gregory and Patricia for mentor-ing me and encouraging me through the final stages of editing and publication. Thank you one and all for your influence and encouragement.

CONTENTS

PART ONE: THE MAN

Chapter One

The Crash

Deep in your blood or a voice in your head
On a dark lonesome highway it finds you instead
So certain it knows you, you can't turn away
Something or someone has found you today.
I don't remember a voice on a dark lonesome road
When I started the journey so long ago

I was only just trying to outrun the noise
There was never a question of having a choice
Jesus or genie, maybe they've seen me
But who would believe me, I can't really say
Whatever the calling, the stumbling or falling
I got through it knowing there's no other way

– Mary Chapin-Carpenter.[3]

IT'S THE CRASH, I said silently to myself as I heard the muffled sound of the Subaru car door slam in the driveway. That instantly recognizable "thunk" was a sound that would strike equally instant panic at the core of every deeply boxed cross-dresser. My wife was home.

As I hurried to the bathroom, I stole a glance in the mirror hanging on the back of the bedroom door at my full length reflection. Who was I? What the hell was I doing dressing up like a woman every time I was alone?

I hurriedly stripped and hid my jeans, burgundy knit top, pumps, jewelry, bra and panties, falsies and wig under the sink. I was still wearing make-up and perfume, so I would have to shower, as likely excuse for locking the door as any. Why the hell was I so afraid to let Peggy know all of me?

It was five o'clock and I had just told my friends in the internet cross-dresser chat room that I had to go. "The witching hour is upon me." How prophetic that quip would prove to be. I expected Peggy home at 6:00, but on February 16, 2006, she came home early without warning. I was caught unaware in marked contrast to my usual precaution of knowing her daily travel plans. I had dreaded this moment for the last several years, but deep inside feared that it would never come. As I stepped into the shower, Peggy knocked.

"What are you doing?" she asked with an odd mix of irritation and curiosity in her voice. I mumbled a childlike "nothing" in reply to her searching inquiry.

"What's going on?" she insisted.

"I'm taking a shower," I said, matching her annoyance. At least that would sound normal.

Peggy wanted answers. I did not have them. As the hot water steamed over my head I furiously rubbed at my make up as if to wash some secret stain away. I let the mascara run down my face, and knew some residue would remain. I could never get clean enough.

I wept with the realization that forty eight years of secrecy were colliding with reality like an ice jam on the Madison River during a mid-winter thaw. No power on earth could hold back the waters. The truth would inevitably, relentlessly spill, and I would not be spared from the flood which was to follow, one which only weeks before I had actually prayed for.

"God, please allow my secret to come out without ruining my marriage, career and family," my very life.

I had given up hope of God ever removing my affliction as I had strenuously asked for so many years. Instead, I asked God that if he would not remove this lifelong curse, that he would let it come to the surface.

I had looked into the dark face of suicide and decided that I wanted to live. But, that's not quite right. I wanted to let the woman inside me live even as I had no hope that it could be. Yet, I was torn with the thought of hurting my wife and children. Everything they had come to know about their husband and father, good and bad, would seem a terrible lie. They would be subject, as would I, to public ridicule and contempt. Even as I was polarized with fear, Peggy was here and the moment was now.

How could I tell this woman, this mate, whom I loved and had promised my whole life to that it really wasn't quite so, that there was something more? It would seem like betrayal. Yet, there was this other side of me. I wandered in a gender wasteland for many years. I was adrift in self-centeredness and desperation. I was not sure who I was or that I could accept what I was beginning to realize was true; that I was transsexual and that it would not go away. I was depressed, alcoholic, borderline anorexic and close to suicide, a regular poster child for the DSM-IV. I could not live, and I could not die. So, I continued to ask God to do it for me, to just take me. I often fell asleep at night praying between tears that God would. God did take me, but not the way I expected.

As the first days of the new-year arrived and I sank deeper into emotional dysfunction, I fell to my knees on the living room floor, holding myself as I sobbed. No one else could know or understand the pain of my secrets.

"God help me, just help me," I prayed, even after cursing God the night before.

I call such prayers of hopelessness "Warren Zevon prayers." "*Send lawyers, guns, and money {God} get me outta' this.*"[4] God must listen intently to those prayers of desperation and brokenness, stripped of pride and anger. I began to get honest that day, and open and willing to rely on something outside myself to make sense out of my life.

Sobriety and transition had begun that day, though I had no way of knowing. My living room in Jefferson Acres just south of Silver Star, Montana was not a dark lonesome road. However, when I started this journey I was truly just trying to outrun the noise. That noise was the voice in my head that told me I could never be my true self; that told me I would be better off dead than to continue to live in ambiguity and secrecy. While many may disagree, there was never a choice. The calling I heard soon became a refrain. Transition or die, and whatever the stumbling or falling, I followed it knowing that there was no other way.

For as long as I could remember I had been searching. U2's "*Still Haven't Found What I'm Looking For*" was my theme song. When I first came to Montana my boss told me,

"You're searching for yourself."

It sounded cliché as I answered, barely concealing my disdain.

"I think I know who I am."

All these years later, I realize that he was right. There had been an ever deepening void that I was seeking to fill. Nothing could fill the emptiness of not knowing who I was, or rather, refusing to accept the truth that inwardly I could not escape. I believed that all the things I tried over my lifetime were means of discovery. I now realize they were means of avoidance.

The truth that I knew about myself I refused to accept. I repressed it and rejected it as fiercely as I could. It was so foreign to everything I had been taught about how I should be, and what I was expected to do. It was a fight no one could win. For all my efforts I could not escape the truth, even to the point that the only way out seemed to be death. I did not want to die. I wanted to live. To do so I had to stop searching and begin to accept the truth about myself. I had to acknowledge that even though born biologically male, I was a woman. I had to stop repressing and rejecting my sense of self. I had to embrace the woman inside, honor her, let her live.

I got out of the shower and walked past the boxes of women's clothes, shoes, wig boxes, make up and jewelry still lying on the bed, the proverbial elephant in the room. I tip toed around them just as one would in the presence of something large and beyond one's control. I retrieved more wood for the stove from the stacks out back, wood that I had cut in the hills and brought home and split. What could I do? The crash was upon me, the boxes in plain view. I would not return to my box.

I sat down at the kitchen table, one I had made for Peggy with pine dimension lumber and commercially turned wooden legs. I had been intimidated by a recently purchased router, but after a little practice, was shaping everything with a Roman Ogee.

"Are you going to tell me what's going on?" Peggy asked.

I could not speak, which was odd for a lawyer who makes his living with words. There were no words into which I could put the truth of my life. I had no practice upon which to rely, as I had never told another living soul. I wanted to tell her, as if I was a criminal long burdened by the weight of my wrongs. But what could I say of the fear, shame, guilt, anger, confusion, desperation and loneliness I felt, about the love I had for her, even though it would look more like betrayal? I cried.

Peggy said, "Don't cry," as her characteristic compassion kicked in.

"Why are you crying?" she asked comfortingly.

"It's the crash," I muttered through sobs.

"What?" she asked, having no idea that I meant that our worlds and lives were relentlessly colliding.

I could not predict the collateral damage that was sure to come with the crash. I had no hope of her understanding or acceptance in that moment, so I hung my head and cried. Peggy held me, a gesture truly representative of her capacity for compassion and giving. It did not matter that we were on the verge of collapse. What mattered to Peggy was that I was in such great anguish. She offered comfort, and I will forever be grateful for her presence of mind and heart in that moment.

As the Serius Satellite radio softly droned on in maudlin blues, I regained my composure. The "Coffee House" had been my favorite channel since Peggy bought me the radio a few years earlier. It featured acoustic renditions of both favorites and lesser known tunes of artists like the Indigo Girls, Sarah McLachlan, Emily Lou Harris, David Gray and others who wrote equally sad lyrics rendered almost holy by the magic and purity of their voices.

"I am the proverbial woman in a man's body," I blurted out.

It was cliché I knew, and told little of a lifetime of duality and secrecy, of hiding, fear and loneliness. Her first questions were equally cliché.

"How long have you known?"

"Have you told anyone?"

"I started dressing when I was ten, and I have never told another living, breathing soul," I said.

Later, in therapy I unraveled deeper, hidden truths from my early childhood.

"How could I tell anyone?" I ventured?

"They would not understand."

"They would think I was kinky or perverted and reject me," I insisted, in keeping with the rhetoric I had told myself over the decades.

Many of us are so afraid to tell people the truth about ourselves that we make up a certain plausible, albeit false, rhetoric to explain. I was a true believer in my own shit. But as I described my life of silent agony, Peggy's great capacity for compassion buoyed me. She could have been angry and hurt and thrown me out of the house. However, she was not thinking of herself and what this would mean to her and our marriage. She selflessly took care of me. She believed in me.

I felt as if she took the lid off my wig box and flung it to the far reaches of the globe never to be seen again. In an email I wrote later to my surgeon, I suggested,

"It's as if I had been stumbling around in a dark room for many years and came upon the light switch. Once exposed to the light, I would never go back to the darkness."

I was ecstatic on one hand, like a prisoner released from a life sentence. Another human being had heard my greatest, dread fear and did not reject me. On the other hand, though, I had clung to fear and anxiety for so long that I could not manage to shed them as we continued to talk. It was surreal.

Peggy Lee Probasco was born in 1952 at the career height of her namesake jazz singer, actress, songwriter, Peggy Lee. For her parents she was an afterthought, born several years after the youngest of her five siblings. The doctors had referred to her as "gas" or an ulcer. Peggy's Mom knew better and told them so. With the same dogged determination she instilled in all her children, she prevailed upon the doctors to treat her sixth pregnancy. Peggy was as loved, perhaps more than her siblings.

Peggy's father had given her a love of fine cuisine, introducing her to all manner of good food, even though they were a family of modest means.

"Daddy and I would crack crab legs on the living room floor with a big bowl in front of us," she had reminisced.

"If Mom and Dad had t-bones, so did we," she claimed with admiration.

Her love for her father was a palpable thing that I could not understand as I had never revered mine in such a way.

Peggy grew up Lutheran in Ogden, Utah, the very heart of Mormon country.

"It is by grace alone that we are saved," she asserted inappositely to my Catholic training, which insisted upon "good works" as well. When I met her in her early forties she was the beautiful swan incarnate, who had been the pudgy girl with thick glasses and too-curly hair that would never behave. The curls had given way to waves of auburn. She looked as if she could have been an Irish lass on a country hillside in the fall. However, Peggy said with pride, "I am Basque."

"Have a care for my heart," she had stated succinctly when our relationship turned serious in the fall of 1992.

She had been deeply hurt by her first husband and sadly disappointed by subsequent lovers. She feared having to endure the trauma of love yet again.

"I am looking for someone to grow old with," I responded, and earnestly believed it was true.

After six years of living, loving, laughing, eating, drinking and fighting together, I promised to do so, and said "I do" before the Reverend, Phil Wold at Gloria Dei Lutheran Church in Butte on June 20, 1998.

June is the monsoon season in Montana, and after fifteen straight days of sprawling dark clouds, they parted as if on cue as we left the church aboard a horse-drawn wagon for the uptown reception and the first day of "old" together.

The deed to the home we bought in 2001 called it a "manufactured home." We called it a "mobile home" because it arrived on wheels. My friend called it a "Montana Dream Home" due to the large number of Montanans settling for this more affordable mode of housing.

Manufactured homes often have aesthetic features which, though built with cheap materials, are designed to add a touch of class. The vaulted ceilings, chandeliers and false front hutches in ours were incongruous with the wheeled designation, but fit the dream home description handily. The vaulted ceiling allowed me to mount the skull of a bull moose high on the wall. I had shot it the year we were married in the Upper Ruby River drainage along Coal Creek descending from Eureka Basin. It was a "European" mount which meant that it garishly displayed only the skull and horns, much like the Georgia O'Keefe painting of a mule deer mount.

Our oak entertainment center with TV and other electronics sat just beneath it for a time. I often arranged the family photos and candles on top. When I lit those candles in an otherwise dark room the mount became a ghastly apparition with large pointed shadows that flickered back and forth.

Peggy is a gourmet.

"She is the food queen," I had said countless times, as I tried to stump her at gatherings on some question about exotic foods.

"What do they put in Thai peanut sauce to give it that rich, creamy texture?"

"Coconut milk," she said without hesitation.

Peggy cooked with herbs and spices like cilantro, star anise, curry and basil, and I was the happy beneficiary of her culinary prowess.

"I'm going to start dinner," she emphatically stated, as if to signal her acceptance of my revelations through a return to normalcy.

But, like that universally defining moment now memorialized as 911, we both knew it would never again be the same. I seized upon the opportunity to press my advantage. Since the door was open a crevice, it might as well be as wide as Montana's expanse.

"Do you mind if I get dressed?" I impishly asked.

I had been on a road trip through Billings months before and begun a habit of dashing into stores and surreptitiously purchasing an article or two of women's clothing, shoes, jewelry or perfume and make-up. I had purchased perfume for Peggy for Christmas, and when the clerk threw in extra samples, I kept them for myself.

I took my time in Dillard's, though, and selected a pair of jeans in the misses department I thought would fit. The clerk asked suspiciously,

"Are you sure those are the right ones?"

"Yes," I said as calmly as possible while hiding my embarrassment. Still, I was pretty proud that I could get into a size 6.

That had gone so well, I dashed into K-Mart too. There I selected a beige, cottony flower-child sort of blouse with a leather tie around the waist. I bought some blue eye liner and suggested to the clerk,

"I use it to hand color photographs."

He was bemused. I hurriedly put on the make-up I had just as hurriedly removed not an hour before and doused myself with perfume from one of the samples. It was way too much I knew, but I could hardly resist the temptation to pour the entire vile over my head considering how cautious I had always been before with the potent smelling stuff. Not only did I want her to know that I was wearing perfume, but I wanted her to know the brand name from across the room.

It was Jessica McClintock, sweet enough to make me feel young and pretty without making me smell like a teenager on her first unsupervised trip to the mall.

"It's too much," Peggy pointed out the obvious with emphasis.

"The eye liner does not look right," she said.

She was right, but I was happy, relieved to finally be out of the box, the gender box in which so many trans people hide.

I remained dressed that evening as I spilled the details of my other life to her like wine flowing from a too-long corked bottle. The cork was gone and the flow would not cease. There was no going back, no matter what the consequences. There was nothing left to hide. She listened intently with great kindness and compassion. It took some time for her to grasp that the virile man she loved was really more a woman.

"*Angel*," by Sarah McLachlan came on the radio. Her plaintive soprano melancholy swirled inside my head as it dripped honey-like from the speakers on top of the decorative "Montana dream" hutch. *You were pulled from the wreckage of your silent reverie . . . ."*5 I had hoped for years that Peggy could see my dark, cold box and pull me from the wreckage of my secret, silent life. I realized that she could not unless I asked her. That, above all else, I could not do with anyone my whole life for fear of loss and rejection.

I believe that God in God's kindness and grace saw this and nudged the two of us into that moment of truth. The crash is never as bad as we fear, and we are often remarkably spared from its carnage. Although Peggy did not presume to understand, she said,

"I want to know all about this."

"All right, I will tell you everything I can," I promised, although I knew very little of what was coming.

I had been wrong about her and perhaps so many others in my life before her.

"Why didn't you tell me before?" Peggy asked as if her realization of my betrayal of marital trust was beginning to dawn.

I reasoned, "I couldn't. I was afraid you would reject me, and I really believed you could save me – from myself."

I tried to explain in so many words what my lifetime of dysfunction was like, but the fact remained; I had suffered in silence at great physical and emotional cost for no good reason. It was fear and fear alone. Yet, I had come by my fear honestly. I had earned my fear through years of a compulsive search for approval and acceptance.

I looked for all appearances as if I was doing well. I had a good job as a popularly elected public official, a wife and children, a home, two cars in the driveway, a couple of dogs in the yard and just about anything I wanted. Yet, I gave it all away. This is my story.

Chapter Two

Oh Montana

Oh Montana, give this child a home
Give him the love of a good family and a woman of his own
Give him a fire in his heart and light in his eyes
Give him the wildness for a brother and the Wild Montana Skies

-John Denver[6]

Montana is at once unforgiving in its diversity and vastness and brutal in its honesty. No blue is as blue as a Montana sky. And you realize that it is so because the air is clear, so clear that you want to breathe it in deep and long. Once at home, you do not want to leave.

Montana has been an enigma for me. It is both beautiful and barren, the perfect metaphor for my soul in years past. As the fourth largest state in the country, Montana is vast. The Helena *Independent Record* reported on December 13, 2009 that Montana covers 147,000 square miles, a land mass twice that of all New England. In its vastness, Montana covers many sins.

Its open space is unrelenting in what it can hide. I had been told I came here to find myself, but, that failing, I hid my true self away. Montana taught me desolation and loneliness. Through much pain, it gave me the certain knowledge that I could no longer hide and live. I had to confront the reality of self in order to be. I did. I am. Montana is still Montana, at last forgiving. It is beautiful, but painfully real. For me it is without romance or pretense.

I was young in the summer of 1980 when I arrived, twenty-two and just graduated from the University of Dayton. I was idealistic and set to save someone or something. I had come to Ashland as a leap of faith. The journey to self is a leap of some sort after all.

I arrived late on an August night. I was unaccustomed as a Midwestern boy to the hot, dry breeze that blew through the open windows of my Herbal-Essence-green Volkswagen Bug as I drove across the "flats" just west of Ashland in far-eastern Montana. In the light of day, you could see low-lying hills with names like King and Cook Mountain, and the Pumpkin-Otter divide twenty- five miles to the east. The Tongue River wound its slow, muddy course in the valley in between. Two weeks earlier I had watched Richard Windmark in *"Cheyenne Autumn,"* the story of the desperate flight of a band of Cheyenne Indians that splintered away from their tribe in Oklahoma to form the Northern Cheyenne tribe near this very spot.

I stayed in the Friary, the residence for the Capuchin priests and brothers of St. Labre Indian School, known locally as "the mission." It seemed more of an oasis or resort. I fell asleep watching the red glare of a light out on the airstrip, wondering where I had landed.

I was to begin a year of volunteer service with the Jesuit Volunteer Corp, Northwest, just off the Northern Cheyenne Indian reservation in Southeastern Montana. I had few concerns about simple living with two women in a spiritual community while we served. If they knew then what it has taken me years to unravel? Ah, perhaps they did. They left after a year or so. I stayed for nine years, met and married my first wife and made a life.

Both my children were born on the reservation, or reservations I should say. Meghan was born on the Crow reservation on May 10, 1982, and Shane on the Northern Cheyenne reservation on February 29, 1984. Meghan's birth day was snowy and cold. I drove with her mother, Joanne, and Joanne's friend, Colleen, wildly in a borrowed van intent on reaching the Hardin Hospital seventy-five miles away.

At Mile Marker 14 on Highway 212, Colleen screamed as she pulled Meghan from Joanne's womb and placed her on Joanne's chest.

"Stop, stop," she cried.

"What should we do?" she desperately asked.

I had grown used to Colleen's habit of strong reactions and my equal and opposite ability to downplay her worries.

"We've got to keep going," I suggested.

"We're in the middle of nowhere, and no one will stop anytime soon."

I later tied a pink ribbon around a road sign there. It remained for several years until the ravages of Montana weather set its tattered remains adrift in some unseen, yet deeply spiritual way. We stopped at the Indian Health Service clinic in Crow Agency, and they took Meghan and her mother on to Hardin by ambulance. Her birth certificate says "BOA" for born on arrival. Later that day, I held Meghan in the palm of one hand, small and pink at three weeks premature.

"She looks like a puppy," I offered.

But Joanne, in a truly maternal fashion born of love like God's for creation, could see only the wonder of this little life.

"She's beautiful."

A nurse clamored in, not intending to destroy a tender moment shared between virtual children just crossing the threshold of parenthood.

"I need a name for the birth certificate," she demanded in a reflexive tone more indicative of her redundant tasks than any urgency.

Joanne and I had discussed names but could not agree.

"Jordan is a good name," she had pleaded.

"I want something Irish," I countered.

"Megan," I insisted, but Joanne provided the Irish spelling – "M-e-g-h-a-n."

"Mehgan," I blurted to the nurse, then spelled it out "M-e-g-h-a-n" before Jordan had a chance.

Six weeks later Meghan accompanied her mother down the aisle as we were married in a big Catholic Church in Delaware, Ohio. A priest friend from high school celebrated the Mass. It was a small wedding, just family and a few friends. My sister, Kathy and her husband, Newt, stood up for Meghan at her baptism the following day.

Shane was born a native Montanan too (which is important in Montana). The drama was just as high with his delivery, perhaps more than with Meghan. We made it only the twenty miles to the Lame Deer Indian Health Service Clinic this time. I was astounded as Joanne shot water across the room.

"Whoa!" I said.

It was a mystery of womanhood that I never would know. And there was Shane, small and purple. At seven weeks premature his lungs were not yet fully developed.

"He's not breathing," Doctor Krivchenya said with alarm, instantly turning my joy and wonder to anxiety. I had no way of knowing just how close to death he was.

"What are his chances?" I asked the life flight attendant just arrived by helicopter from Billings, 100 miles away.

"Ninety-five percent that he won't make it," the attendant opined, oddly detached, as if reciting academic findings before a group of scientists

It took me months to get past that trauma enough to accept the fact that my son would live. Just like that, I was a husband and father. I had a family, a home, a job and a place in the world. It was just what I had always wanted, so I thought. Still, something was not right with me. I said to my friend, Scott, a teacher a Saint Labre,

"I feel like I'm sneaking into a gold mine for one last haul before the roof caves in."

The treasure was not what I sought, but I took it anyway.

Joanne and I could never love one another in a way that made sense to me. Scott asked me once if I loved my wife.

"It's a *Fiddler on the Roof* sort of love," I had responded.

I felt like Tevye, when he sings, "Do I love you?"

We made children, had a home and a life together. If that was not love, it became so in time. Still, the innocence of our children was magical. It was a tonic, a salve for that something inside that I could not place. They wonder now about me.

"Did we ever really know you?"

"Did you ever really love us?"

One true thing as I write this, for I am unable to tell them, is that I have always loved them. Even though they are no longer in my life, I will always hold them and that time in my heart. Being their father was worth every moment of pain, loneliness and self-doubt. It was worth the ambiguity and duality, the not knowing who I really was or where I fit. I tried so hard to be a normal man, a good husband and father. But how could I give myself to something fully when I could never fully be myself?

I clung fiercely to images of self. I believed that even though I held deep secrets that would ultimately betray those closest to me that I was honest and kind. I did not realize that, although I managed to do some nice things, I was self-centered and dishonest. I would not admit that even the good things I did were more attempts to affirm my goodness in the face of mounting evidence to the contrary. I was severely deluded, plodding miserably through life all the while wearing a smile and acting self-assured.

I had visions too of what I thought I should be as a son, husband, father, brother and friend, yet I was equally deluded, believing that each of those roles were the true me. They were not ever me. The man was more like a garment I learned to put on from earliest childhood, one that I could change or replace as circumstances warranted and people demanded. The choice to be false and incongruent was mine to make, but driven as I was by fear, I chose to live the images, not the person.

My earliest images did not involve gender at all, as much as they involved emotion. I felt, not as a boy feels, but as I believed a girl thinks and feels. Snails and puppy dog tails held little fascination for me. I much preferred sugar and spice and everything nice, and why couldn't people see that? I wanted to play with Barbie, yet I came to covet a Tonka truck. Mine was the Yin, yet it was the Yang that I wore. On came the garment as a grain of sugar slipped away.

It is hard for me to say what the forces of fear, shame and uncertainty will wreak upon the psyche of a child. I believed that I should not be the person I felt inside that I was. It was wrong. I was wrong. I was born wrong, and the only thing I could do to change that was to try and be the boy that I was supposed to be, to live the images given me. All might have been well if I could have pulled it off. I could not, as the girl inside would never leave. Though the grains of sugar may have all slipped away, the spice remained.

When I was very young, at that age when memories first begin to form, I had thoughts about girls. They were not sexual thoughts, as I had not yet reached that age. As I lay in bed with the covers pulled over my head, I thought I was a girl, should be one, or at the very least wanted to be one. Dr. Sidney W. Ecker of Georgetown University School of Medicine hypothesizes that the transgender emerging child will have "transgender thinking."[7] I knew not why such thoughts occurred to me, or that any reason existed that they should not occur. The fact is that they did occur.

I was sensitive to the women in my life, although I suspect my sisters would take issue with this. I wanted to be just like my older sisters. I thought too of the girl next door, her lithe body, her voice, her walk and her clothes. Oh, the clothes. But, I am getting ahead of myself. I wanted to be like the girl next door especially.

I liked being around girls and enjoyed the company of women well into my forties. I just liked the feeling of being with the girls. I watched them keenly, the way they spoke, their gestures, a turn of phrase or body. I looked at their faces, the clipped brows, the hair and make-up. I noticed slender fingers as they brushed long hair away from the face with a slight shake of the head. I noticed a wisp of hair, a smile, the lines of the neck and shoulder. I looked and I learned. I saw waves, curls and color with more than a little jealousy. I stored the information unwittingly against the day that I might become what I saw.

One thought from perhaps my first Christmas of memory was like that. As all families do, ours had its holiday traditions. One was to gather around the black and white Zenith television, an occasion that usually found me close to my mother, and watch *White Christmas*. The movie starred the infamous duo of Kaye and Crosby, and featured the leading ladies of sultry singer, Rosemary Clooney and dancer Vera Ellen. She, the least infamous of the voices harmonizing in "Snow," was the one that always caught my eye. I can see even now her thin legs and Barbie-like torso, as well as her graceful arms and fingers while she danced. She moved with elegance and beauty. I wanted to be her.

Those feelings had always been with me, and yet I ignored them. I never tried to figure them out. I was afraid of what they might mean and where they might lead. Truthfully though, fear was more at the very core of me than I would know for many, many years. I knew I carried the scars of my childhood into adulthood. I just did not realize how deep the cuts had gone.

I have so few good memories of my father.

"Look at me when I talk to you!" he screamed, his twisted face inches away from mine.

Spittle formed at the edges of his mouth as he stooped from his full six-foot height to my slight frame. His hot breath came out in spurts like a beast winded from the attack and brushed against my cheeks. I could think of my father only as a monster with that image seared forever into my four-year-old psyche.

"Terry, Kathy, Andy, Bobby, Michael," he belted out, then paused for breath, "Maryann, come here, now!"

He called his charges in descending order of age like a drill sergeant expectant of orderly recruits marching lock step to his commands. We obeyed, not from a sense of duty or respect, but from one of fear.

Dad was a complicated man. At 6'2," he seemed so tall to me. My brothers got their curly-to-kinky hair from him. Mine was always straight and blonde. Most of the Zenker children got his long, hawkish nose. Now it seems we all need glasses like him as well.

He could be jocular when in a good mood. He once pushed those glasses down on the edge of that long beak to tell us a joke. He wrote down on a piece of paper this code:

"F-U-N-E-X," and asked us to say it "F-U-N-E-X?"

He said it again in a contrived German accent, and after the third or fourth time we figured out he was inquiring about eggs. I loved that side of him. The side that left its mark on me so profoundly, however, was darker.

He was so easily enraged. The slightest offense would send him screaming into orbit. While I would continue to fight that man for the next fourteen years, I knew intuitively then, before I was even capable of any cognitive awareness of gender confusion, that I must hide my true self inside just as deep as I possibly could.

I could not do math. I failed the fifth grade because of it. At forty-nine years old, I was finally diagnosed as having a learning disability. It was of little consolation. Once Dad got angry that I would not do my math homework.

"I forgot my book at school," I pleaded.

"Do your homework," he spit the words at me.

I hung my head in shame.

"I can't do it," I admitted.

Dad was so angry that he sat me down at his big maple desk to make me do my homework. The hardwood antique sat stoically in an extra room on the main floor we called the dining room, though no one ever ate there. I loved the desk for its solidity in my turbulent world. He stood above me.

"Do your homework; do it now," he commanded, always the drill sergeant.

It wasn't that he did not love me. I never doubted that, choosing instead to believe almost defensively for his sake that he did not know how to love. His father died when he was seven. Yet love and pity for his fatherless childhood were far from my mind as he screamed,

"Do it, or I'll make you do it!"

Still, I merely fumbled with a No. 2 lead pencil, feeling his presence behind me as his arm swung silently up and back.

"Goddamn it," he screamed, "I'll beat math into you!"

"Whap!" sounded in my ears as they began to ring, and a flame-like sting spread across the back of my head.

"I'll make you learn it," he added, underscoring the senselessness of his act.

"Whap!" he slapped the back of my head again for emphasis.

"Whap! Whap! Whap!" for God only knows what reason.

Then, everything went black.

When I came to, my father's tone had changed. He was consoling me and I was indeed relieved to have survived the assault. I think it scared him more than me, though, as he did not strike me again for many years.

My parents were very concerned about my academic failings. They took me for medical tests that I did not understand. I felt special though, because I was getting a lot of attention. The doctors all pronounced me healthy. In 1960s Columbus, Ohio they could not have been expected to unravel the layers of fear and confusion that hid the mysteries of gender dysphoria in a prepubescent boy.

As powerful as fear is, it is small wonder that I had no true sense of self until so many years beyond my youth. I never wanted to be the boy Dad wanted me to be. I resisted him and felt very bad about myself because I could not, or would not, be that boy. The two central themes of my early childhood were a hidden sense of femininity, in spite of male physical characteristics, set against a mortal fear of my father.

I knew intuitively long before I was capable of reason that for safety's sake I had to hide feminine urges and feelings and adopt a male role and mannerisms. For example, I would have enjoyed playing with Barbie dolls and jumping rope with the girls next door, but took Barbie's arms off instead. Fear kept us all, my siblings and me, from learning healthy ways of openly and honestly talking about ourselves. As for me, I hid and repressed my sense of self just as deep as I could, where it successfully remained in hiding for decades.

I hated playing sports even though I excelled at them. I absolutely hated the boys' locker room. It was not just the odor, although that was bad enough. I was embarrassed by my own body, as many kids are. Only mine just did not feel like the right one. It was the penis. I did not want anyone to see it and did not want them to know I had one. I certainly did not want to see theirs. So, I put my head down and went about my business.

Even though I learned what to do and how to act, I was never at ease in the boys' locker room. Guys would walk around naked showing off that uniquely male part as if they were Adonis himself. I would just sit there, innocuous as possible, and join in their hilarity so as not to appear different or, God forbid, queer.

Sports became my release, my escape and means of recognition and affirmation. Still, I felt somehow different and inferior. I had all these impulses toward feminine things like wearing girl's clothing or just holding and taking the feel of them in my hands, too afraid to actually wear them. I once (or twice) stood in my Mom's closet beneath her hanging clothes with them draped over me dreaming about what it would be like to wear them. What was I searching for? What did I want? I did not have answers then, but I was driven.

I would comb my hair in a certain way that looked more feminine.

"Look what I can do," I had once remarked to my brother.

"You like just like a girl," he replied with mild enthusiasm while I was elated.

I could contort my body in front of a mirror for the same effect. I could stuff my penis back between my legs, cock one hip to the side, and look girlish enough. It helped that I never did have much body hair. I would look for feminine products in the bathroom closet just so I could smell them and dream about putting them on. I would inhale deeply, grasping again for something or someone I had no hope of ever becoming.

It is hard to be certain about what I may have felt or believed as a child, but I knew that all these feminine things would not work in a boy's world. They certainly did not fit in with my Dad's vision of youthful masculinity. He was very hard and wanted me to be tough.

"That's the way to raise boys," he had said almost apologetically, although I do not recall the words "I am sorry" ever crossing his lips.

I don't remember any positive, nurturing physical contact with my Dad, except that when he was in a good mood I loved walking around on his toes as he held my hands when I was very young. I liked doing that with my own children and always thought of Dad when I did. Dad could not have known to allow more tenderness. Even if tenderness was there, all I could see was the rage, the angry man who we thought was crazy.

Dad would begin to yell as my brothers, my sisters and I ran through the house to close all the doors and windows. He would scream and throw things for what seemed liked hours. We closed ourselves in to hide a most fundamental truth. We were ashamed of our father. I learned to hide my shame, to bury my feelings deep within. I was ashamed that I felt more like a girl inside than a boy and would not open the doors or windows to allow the light to shine on that truth for many years to come. By the time I was ten, fear and shame were deeply embedded in my character. Slowly they churned and boiled over into anger. I was a very angry little boy. Playground sports became my outlet, and I played, swore and fought as hard as I could.

St. Michael's Catholic Church stood like a fortress at the top of the hill on East Selby Boulevard in Worthington, Ohio. The pastor, Father John Patrick Byrne once unleashed his anger upon the entire congregation when some rascal broke the tip off of St. Michael's nose as that archangel stood vigilantly guarding our souls in front of the new brick church. I never could grasp the relationship between ornate, ostentatious architecture and faith in a loving Creator, and St. Michael's church only made it worse.

The church had spared no expense (funds no doubt generated in some measure off the bingo and bake sale backs of parishioners). Hardwood pews and covered wooden kneelers rested on slate floors. Towering marble pillars lead to heavy wooden cross beams with enormous bolts holding them together, and large chandeliers lit our souls and misslettes.

We lived at the bottom of the hill on West Selby Boulevard just across High Street, Route 23 that ran the length of the state from southeastern Ohio through Columbus and on to Cleveland. All the trees between the church and our house had been cleared for the new subdivision, called "Worthington Woods," so we could look reverently up to the monolithic bell tower of St. Michael's from which the Angelus rang twice daily, dependably at time intervals that involved a meal and required my presence at home.

I met Sr. Archangela (pronounced tar-ran-cha-la) on the first day of school at St. Michael's grade school. Having been pronounced too smart for kindergarten at five years old, I bravely ventured towards my academic destiny a safe distance behind my older brother. Andy took me to school early that day to show me the ropes. Where Andy led I followed, even if it was not consistent with what I felt. He was husky and tough. When I mouthed off, which was often, I got slugged. Eventually I learned the inverse relationship between knowledge and pain. The more I learned, the less I hurt.

I have always had an overactive bladder, both as I slept and all the livelong day. So, of course, the boys' bathroom was the first stop on Andy's tour. Public restrooms at that time were still unusual for me, but from that very moment I wanted to use the girls' restroom. I was always more comfortable sitting down to pee than that more traditional male urinating posture. We must have made considerable commotion at 7:30 a.m. that first day of school, or as much as a five-and-seven year old could together muster, for Sr. Tar, er, uh, Archangela stood at the door in all her heavily habited black and white glory bidding us forth in no uncertain terms.

Evidently, Andy was already well versed in the proper school house etiquette for young saints. He let me go first. Sr. Archangela pulled me by the ear down the hall proclaiming,

"If I catch you making trouble again I'll pin your ears behind your head," as surely my father would approve.

I never doubted the validity of that statement and most assuredly never challenged that holy monstrosity. I believed that she was in league with the monster I called Dad. And so I became afraid of school too.

The school years passed with plenty of incident, too many to recount here, except that in retrospect they were the prototypical escapades of a troubled child. When I failed the fifth grade, my parents determined to discover the source of that trouble with all the innocence of loving guardians, guiltless certainly of any parental deficiency and possessed of the notion that there was something wrong with me. I never doubted the validity of that notion either.

By then I had so suppressed my gender questions that I could not have said just what was wrong with me. I knew that something was, and it dogged me for decades. Of the tests my parents took me to receive I have little recollection of any except an EKG. That procedure intrigued me. Surprisingly, I was unafraid. I thought the electrodes were cool and secretly wished that the test itself was somehow more than a diagnostic tool. I hoped that it would transform me, that with one zap it would fix whatever was broken inside of me. While it was interesting, it produced no lasting cure. I could not be fixed.

My seventh-grade teacher at St. Michael's grade school was Sr. Kathleen. She was reputed to be the only girl among several boys in one of the many "good Catholic" families in our town who did their level best to populate the throng of John, XXIII. I think Sr. Kathleen must have played a lot of football with her brothers. She looked like a half-back, tall and muscular with bowed legs. She showed the kind of toughness that could only be learned by necessity, by bearing up under the toughness pressed upon her.

I had learned by then that in order to get people to like me I had to be funny. I must have reasoned, perhaps subconsciously, that when people laughed at the things I said or did that they liked me. I had a great need to be liked. I suppose that by the seventh grade I had a reputation to boot - class clown.

I was certain that teachers spent the off season, as it were, discussing students like baseball managers discussed players at the winter Major League Baseball meetings. When it came to Bobby Zenker, I suspect they passed warnings amongst themselves.

"He talks out."

"He can't sit still."

"He's a trouble maker."

If it were football, I would have been high on the Oakland Raiders' list. At any rate, Sr. Kathleen was ready for me the first day of seventh grade.

Like the alcoholic I would later become or was perhaps born as, I swore to myself that this year would be different. I would behave. I would do my homework. I would not get in trouble. Yet, as I sat in the back of the room that first day, all the resolve in the world could not have spared me from the patterns that had already taken such a firm hold on me. I was simply a troubled kid, and no one would ever figure out why.

Girls sat on either side of me in the back of the class that day. I liked it, liked feeling a part of what they did and said.

Kristy asked, "Can you give this to Peggy?" as she handed me a note.

I liked having the paper secrets in my hand. They represented so much more than mere words passed between school girls. Those words possessed something so far beyond my understanding that it would take almost another forty years to grasp. It was the language of girls that I wanted, for it was the gateway to who I was. I didn't know it at the time, but it was the something that I lacked and yearned for. It was the something that was wrong with me. I was a girl but had not learned the language.

Oddly enough both of those girls and I would "go" together at different points that year, which consisted of asking a question like, "Will you go with me?" exchanging some sort of cheap cosmetic ring and me never having the guts to speak to them.

I was just passing the note when Sister Kathleen walked into the room. She announced with a tone that suggested she would not put up with my shit,

"Bobby Zenker, get up here!"

My legs were weak as I advanced to meet her by the door. My face burned, but not nearly as red as it soon would be. I thought maybe a trip to the principal. That would be no big deal, as I had been there before. But Sr. Kathleen was different. She simply grabbed me up by the scruff of my neck and smacked me a few times. I was angry and ashamed. The playground was my relief.

In Columbus, Ohio, the home of the perennial top ten caliber college football team, the Ohio State Buckeyes, boys played football. I was no exception. We played at school and at home every chance we could get. I was quarterback and I played hard. I swore and I fought with equal vigor. I did not realize then, but I must have somehow felt that with the few outlets I had for my brewing temper, a football game was the place to let it all out, no matter where the game was played.

Sr. Kathleen did play football, and she did not approve of my language. She was a nun, for Christ's sake (quite literally). The day she played with us at recess, giving in to our begging, was a new lesson for me in the ways of discipline and teaching. She let me cuss a little. After one play, she said casually,

"Bobby, come here a second."

With her arm resting around my shoulder she spoke in a hushed, but firm tone that I was completely unaccustomed to.

"I know you get excited out here, but you can't talk that way."

Suddenly, I wanted to do what I was told, not out of fear, but for some other as yet unknown impulse. An adult had treated me kindly as if I was worthy of kindness, leaving me with an expectation I happily met, at least for the rest of seventh-grade. But I was still angry. Late that seventh-grade school year, Sr. Kathleen took me and a girl from my class to see James Taylor in concert. She must have sensed that I needed something extra, and though it would not bear fruit for many years, she planted seeds of empathy and compassion.

For all the brutish discipline and dogma that was my Catholic education, I have never really begrudged it. I did come to know God there, as much as I could in my fearful, ashamed, angry and wrong little life. I did not blame God for these, as much as I just came to know them as part of who I was, the way of my life. I learned to pray, most often for things, like winning basketball games, and other stuff. But, I also turned to God when I was afraid. I often relied on that most Catholic of prayers:

Hail Mary, full of grace, the lord is with thee
Blessed art thou among women,
And blessed is the fruit of your womb, Jesus.
Holy Mary, mother of God,
Pray for us sinners now
and at the hour of our death, Amen.8

I captained our Saturday morning grade-school basketball team one year.

"Hey, huddle up," I yelled at the other boys as I gathered them in a team circle.

"Get your hands in," I said as I torridly ripped through that prayer to Our Lady of the Hard Court, as if she would replace her powdery blue graciousness with gym shorts and guide our every shot to the orange rims and nets of basketball heaven. After so blessing ourselves for battle, we would break with a yell. We did not win much, but the prayer stuck.

I became an altar boy. Mostly I succumbed to pressure from the priests and my mother. "You live only one block from the church," Father Kunkel had pleaded.

Mom pointed out, "You are up early enough with your paper route to serve 6:15 a.m. Mass."

I had been double teamed in a conspiracy involving the church and motherhood. I didn't stand a chance. (I must say here that no priest ever said or did anything untoward to me or in my presence.) Even when looking for all of me like a caricature of an extra from *The Bells of St. Mary's,* inside it did not fit. I listened to what the priests said about faith and God, and I argued to myself, a skill I would later come to perfect in committee fashion as a fully credentialed alcoholic.

"It should not be about the threat of eternal punishment as a motivation to do right," I reasoned.

"Hellfire be damned!"

To me even then, God was a loving God. God was comfort, strength and hope for my troubled soul. He just had to be.

I had a morning paper route from the time I was ten until I was sixteen and old enough to get a real job, like in a restaurant. One particular morning during a thunderstorm, I took refuge on a covered porch. I could not have been older than ten or eleven. There in the dark I cried, feeling empty and alone. But I did know where to turn. I repeatedly, earnestly prayed the Hail Mary and the Lord's Prayer until the rain stopped. I believed.

My mother is a sainted woman. She had to be to live with my father and put up with six children and eight years of nearly continuous pregnancy. Though my mother got angry and yelled at me, it never lacked loving kindness. Where my father's rage went beyond all reason, my mother's indignation bore a definite righteousness with which I could seldom argue with a straight face.

My efforts, therefore, were to simply ignore her protestations and escape the strictures of her supervision. Mostly I thought of my mother as an island of safety in a very troubled sea. She gave me loving comfort. I hid in her lap during scary movies, and she often made an effort to comfort me at bedtime. She intuitively knew that I needed it. Mostly though, it was my mother's inclination toward abiding Christian faith that sustained me and stuck to me like honey. It was sticky stuff alright, but too sweet to wash away.

Throughout my life I did, or performed, all the things I thought a guy should do. I likely overcompensated for great feelings of inadequacy by doing all the manly-man things. Once I was in Dad's shop with Andy and Dad.

"Andy, come here and hold this board so I can cut it," Dad instructed.

I quickly volunteered, "I'll do it."

"No, you're too small," Dad replied.

Lights came on. To get recognition from Dad I should not do things like my older sister whom I idolized. I should make myself bigger and stronger so I could do "Andy things." I lifted weights and ran punishingly hard for many years. I worked out and built a strong body throughout my teenage and adult life. I even began to enjoy the feel of my own strength, although that may have been the testosterone talking.

The other "Andy thing" that stayed with me for years beyond Andy's interest would linger was baseball. I already knew that "Andy things" were big when he went out for baseball.

"Dad, I want to play too," I had begged, even though I was a year too young.

The argument was short lived, however. Much to my surprise, Dad *wanted* his boys to play sports, believing that it would help develop strong, healthy lungs. As an asthmatic, healthy lungs were something he did not have.

"The sooner you start the better," he reasoned.

I started baseball at seven years old, a year younger than the league allowed. For some reason unbeknownst to me, they made an exception. Dad didn't get to play sports when he was a kid. Every father lives to some extent vicariously through his children, but when it came to sports, perhaps Dad lived a little more through me.

I was blessed with an athletic, if not skinny, body. I was quick and agile. So, I played sports like all the other boys in my neighborhood. I was better than most. I played football till I broke my nose in the ninth grade. I played basketball some in high school. And though baseball was my passion, I often felt like I was playing just to prove myself to my Dad, or to someone, the world, or maybe just myself. Sometimes I think I pushed myself hard just to say to myself,

"See, I am a guy."

I was not the sort of trans child that *wanted* to be the other sex. I tried desperately my whole life *not* to be a girl. Though sports were a great way for me to repress feminine urges, the girl would never leave. She would not lie dormant. In fact, the persistent drive of my female persona lay just beneath my troubled surface, always needling me in one way or another. She just wanted to be. She would not be denied.

The fear of my father was compounded by the fear of discovery. Looking back it seems all I knew was fear. That fear lead to chronic, prolonged anxiety that remained with me well into my thirties. Of course, growing up Catholic exacerbated everything. Religion induced lasting, great shame about how I felt inside and led to further denial and repression. Perhaps it goes without saying that the manifestation of my urges produced boatloads of guilt. The guilt and shame have lasted almost to this day.

Thus, I was drawn by a need for relief to alcohol and drugs. I began abusing both as soon as I started at age thirteen, and continued abusing alcohol for the next thirty-five years. A secret brings its own punishment. The longer the secret is kept, the greater the punishment.

I met a girl when I was thirteen. Maureen was pretty. Her eyes were dark, as was her long, wavy, almost frizzy hair. She had a few freckles for good Irish measure. I liked her mostly because she liked me. Plus, when we kissed I felt it between my legs, as did most testosterone driven beings at a still young age.

"I'll turn 'ya on," she had said teasingly.

I knew she meant marijuana, but I was not quite sure I wanted to take that jump.

"I don't know," I said, more out of a sense of uncertainty than right and wrong.

"C'mon, it's really cool," she insisted.

"Well, what's it like?" I began questioning Maureen, stepping closer to the ledge.

"You don't get high the first several times," she informed me.

"But, when you do, you laugh a lot and get a really dry mouth – 'Cotton mouth,'" she called it.

"Then you get the munchies."

Maureen did teach me how to smoke marijuana, but, much more than that she introduced me to the experience of mind altering substances. The simple truth was that when I was high I felt good, unlike the rest of the time. "I go flying so high," Harry Chapin suggested in his 70s classic song, "Taxi," "When I'm stoned."[9] I flew beyond my demons.

Drugs became my companion, amicably enough at first, but like an evil twin, they ultimately turned my life inside out. However, at the beginning, drug use and the culture that surrounded it brought me something I had not yet been able to feel. I got acceptance and recognition. I fit in.

I took every substance that was put in front of me. Fortunately, the drugs available in Worthington, Ohio in the early seventies were relatively harmless. Window Pane, Black Beauty and Mescaline were a few of my favorites. Once when I was doing speed I had a long, loose conversation with my Dad.

He said, "I do not know what you are doing, but I wish you would do it more often."

I said, "Okay."

Like most of my companions I smoked cigarettes too. We washed it all down with alcohol. I took a great many risks in those years with an aura of invincibility cloaked in youthfulness. I see now that it was just plain ignorance. I had not yet been beaten down by enough consequences to suspect anything amiss in my conduct, and doing wrong just seemd to coincide with my being wrong.

I was lucky, or somehow protected, to have survived my teenage years. I used to hitchhike everywhere before I could drive. Several men made passes at me, as I was slender and fair.

One said, "I don't really care who gets my rocks off."

I fidgeted as I said, "I'm not into that."

My sexual orientation then, as today was toward women. No man ever touched or forced himself upon me.

Perhaps the greatest threat to my safety, however, was driving while under the influence of both alcohol and drugs. Fortunately, the car usually available to me was a Volkswagen Bug. It did not go very fast, like the muscle cars of the 70s, and it was hard to roll over due to its shape, which placed most of its weight at the bottom. I had several close calls in which I lost control, but I never wrecked. That was surely by the grace of God alone.

It is hard for me to recall exactly why I liked drugs and alcohol so much. It seems like it was as much for the persona their use allowed as it was for any effect they might have had. I looked forward to using them for days in advance, as if the opportunity to use was the event itself, rather than the social situation that surrounded that opportunity. I prided myself on the fact that I got stoned every single day of my sophomore year at Worthington High School. I used to say,

"Why do you think they call it 'high school'?"

I was an addict.

When I was sixteen, I ran away from home with my best child hood friend and a couple other guys. We hitchhiked across the country to Phoenix. Again, we were blessed, and by the grace of God no evil befell us. An old hippie in an even older car pulled over somewhere outside of St. Louis. He reminded me of Cat Stevens with his long black, curly hair and thick beard.

"Where 'ya going?" he asked.

"Phoenix," we offered in unison.

"Hop in, I'm going that way," he replied, evidently having no particular destination. The car was a large, chocolate brown 60s model with big fins, a Lincoln Mark IV. Its key characteristic was a rear window that slanted inward at the bottom and electronically moved up and down at the flip of a switch up front. Every time we lit up a doobie, down went the window. When the joint was through, the window mysteriously raised.

"Whoa dude, did you see that?"

"It went up by itself."

We rolled with laughter.

That old hippie had some great pot, and we washed the cotton mouth blues away with Coors beer. That was the first time I drank Coors. It seemed like some sort of treasure mostly because it could not be found at the parties I went to in Ohio. Suddenly, we were Rocky Mountain bound, although traveling through Kansas gave us no clue – other than Coors beer. I suspect that old hippie was looking for company and in truth looking out for a bunch of wayward teenagers. For our part, we accepted his generosity and care without looking back.

My friend Doug and I did not care for Phoenix and the prospect of scooping poop at the dog track for a living. We decided to hitchhike to San Antonio to engage a higher calling of shoveling elephant poop at the zoo that his uncle managed. I first saw the Rio Grande River as we moved through El Paso. It was November, and the river was merely a trickle that you could walk across.

"Let's go across," I said.

"I want to be able to say that I went to a foreign country."

"Na, we better not," Doug advised with a cautionary tone.

"Ah c'mon, no one will see us," I insisted with a kind of half logic that made full sense to me.

We compromised instead and tried to throw rocks into Ciudad Juarez.

That night after trying all day to hitch a ride away from that hot, dry enclave, an old couple driving an old pick up stopped. It was a 40's or 50's model Ford. I am not certain, but it had those overly pronounced wheel wells in front. I guessed the couple was Mexican as they did not speak English. I had taken some Spanish as my required foreign language my sophomore year, you know, the one where I was stoned every day. I got a hard earned "F."

We tortured the teacher as many of us were stoned every day. I thought it was clever when I tossed my book out the open window, but that only got me a paddling from the principal. I remember that spelling because he was supposed to be my "pal." He was anything but as he went through his cabinet of wooden paddles. He selected the one with holes cut in it to diminish wind resistance. He told me in a calm mannerly voice to stand. I said I would rather sit without intending to be smug. He gruffly insisted that I stand with my hands clasping his desk. I did not question his resolve a second time. I thought one swat was sufficient. Three had me in tears. I had enough of "high school," but I did recall on my way to San Antonio in the back of that old pickup with the cold November night wind whipping right through me that *me yama est Roberto*.

When we got to a country crossroads outside a small town called Alpine of Steve McQueen fame in the movie, *The Get Away*, they dropped us off as we did not want to go on to Mexico. It was cold on the outskirts of town late at night with no traffic in sight as we hoped to hitch a ride towards San Antonio.

"Let's crawl into our sleeping bags," Doug suggested.

"I don't know," I said, worried that we might miss a ride.

"C'mon, I'm freezing my ass off man!"

"We can climb out if we hear a car coming. Probably won't be any more tonight anyway."

His logic and the cold winds sealed the deal, and our fate. We were soon asleep, only to be awakened by police lights and staring handguns. It seemed that officers from several agencies including city police, the county sheriff's office and the border patrol, had gathered to investigate the threat to international security posed by two youths in sleeping bags by the side of the road. They stuffed us in the back of a patrol car. One deputy drove as the other stared at us all the way back to the station.

"Do you have any drugs on you?" he demanded.

"No!"

I lied as I realized with horror that I had joints stashed in my pack of Marlboro's in my jean jacket pocket. I could not remove them as long as his eyes were on me. They never even blinked.

I had not told anyone at home that I was going, and when I called my Dad from a county jail in Southwest Texas to tell him I had been arrested, he was a broken man.

"Dad, it's me, Bobby. I'm busted," I meekly explained.

Getting "busted" had only one meaning in 1974 - drugs.

"What happened?" he asked with great struggle.

The pain and hurt I heard in his voice struck me hard, as I had never pierced another soul so deeply.

"We were hitchhiking through Texas, and I had joints in my pocket."

He wanted the details of my ten day hiatus, but I was too ashamed to speak.

"Put the officer on," he said.

They housed us in separate cells, and Doug began screaming in pain in the wee hours of the night. I knew it was not drugs as we had only smoked some pot.

Doug said, "It's my appendix," but we could not convince the jailer of that possibility.

It was the same cop who had eye-balled me all the way to the jail.

"What's he on?" he asked repeatedly, as if drugs were the only possibility.

"He's not on anything," I insisted.

"All we had is the pot, and we didn't smoke all day."

I believe that Doug may have died but for the young Mexican janitor whose rational pleading prevailed.

"Maybe he needs to go to the hospital," was all he said, but with great rational, imploring force.

Doug recovered from his appendectomy in the comfort of a hospital bed and got a plane ticket home while I sat for days alone in a jail cell. Its lone barred window overlooked a school playground. I can still hear the sound of children at play juxtaposed against the loneliness and fear ringing in my ears.

A teacher told them, "Do not look at the criminal."

I cried. I was as alone as I had been since I took cover on that porch in the early morning darkness to wait out the thunderstorm. I looked around for a rope, wire, or something, but the cell was clean. I prayed "Hail Marys" instead.

The food was Mexican. It was not good. I complained to my new found friend, the janitor,

"These beans are so dry that I can blow dust off the top."

He merely laughed. I liked Spanish rice so subsisted on that for four days. They did not know what to do with such a youthful law breaker, so decided to put me on a bus to Columbus with a stern warning,

"Do not get off!" as if I might have somewhere to go.

As I sat silently brooding on the Trailways coach, a pair of golden eagles flew close to the highway when one of them smashed into the front of the bus. I watched as the other flew away and thought I knew how the wounded bird, left behind, felt. When I arrived at the station in Columbus, Dad was there to greet me. He cried, and said,

"Welcome home, son," as he hugged me, his prodigal son.

I wonder now if he would so readily embrace his prodigal daughter.

My impromptu sabbatical resulted in expulsion from Worthington High School. That left only the local Catholic school for enrollment. A former girlfriend and all my grade school chaps attended Bishop Watterson High School, as well as my older sisters. The transition was not all that dramatic. Still, given my forays over the previous three years into drugs and other decidedly non-Catholic behavior, as well as that last escapade, it was hard to fit in.

It was not long before I made a wise-crack, trying desperately to be liked, to a big strong underclassman.

"You're doing a great job," I quipped as he was mopping the gym floor for basketball practice.

"What did you say?" he replied angrily.

"I was just joking," I half heartedly stated.

"Not enough tough guy," he said as he sucker-punched me.

We sparred a few moments until I managed to get him in a head lock as I leaned back against the roll-away wooden bleachers. I thought about smashing his head against them as the basketball coach walked in.

"Hey, hey, hey, c'mon fellas," he yelled across the empty gym.

The fight was over shortly after it began, but I was bruised inside and out. The kid put a big knot on my noggin, and I cried terribly. Coach Straub tried to comfort me, but he had no idea what he had stumbled into. I had only been in a few fights previously, but the result was always the same. I cried. I did not know why but do not wonder if I was far too tender inside to portray such macho characteristics.

Later that junior year, a priest befriended me. Fr. Paul would stop and chat during study hall and did not expect anything of me.

"Hi, I'm Father Paul," he had said nonchalantly.

"And you are?" he had to ask, as I wasn't sure about how cool it would be to talk to a priest.

He seemed to be actually looking for the person behind the facade. I wish now I could have revealed myself to him, or anyone, but that would take a few more decades.

I do not recall much of the following summer. I was seventeen, working and playing without much direction. I still used drugs and alcohol. I was still angry, ashamed, afraid, and probably more than a little depressed from the lingering effect of those ugly, painful emotions that I could not escape or drown. I often used only one phrase when talking with my friends,

"Ah, fuck it!"

Early in my senior year at Watterson, Fr. Paul suggested I attend a retreat called "Teens Encounter Christ." I was ripe. I went, and I did encounter Christ. It was then that I first understood that God knew me and loved me. When I got home, I flushed my drugs down the toilet. I lit a candle and prayed for forgiveness. My older brother burst in and commented sarcastically,

"What is this, mellow out time?"

I suppose it was.

I went to morning mass every day the rest of my senior year. I began a faith journey that has been up and down, not unlike many Christians. Yet, like weathering the storm on that darkened porch years earlier, that faith has been with me all the while. It did not keep me necessarily sane or sober. It kept me alive.

I always thought that the urge to dress, mimic or just observe women was simply a character trait that would someday vanish. I believed I would outgrow it, and I waited a very long time for that to happen. It did not. I was convinced that this feminine thinking was sinful. So, I did what most Catholics do when they feel guilty. I prayed mightily, as if the sheer effort would bring redemption. I went to church. I drank.

I made a pact with God, asking him to make me sneeze every time I indulged in such thoughts. I sneezed a lot, but the guilt remained. In my guilt, fear and shame, I asked God many, many times to take this sin away. God always hears and answers prayers. Sometimes the answer is no. Sometimes it is maybe, and sometimes it is maybe later. After forty-eight years of confusion, fear, guilt, shame, doubt, ambiguity and uncertainty about something as fundamental as self, I decided that the answer was probably not maybe or maybe later. God did not remove my gender identification dysphoria. Instead, like Moses and his followers, I wandered in a gender wilderness for forty-eight years.

Reasonable minds may disagree, while unreasonable minds will judge and condemn. Thank God that I have learned that what other people think of me is none of my business. At some point, I stopped asking God for forgiveness for who I am. That was when I asked God to bring about disclosure in a way that would not bring shame and ruination to all those around me. Ironically enough, that simple prayer may have been the only thought I had in the previous ten years that was not entirely based on self. The answer to that prayer was "yes."

Chapter Three

Got Your Back

Well, I did it for kicks and I did it for faith
I did for lust and I did it for hate
I did it for need and I did it for love
Addiction stayed on tight like a glove.

- Emmy Lou Harris[10]

I could not hide even in Montana's great expanse. My true self assuredly remained, and although intermittently benign, it would not be so forever. Most Montanans go through their entire life never wondering about their "true self." Self assurance is their birth-right. They know just who they are. I am not like that, and not merely because I am not a native Montanan. I was plagued for most of forty-eight years by questions about self. I did not ask whether I was a man or a woman. I dared not for fear of the answer. But why couldn't I be the man I tried to be? Why did I have so many insecurities and doubts around other men? Why did I try so hard to stack up and never feel as if I could?

Perhaps other men ask those same questions. Perhaps they find answers. Maybe the truth lies in self acceptance. I tried that route too. It just did not work. My doubts and fears would not go away. At the same time, I began to think about and indulge more and more in my feminine side.

It became an unhealthy pre-occupation. Yet, hard as I tried, and fervently though I prayed, it would not go away. The woman inside persisted.

Was she thirsty, or was it me trying to drown her out? Whichever it was, I tried to satiate the need. Many say that alcoholics are just trying to fill in a hole inside of them. They obsess in their minds over the manifestations of emptiness. They are seekers. And, in seeking, alcoholics are never satisfied. They can never have enough of anything to which they turn their attention. Their obsession of mind soon turns to an allergy of the body, and before you can say "how about another," they are addicted.

I was thirteen the first time I got drunk. I snuck out on a summer night with my brother and some friends. It was warm, but not hot, probably in the low seventies. The oppressive Mid-western summer humidity seemed to sleep as well. Katydids and crickets sang a sweet summer cacophony, and the lighting bugs seemed to dance a sort of phosphorous refrain. It was dark, so mixing the warm Coca Cola with Southern Comfort in Doug's driveway would be a trick.

"Why don't we drink a little first and make room for the Coke?" I suggested.

"Whew!" I said as I shook my head, feeling the burn all the way to my toes.

We all, Doug, Mike, Shane and I took a ridiculously macho swig for one thirteen-and three eleven-to twelve-year-old boys.

Doug poured the Coke while Shane held the bottle.

"Hold still," Doug demanded as he half laughed and half giggled.

The Coke fizzed as it mingled with the Southern Comfort but settled into a dark elixir that we soon swilled, gulped and sipped till we were stupid.

"I've had enough," Shane said.

"Ah c'mon, don't be a wimp," I encouraged him.

But Doug chimed in too, "Yea, I've had enough."

"But there's still some left," I insisted.

There being no other takers, I drank it till it was gone.

We went about our morning paper routes, and on the way home I found my brother lying on the street curb. He had vomited.

"Mike, get up. It's me, Bobby. We have to finish your route."

"Huh," he said, not even close to conscious.

"C'mon Mike," I insisted, half pissed off by now.

He finally came around enough to function, and we finished his route. I have always loved my brother dearly. I watched his back, even when he did not realize.

When I had my first route, before he had taken one, I took him with me one morning. "C'mon Mom," we begged, "It's summer. We don't have school tomorrow."

"Alright, but go straight out and come right back. No fooling around!"

"But *that's* the whole point," I whispered under my breath.

If Mom heard me, she merely shook her head and said with that almost authentic Irish brogue of hers,

"Ah go on with 'ya."

It was an average size route, about fifty papers. I could do it on a bike in about a half hour. Walking took longer. I had twin canvas bags sown together like saddle bags with a hole cut in the middle so they could be worn over the shoulders, like a sort of poncho with a bag in front and another in back.

I wanted to hurry, though, partly because that is my nature and partly because my route took me along a short cut through the cemetery. I would walk through the cemetery at night with a half moon shining through intermittent clouds. It was dark, but still light enough to see shapes and shadows, likely just grave stones and shrubbery. I could never be certain, though, so I hurried.

I was not sure I believed in ghosts, but, like my thinking about God, I decided to hedge my bet in favor of their existence. I did not want to risk a ghost's ire by refusing to acknowledge its very existence. I never did see a ghost. Perhaps I had enough of my own skeletons to keep the spirits at bay.

On the morning Michael joined me, I had him deliver papers to houses on the opposite side of the street, and we would meet in the middle for the next round. A kid I knew from school lived on my route. He had an extra thick corrective sole on one shoe. It looked like a club foot, though it was not. He was different and I befriended him. I have always had a soft spot for the underdog. He was taller than the other boys, so did not have to suffer much teasing that I was aware of. He walked with a limp and ran with a side winder limp. I never saw it stop him.

On this morning his dog began to bark as Michael approached his porch. I had always managed the dogs by speaking to them as gruffly and firmly as a ten-year-old can and not backing down. I had given Michael the admonition,

"If a dog runs out at you just yell at him, and DO NOT RUN!"

He ran and, of course, the dog chased him.

I do not know what possessed me. I only knew that my little brother was in trouble and I had to help.

I ran from across the street yelling "Heyyyyyyyyy!" at that dog with a voice much gruffer than ever before, no doubt fueled with a lethal dose of adrenaline.

"You get outta' here!" I screamed.

I had a rolled up paper in my hand and more in my bag. Mike was yelling and running, and the canine was at his heels as I ran head long into them with no idea what I could do to influence Michael's fortunes. I threw two or three papers at that dog as it turned and scampered off with a yelp. I have always loved my brother.

I hurried through my paper route for another reason too. Just before entering the cemetery, I delivered the morning news to the locally notorious house of the woman known only as the "No Lady." I never did actually see her, but, I heard her often enough in the wee hours to become accustomed to her moaning cry,

"No-oh. No-oh. No-oh."

I never knew what tragedy befell her or evil spirit gripped her. It is painfully clear as I think of it now that she experienced a serious mental illness for which she likely could have been committed.

The "No Lady" lived in an old wood and masonry house on the hill at the end of the street, right across the dirt road from the cemetery. That location only fueled the speculation surrounding the nature of her tragedy. Ivy grew high along the stone portion of the house, and the whole property was surrounded by a stone and wrought iron fence. But, in the light of day, the house was only marginally spookier than other houses along the street.

Still, when I came to collect payment for the papers, I approached the door warily, as I could still hear the "No Lady" now softly moaning for some hidden pain or grave misfortune. The screen door was metal, and a door bell was mounted nearby. Thus presented with a choice, my learned practice was to bang hard on the loudest instrument, the bottom of the screen door. A surprised customer was less likely to pretend that they were not home when they were shocked into a response before having time to think. A younger woman answered the door, which I guessed was the "No Lady's" daughter.

"Paperboy, can I collect?" was my usual greeting.

"Oh wait a minute," the woman said, "I'll have to find my pocket book."

She was still dressed in her night-gown in the middle of the afternoon, and her eyes looked dark and worn. She had only a few wrinkles, but to me anyone over thirty looked old. Her hair was dark with streaks of gray and hung in frizzy disarray.

"How much is it?" she asked.

"Two ten," I responded, hopeful of payment as my earnings came from what I was able to collect.

Between collections and tips, I might earn a hundred bucks a month.

"Here you are," she said as she handed me bills and loose change, "Keep the change." After a quick count I looked up to read her face, but she had already stepped behind the door. It was only a quarter extra, but I could not begrudge her. The difficulty of her task of caring for the troubled soul that was her mother was not within my grasp, but then again, I did know a thing or two about craziness. At the tender age of ten I came to understand empathy.

The laughter and jokes between my family and friends surrounding the "No Lady," however, did not belie such an understanding. While it was probably cruel to make merriment over someone else's tragedy, we had tragedy of our own, and humor sustained us. Our tragedies may have paled in comparison, but pain is not relative. We each feel our own measure, and in the depths of our pain, we seldom see that of another. So, we laughed and we fought. We survived.

I have lived in Montana for nearly thirty years. The myths of boundless beauty and freedom have long since slipped away like the smoke of so many summers' forest fires. Though a fire might be far off, its smoke seemed almost a living thing. In August, with temperatures in the nineties, it seemed less a metaphor than it did the reality of hell. Then, with the cool September rain the fires would be gone.

At first all I could see was Montana's beauty. I would look at her snow-capped peaks, and green forests as if that were all there was to see. The truth that Montana is mostly prairie was lost on me. While there are many trees, there is more grass. Montana is a place where you notice it turn green and speak of it almost reverently as an event. "Green up" is too often short-lived, and gives way to the brown coat Montana wears most of the time, less a Carhartt brown than an Andrew Wyeth brown. Those images from hell-like summers and brown, dry hills became the metaphor for my soul. What spirit that I had not burned in hopelessness was lifeless or desperately in fear of becoming so.

The soul is the place for the spirit. If the spirit dies, the soul is an empty shell like so many long abandoned Montana homesteads. I once went antelope hunting with my friend in southeastern Montana near Sayle Hall or Biddle or some such other long forgotten Montana place, its spirit carried away on the winter winds. The sign at the landowner's gate read, "Landowner Permission Required. M. E. Lloyd."

I stopped a few places in search of this M. E. Lloyd, and discovered that he lived in an old log house up the road. There was only one such house in the locale. It was fronted by a driveway sign bearing the shakily handwritten name, M. E. Lloyd. I crossed the wooden porch and knocked lightly on the wooden framed screen door. An elderly woman I took for Mrs. M. E. Lloyd, later introduced as the same, answered the door.

"I'd like to go antelope hunting out on your ground," I confidently asserted, suggesting the hopeful response to my question.

"Wait just a moment," came the soft reply. "I'll have to get Mr. Lloyd."

A sprightly old man came bounding to the door and immediately invited me and my hunting partner in.

"C'mon in fellas," he beckoned.

"Mr. Lloyd," he stated with an outstretched hand as we extended ours.

"Have a seat, have a seat," M. E. Lloyd insisted.

My partner, Tony, was the talker between us, but he may have met his match in Mr. Lloyd, who immediately began to regale us with stories of the old days.

"Would you like some coffee and pie?" he insisted.

No, I mean he *insisted*. I had not understood that a request of any sort in that neck of the woods, or prairie, as it were, was a request from a neighbor and an occasion to visit. It was lost on me that during Mr. Lloyd's formative years visitors were seldom and few. The coffee was hot and the pie delicious. We would be there for a while.

"I have something you boys may want see," he said, but apparently only after we heard the tale of how it came to be.

"These two old bucks were fighting and locked their horns," said M. E. Lloyd.

"So, I shot 'em both. It was not in season, but they would have died anyhow."

"Oh really," I responded with feigned surprise, thinking I knew BS when I heard it.

Mr. Lloyd had apparently been to this rodeo before, as he truly surprised me with the proof.

"I hung it in the corner with one head on this wall and the other on this one," he said as he held his hands at a right angle.

"C'mon, I'll show you."

And he did.

"I was born in this country in 1903," Lloyd now told us.

He had our full confidence.

"In the two story log house down the road," he said. I needed no proof this time.

"Yea, I saw that on the way in," I blurted out like an excited kid warming to the story.

His family had been homesteaders under the Homestead Act of 1862, established to populate the country west of the Mississippi River.

"My dad built that with his own hands," M. E. Lloyd recounted.

"There were too many of us for the old place," he said.

The two story log house was the *new place*, yet leaned precipitously to the northeast, having withstood more than eighty years of prevailing Eastern Montana winds.

As we drove back north to Ashland, we looked at it with a new sense of respect but could not see the life in it that M. E. Lloyd had described with vigor. The sense that something vibrant once was there was inescapable, though only the residue of livelihood remained. The logs by now have likely fallen or rotted from dryness. Yet, the remnants of structure and function sit squarely on the land. Where once there was life, only a shell remains. That was my soul as my spirit seemed to dry too with each passing year.

As with green up, Montana has a way, when the winds of April give way to the precious, early warmth of May and the rain of June, of letting life seep into its soul. Though my soul laid in ruin, it was not dead. I could not kill it, as I wanted to live. Somewhere inside of me the ember of spirit wanted to blaze again with hope.

Chapter Four

My Only Sunshine

My baby needs an Angel
She never learned to fly

- Emmy Lou Harris[11]

The Swift Hawk group home for troubled Indian teens stood like the palisade walls of an old fort half way up the hillside above St. Labre. I worked there as a houseparent/counselor in the early 80s. It was a live-in position for a four day stint with three days off. It was exhausting, but, thinking that I had overcome my own troubled youth, I concluded that I had something to give. Perhaps I did. I was a young daddy with a beautiful new baby daughter. During my three days off, I was Mr. Mom. I fed Meghan, changed her diapers and sang to her as she slept in my lap,

"You are my Sunshine, my only sunshine. You make me happy when skies are gray. You'll never know dear how much I love you. So, don't take my sunshine away."

And I will be damned if she did not do just that. She has not uttered a word to me in years. She daily breaks my heart. Yet, I must admit that I more likely drove her away, or gave her away, with so much else in my transition.

She was petite and fair as a toddler. It took her three years to grow hair.

"Oh, what a cute little boy," people would say in stores.

"She's a girl!" became our constant refrain.

"Maybe we should tape a pink ribbon to her head," I suggested to Joanne.

People still called her a boy. Once she did grow hair it was blonde. And we let it grow as much as it would for several years. Joanne took great pains to curl Meghan's hair and keep it pretty.

Despite the blonde hair, Meghan was genuinely Irish. She had this fierce, stubbornly independent streak. Once, when she was about four and playing industriously with her dolls,

Joanne said,

"Meghan, I want you to go clean your room."

"I'm busy, and don't bother me either," Meghan earnestly responded.

We looked at each other and laughed. What else could you do at such a Reader's Digest moment? When Meghan's mind was fixed, I did not bother her. Perhaps I should have. But it was not in me to force her into confrontation. I was too afraid of becoming my father.

Children learn what they live and live what they learn. By the time I became a daddy, I thought of myself as all grown up, certainly mature enough and emotionally adequate to the task. I was wrong. I was still ashamed, fearful, angry and depressed. Those emotions kept me in sharp focus on my-self most of the time.

The image that looked back at me from the mirror was pretty shaky. It was not just my body that gave me such discomfort. It was the persona, the way to live life as a man, that left me ill at ease and questioning who I was. This holistic image of self, body in concert with persona is an apt description of what it means to be comfortable in your own skin. I was not.

Shane could be independent in his own right. However, I suspect that in the end he found it easier to follow his sister's lead. She felt that her rightful place as the first born was to be in charge, and in that way the two formed a symbiotic relationship which probably drives both of them still.

Shane was born on leap day, 1984. He was seven weeks premature. His lungs were not yet fully developed, and he could not breathe on his own. I shudder to think what would have happened if I'd decided to continue on to Hardin, another fifty-five miles away, instead of stopping at the Indian Health Service (IHS) clinic in Lame Deer, the seat of sovereignty and the U.S. government services on the Northern Cheyenne Indian Reservation.

Shane needed to be on oxygen, and the IHS clinic did not have air hoses small enough for a premie baby. They used what they had and scarred his trachea in the process. It caused him to bark like a dog when he coughed for his first several months. It was especially difficult at church, where people would look at you as if you were neglecting your child. At least that's how I perceived it. We took him to Denver to have it fixed by an ear, nose and throat specialist.

They had no incubators in Lame Deer either. The doctors improvised and calmly placed Shane in aluminum foil under a heat lamp until the HELP helicopter from Billings, 100 miles away, arrived to life flight him away. His mother went with him in the helicopter, but I had to drive. As I drove, I cried and prayed. I knew his stake on life was tenuous, but I had no sense that my child might not live.

Shane survived his traumatic arrival after a month in the infant ICU center at Billings Deaconess Hospital.

"He looks like a frog staked out like that," I commented to Joanne as Shane laid on a lab table with all the tubes and wires hooked up to him.

She disagreed, but that was expected of his mother.

Joanne stayed at the Ronald McDonald house in Billings that entire month, while I commuted back and forth from Ashland on weekends. As he clung to life, I felt it important to spend a significant part of those weekends observing the television spectacle known as "March Madness," the NCAA men's basketball tournament, as I continued to do throughout his life at home. Sr. Kathleen's lessons about cussing at sporting events had long ago vanished. For years, I yelled and swore at a lifeless piece of electronic equipment for nearly the entire event. I had no sense of enjoyment and scrutinized each contest for the quality of officiating, the oxymoron notwithstanding. To this day, I am uncertain how to characterize that insanity. Was it all the pent-up emotions finding their way violently to the surface? Was it alcoholism, or did I drink to take the edge off? I do not know, but I fear that for Shane that is my legacy. It all sort of ran together and could be added to my growing list of dysfunctions.

In his early years, Shane was happy-go-lucky. He had those "uptosomething," smiling Irish eyes and devious grin to match. He was clever even at a very early age. When he was two or three, we played the animal sound game with him. He could make the cow, dog and horse sounds easily, so I thought I would stump him.

"What sound does a deer make?" I asked, thinking it clever, as at the time I thought deer were non-verbal.

Shane looked at me quizzically and thought so hard you could see those wheels turning. He said nothing but leaned his small head far over to one side as if hanging upside down and stuck out his tongue. It dawned on me then that though he had seen many deer in the wild, like most Montana boys, the thing that left an indelible impression on his very young psyche was the deer hanging in the garage.

When Shane was a toddler his sister wanted to take care of him. That meant he should do as she said. And he would to a point. However, when that unspoken line was crossed, Shane went his own way, much to Meghan's chagrin. Meghan needed to be in charge, and I suspect that she developed her own methods of obtaining Shane's devotion. But, get it she did.

When Shane was seven and Meghan was nine, I went to law school. In the spring of 1989, as I drove off the St. Labre campus in my Jeep Comanche pick-up, I broke into a grin. I opened the official-looking envelop from the University of Montana School of Law and quickly scanned it for the words, "You have been accepted." There had been few moments of real joy and pride to that point in my life, like the days my children were born, but acceptance into law school was one of them. I could not have known how the decision to move across the state to Missoula would affect the course of our lives, but our family would never be the same. It was the beginning of the end of innocence.

The cultural shock of moving from Ashland, a small, rural, politically conservative town in Southeastern Montana, to the bustling, urban, politically not conservative city of Missoula, was profound. I could not have adjusted quickly if I had wanted to, and I did not. I could not see the effect that nine years in a time warp had on me.

I had been idealistic and leaning liberally when I arrived in Montana in 1980. I had voted for Jimmy Carter only four years earlier, and I detested "Reaganomics." Yet, by 1989, I was a right wing, Republican voting, and queer bashing conservative from hell. This persona is not exactly what you would expect to find gravitating toward Montana's version of Cal - Berkeley, where Birkenstocks and dread-locks were common. Just like those days as an altar boy, the committee in my head fought everyone and everything.

The rental market in the late eighties and early nineties in Missoula was very tight. We were displaced in even the first two dives we could find to hang our hats. The third was indeed charming. We rented a beautiful house on North Street while the owners were off on sabbatical. It was just an old salt box wood frame house that had been remodeled and exceptionally maintained. They put a dining booth in the small kitchen just below a large bay window that looked out on the garden in the small, city neighborhood back yard. The basement had been remodeled into a large family room that we made our bedroom, a small bedroom that became my office and a beautiful bathroom completely finished in stained wood. It had the first shower stall with a tile bench to sit on that I had ever seen. I had been running about twenty miles a week and after my work-out would sit on the bench and let the water run over me. A full length mirror hung just across the room and as I emerged from the shower, and I often stopped, stuffed my penis back between my legs and cocked one hip to the side. There she was again.

While we were there for only a couple of years, I finally began to feel at home in Missoula. I put in a garden, as I had every year since moving to Montana. The kids were enrolled in Catholic school where Shane met his own Sr. Tarantula in the formidable persona of Sr. Rosata, his second grade teacher. While she stood all of 5'2", she wielded a mean bar of soap that turned Shane forever away from the strictures of Catholicism.

Law school was grueling. My study habits were not good, and I got through on rote memorization. I did not learn to "think like a lawyer" until in my first law job. My boss, Loren Tucker, the pedantic old school lawyer from rural, conservative Madison County said, "Turn the crank" whenever I came to him looking for an easy answer as I had done my entire life. He held his closed palm at the side of his head as if holding a crank and began to make a circling motion as if turning it.

"Turn the crank, Bob, turn the crank," he repeated, sometimes out of the mere frustration that he had his own thinking to do and couldn't afford to do mine as well.

"Now, you have to do the hard work," he would say as he sent me off to turn my own crank.

I cannot say why I did not want to use what Sr. Kathleen had called a "fine mind," but I was mentally lazy. It may have been that since there were no answers as yet to all the pain in my heart and soul that I did not want to go to a greater degree of analysis. I don't know, but I had gotten by for many years by adroitly piggybacking onto the thoughts and actions of those around me.

I was the chameleon. I could change my stripes instantly to fit in with any person or group in which I found myself. At least I tried. While much of this process was not conscious, it did allow me to avoid the truth about myself and who I was for many years. It allowed me to live without any real self identity for most of my life.

Law school was no different. I hung out with smart people and party people alike. I did not hang out at home. I went to class and lived in the library the rest of the time, except Friday and Saturday nights.

"Weekends are for letting off steam" I asserted to Joanne as I left the family at home many weekend nights, preferring instead the bars downtown and my law school buddies. Some nights, though, when I was home and not drinking we made popcorn and set blankets and pillows out on the living room floor in front of the TV. We once watched *Robin Hood, Prince of Theives*, starring Kevin Costner, as I held Megan on one side and Shane on the other while Brian Adams plaintively sang,

"Everything I do, I do it for you."[12]

I believed it then and shed a tear. I cry now because I had not known how to be that unselfish, and lacked the honesty to admit it.

In law school I learned to drink like a man. I drank shots of whiskey and liqueurs the names of which I cannot even spell. I learned to power drink beer. I smoked cigars with the best of them.

Sunday was left for family, first church and then something with the kids. I treasured those moments, like riding bikes around the campus or looking for deer on Mount Sentinel, rising above the eastern edge of Missoula forming part of a great nest for the inhabitants below.

"You want to go 'deer-ing?'" I would ask Meghan and Shane.

It always amazed me that no matter what activity I suggested, they always were eager to go. I could not see that my children needed a father more than one day a week.

When summer came, I interned, which took me away from my kids for even greater stretches. My internship after my first year was in Helena, a little over an hour away. We needed the money, and I needed to build my resume. I worked in the tort claims division of the Montana Department of Administration. There were two lawyers in the office, Bill and Ann. They were both friendly, and I was comfortable discussing both legal and life issues with one or the other of them. They both remained in government service, Bill eventually becoming the lead attorney for tort claims and Ann rising to the governor's office.

I rented a one-room apartment that summer. It was just off Lyndale, a very busy Helena street. You could hear car traffic at every hour of the day or night, but I was used to city life by then. I clomped up wooden stairs to reach the second floor, opened the door to a bed, small black and white TV with local channels only, a lamp, alarm clock and kitchenette. The bathroom was equally small, but the shower ran hot and hard just the way I liked it.

I had purchased a pawn shop ten speed Schwinn bicycle in Missoula before I left, and tore all over town in the evenings. I played basketball on the court at Pioneer Park by the swimming pool and generally enjoyed my independence very much. But I could not wait to get to Missoula to see my kids on the weekend and raced to get back home.

When school resumed in the fall I peculiarly had time to go hunting every weekend, in spite of the heavy class load and studying required of second year law students. Really, who was that about? It was not about my kids or my spouse, because I never took either along. However, if you suggested that I spent my time selfishly, I would not have believed you. After all, I gave my family one day every week for most of the year. I played guitar at mass. Was that not enough, while also working and going to law school? Add self-righteousness to the list.

After my second year of law school, I interned as a prosecutor in the City Attorney's office. I had found my niche, pursuing the ends of justice and all that. I learned two valuable philosophies there.

Judy, a lawyer who did most of the criminal work, taught me to do the right thing. She never told me what that was. The lesson was that I had to give questions of ethics my full consideration. I had to "think like a lawyer" and in my best legal judgment, do what I concluded was the right thing to do. That advice has served me well over nearly twenty years of practicing law.

Another matter of Judy's dedication to law was the development of legal protections for abused women.

"A man in Montana could beat his horse only once before facing a felony criminal charge, but he could beat his wife three times before facing the same level of criminal sanction," Judy once pointed out to me.

It remains true today.

In a tragically ironic twist of fate, Judy was killed by a drunk driver on September 25, 2009, while returning to Missoula from a domestic violence conference. Judy will forever be remembered as Montana's crusader to strengthen domestic violence laws. Judy did the right thing.

Jim, the Missoula City Attorney for many years, taught me that the prosecutor should always win. Once after a great trial victory on a traffic ticket, I was scrambling back into the office with another intern, pumping each other's back generously and proclaiming the successful barbeque of some hapless criminal.

"Well, the prosecution should always win," Jim said.

"They usually have both the law and the facts on their side and get to decide whether or not to go forward."

"Oh," I said, my pride sinking as the rain of wizened experience began to fall on our parade.

But I never forget the lesson.

The prosecutor singularly has the power and authority to decide whether or not to prosecute a case. That is a choice no defendant has. If summoned, he or she must defend against the charges, while the prosecution may always choose not to file them or to dismiss them. It was a great lesson, as I have seen far too many prosecutors aggressively pursue bad cases for the sake of their own pride, myself included. I pursued the ends of justice, truth and the American way right into a legal career as a Montana county attorney, one of about fifty across the fourth largest state in the nation.

Just before my third year in law school, an old friend from Ashland showed up and offered Joanne a teaching job in Roseburg, Oregon, where he was the new principal. After the requisite deliberations for appearance sake, we both agreed that it was the right thing to do, both for our finances and for our marriage. We could not have been more wrong, for it really was the beginning of the end. But, for the first time in ten years, I was by my self-indulgent self. The plan was that I would finish my last year of law school, take the bar, find a job and bring my family back to wherever I landed.

I had never recognized the onset of clinical depression, but then it was palpable. I quite simply loved my children and missed them more than I could say. I could not say the same for my spouse. It was clear to me then that whatever love I had for her had faded. I suspect that if she could have admitted it, it was clear to her too. If only I had taken stock then as I do now, but I had not yet fallen as far as I would. We separated, never to seriously rejoin.

Chapter Five

Someone to Grow Old With

So I will share this room with you
And you can have this heart to break.

I met Peggy in a bar where the main feature was a Rhinoceros head hanging on the wall. Rhino's had been a principle "steam letting" institution throughout my legal education. It was funky, and *so* Missoula. The clientele varied from the regulars, working people and washed out hippies to young college hippies, underage teenage girls and all sorts in between.

By my third year of law school, I had actually gotten used to it and Missoula in all its funky glory.

"Missoula is a place, sort of," they used to say.

It was an apt description. Missoulians enjoyed defying definitions and labels as much as they did convention. They were inclusive, beyond surprises from their fellow "zootypes" as I called them, derived from the nickname that I used to refer to Missoula, "Zootown." Other Montanans often refer to Missoula as California North for all its weirdness and that of its inhabitants. By the standards of the rest of Montana's less left leaning populace, it was so. I had struggled greatly to fit in there and feel at home. But, in those days I was still the conservative, tightly wrapped, and religiously right Republican. I did not stand a chance.

Peggy lived in Butte when I met her, having left Missoula the year before. Though she was raised in Ogden, Utah, she fit right in and felt at home. Butte was very different from Missoula in most respects, except its democratic politics. Butte politics had come of age during the golden age of unions. As Montana State University history professor, Mary Murphy points out, Butte was the "'Gibraltar of Unionism,' where nearly every working person from theater usher to hoist engineer belonged to a labor union."[14]   Butte had once been not only the largest city in Montana, but the largest between Seattle and St. Paul. It had been a "'wide open town' meaning that a man could buy a drink, place a bet, or visit a prostitute at any hour of the day or night without worrying about being arrested."[15]

Butte's population during its heyday had been close to 100,000, the majority of whom were hard rock miners and those who served them. Its glory days, however, had long since passed by the close of the twentieth century, and its population dwindled to less than 30,000.   Still, Butte maintained a well earned reputation as a hardscrabble town.

Butte had its own code, or so some of its denizens claimed. While I never heard a precise description of just what that code was, I do not doubt that it did, and does, exist. There were just certain unwritten rules of conduct that a Butte boy was socialized to observe from a very early age and was expected to exhibit in his behavior. They had to be tough and accustomed to hard work. When they drank, they drank hard, and when they fought, someone might die.

Having represented on appeal a man convicted of deliberate homicide for stabbing his assailant by wildly thrusting his knife upward into the aorta of a man kneeling on his chest and pounding his head against the curb outside The Irish Times bar, I know that this is true. Trying to get a guy from Butte to turn state's evidence and testify against someone else was damn near impossible, as it violated the Butte code.

I once prosecuted a man from Butte named Batterman for assault. What is worse is that the victim's name was Deadman. Fortunately, he was not - a dead man. I cross-examined one of Batterman's witnesses about his motive to testify, and he attempted to explain to me the virtues of the Butte code, as if a Madison County jury would accept it as reasonable or some sort of legal axiom. It was lost on me, and evidently the jury as well, as they took about twenty minutes to return a guilty verdict. The moral I took from the story is that a Batterman should never beat a Deadman.

In 1920s Butte, Peggy might have been a flapper or a socialite and would have had difficulty in choosing between the two. During our marriage, her closet, the contents of which I was intimately familiar with, reflected as much. She could dress as the belle of the ball or don the flapper fringe. Peggy could drink and party with the best or dine with the highest officials in the state as the situation called for, with nary a change in her presentation or persona.

Peggy fit in with Buttians because she, like them, utterly lacks pretense. Peggy is real to her core, and, in contrast to me, hid nor feared nothing about herself. I have always been attracted to such utter lack of pretense, perhaps because my entire life had been just the opposite. Peggy is a giver and shares what she has and who she is with anyone who needs her or might take an interest.

The thing that caught my eye that first night in Rhino's was her smile. Her smile is the crown jewel of a genuine soul. It gives her more than the proverbial glow. She really does light up a room.

I saw Peggy again that summer as I was getting ready for the bar exam. In those days, I was running twenty miles a week and doing lots of situps and such. I was in good shape. I loved to feel the warmth of the sun on my bare skin. Since I did not really have a back yard, I suntanned next to the truck in the driveway in my Speedo. I frankly enjoyed more than a few double takes from women who drove by.

One afternoon, as I lay snoozing through torts, or contracts, or evidence, the friend who had introduced Peggy and me drove up with her and his girlfriend.

"We're going up the Blackfoot to go swimming. Want to go?" He asked.

Since I was already dressed for the occasion, I could hardly say no. I spent the afternoon hanging out with Peggy. I think we both knew then the shape of things to come, but neither took any specific move to advance our simmering attraction. Outwardly, we only teased one another in some precourting rite, ambiguously expressing our intentions. However, the seed was well planted in both of us.

I spent six weeks preparing for the test from hell and three days roasting on its spit. While I would not get the official results for several weeks, I was confident that I had passed the bar exam. Since I would not have to start work for another week, there was little else to do but get drunk. I began the evening when the tests were through with shots of Jack Daniels and a cigar. I got sick. I cannot recall the rest of that event. I should not be surprised that, having anticipated the drinking as the main part of every event, I recall little of what actually occurred.

The week after the bar exam, I went camping with my law school buddy, which roughly translates into a three day drunk. Two highlights of that trip stick out in my mind that describe my state of being as I embarked upon my legal career.

"Where're you going?" my friend asked the first morning as I grabbed the ever present bottle of Ten High.

"I'm gonna' take a bath in the stream," I replied.

"I forgot my tooth-brush so I need this mouth wash," I hollered back as I scrambled out from under the canopy on my pick-up and sat naked in an ice cold mountain stream.

If it had been regular mouth wash, I would have spit it out, but I had somewhat of a code too. I would not "waste" booze. Odd, that one, as it had no qualms about wasting me.

The other highlight was fishing. I had not yet reached the point in my drinking career where I was capable of little else. The trip began with shooting our law books with a .357 pistol and watching that bittersweet confetti drift to the ground, laughing as we swilled Ten High. My friend showed me how to catch grasshoppers with my cap.

"Trout just love 'em," he had claimed.

"I'm a meat fisherman," he asserted, meaning that the effort was not successful unless rewarded with dinner.

I too eschewed the Filson pedigreed fly fishermen.

"I only want dinner," I asserted boldly, although the truth was that we just did not realize that we were having the time of our lives.

We went fishing in several places as if left over extras from *A River Runs Through It*. Lots of rivers and streams run through Montana. We both knew that we could never get to them all. But we did go to the Big Blackfoot of Norman McLean's youth.

Another place I will never forget, however, was a secluded small stream called Little Prickly Pear Creek near the Seiban Ranch, about twenty miles north of Helena and just off Interstate 15.

"Max Baucus grew up on that ranch," my friend told me.

I once met Max, Montana's senior senator at a St. Patrick's Day parade in Butte. As I marched along under the buzz of a few shots of Bushmill's at 10:30 in the morning, I almost ran right into him. I was still very much in my tightly wrapped, conservative box but shook his hand anyway.

"I'm Max Baucus," he said in that real Montanan fashion totally devoid of pretense.

I was too dumbfounded to respond.

"I know a 'hidey hole up ahead," my friend said.

We were fully armed with grasshoppers and optimism that only the freshly matriculated can know. The stream was overgrown with brush, so it was cool and shady on that late July afternoon. The water was shallow, but cold, as mountain streams are even at the height of summer. The glimmer of sky peaking through the blowing leaves was strikingly blue as only a Montana sky can be.

I had caught bigger fish on the Bighorn years earlier, but the one I caught that day I especially remember, perhaps because, being a meat fisherman, I got to eat all of that ten inch trout. Or, perhaps because it was one of the rare times I was free of my tension and duality of self enough to merely enjoy being alive in that place and time. I was just drunk enough to lose my fears and inhibitions without losing myself to my disease. That would come later.

We all had struggled that last semester in law school to find a job. It was more than just a job, of course. It was the start of a career, so the pressure ran high.

One of my law professors whom I admired a great deal suggested how I should go about it.

"The way to get a job is to go out and find it."

"You have to beat the bushes and back roads," he said.

I took his advice literally and made arrangements to meet with practicing lawyers across the State from Supreme Court justices to District Court judges, and small firms from Cutbank to Baker.

It was on that trip that I first met Justice Karla Gray, who would later become Chief Justice of the Montana Supreme Court. Karla was an old Butte girl, and though we differed politically and philosophically at the time, I was enamored by her grasp of political and legal thought and our resulting discussion.

I also applied for an opening at the Tucker Law Firm in Virginia City. I got that job. I worked on a few projects in June, and Reid Rosenthal was not the least among them. He would be a lasting nemesis. However, that first project involved a summary judgment brief in a lawsuit he brought to obtain adverse possession of a road that lead to property he was managing. It was then that I first learned that it was not legally possible to obtain adverse possession as against the government. I had started to work like a lawyer, even if it would take longer to actually think like one. However, I did not begin in earnest until August.

On August 22, 1992, my law school buddy and I, along with a few others, packed up a Uhaul with all I owned and headed out for Virginia City. It was snowing as we set out on Interstate 90 East that morning, which in Montana is not all that unusual for an August day or any other day for that matter. My friend was driving the Uhaul behind me as we passed Anaconda. As I began to climb the hill to Butte, I looked back. With a gathering sense of dread, I could see traffic stopping and a commotion in the median strip between lanes on the interstate.

"He's in a wreck," I thought as I cursed to myself.

I committed that most egregious of interstate sins and turned around across the median and headed West. Miraculously, my friend stood there with all of his parts in front of the perilously still standing Uhaul on the slope of the median. It was surreal like the part in the movie, *Who Framed Roger Rabbit* where the animated figures and actors appear together. It was happening, but I could not put it together as real.

"That old beater pick up loaded down like the Clampets just pulled right out in front of me," my friend said between excited breaths.

"I had to dump it in the middle so I didn't crunch them," he blurted out.

"As I went off into the median, the right front axle broke, and the tire lay down as pretty as you please," my friend theorized.

The effect was to keep the vehicle nearly even and upright.

"Did you get insurance?" He asked.

Inexplicably, I had purchased the insurance that Uhaul always tries to sell you and which I usually decline.

While no one had a scratch, we spent the rest of the afternoon unloading the truck of all my worldly possessions and putting everything back on another truck brought out from Butte. Since we were so close to Butte, we decided to go to Peggy's house for dinner. She insisted that we all spend the night, and she would come with us in the morning.

Dinner was great, and as I started to unwind on the couch I noted on an end table a devotional publication called *The Portals of Prayer*.

I had never read it, so I asked Peggy,

"What is this?"

"It's a devotional book from my church," she said.

I realized at once that we shared an important value of faith that was not part of my marriage to Joanne, which, as a matter of law still existed even though we had separated nearly a year earlier. Peggy and I read the *Portals of Prayer* on and off for many years, but that night we talked late about things spiritual.

"I want someone to grow old with," I said.

She agreed and the seed began to grow.

The next day we all went to Virginia City and unloaded at the Tucker Law offices where I would be staying in an extra room until I found a place. Peggy rode the hour and a half with me as we continued to talk, not small, but the kind of talk which searching souls will make. We made arrangements for Peggy to return the Uhaul.

She asked,

"How will you pay for this? I need to know for when I take it back."

"My American Express card for the miles," I responded.

Then, ever wanting to be liked, I joked to the others, "Geesh, she wants my credit card, and she hasn't even slept with me yet."

It was nothing more, or less, than what we both were thinking. I gave voice to our desire, more as an invitation than the errant remark I tossed off.

I had managed to invite Peggy to a music festival the coming weekend. We spent the afternoon in Ennis listening to music, drinking and just enjoying each other's company. She tried the chewing tobacco that I had taken to and immediately turned green at the proverbial gills.

"Excuse me," she said as she ran to the bathroom.

At the end of the day I insisted she stay.

"You've had too much to drink to drive all the way back to Butte."

"I'll take the floor and you can have the bed."

"Oh, you play guitar," she said as I gave her the office/home tour.

"Yea, I haven't played in a while, though."

"Play something for me," she pressed further.

"Oh, okay," I relented.

James Taylor had been a standby in my repertoire for years, so I sang as I finger picked in D with a base run,

"So goodnight you moonlight ladies, and rock-a-by sweet baby James. Deep greens and blues are the colors I choose, won't you let me go down in my dreams, and rock-a-by sweet baby James."[16]

We had breakfast in Butte at the Hanging Five, owned by Martha, her ex-boyfriend's sister. It was Sunday, so we retreated afterward to Peggy's flat on Granite.

"What do you want to hear," she said as we finished the tour of her place, and she walked toward her neatly organized CD collection.

"I don't know. What have you got?"

"Just pick what you like," I urged, hoping to find out more about her.

She picked something called "Sunday Morning Coffee," a collection by Chip Davis and friends which is as light, warm and inviting as it sounds.

Chapter Six

The End Of Innocence

I can tell by the way you're talking
that the past isn't letting you go
There's only so long you can take it all on
Then the wrong's got a' be on its own
And when you're ready to leave it behind you
you'll look back and all that you'll see
is the wreckage and rust that you left in the dust
on your way to the Jubilee.

- Mary Chapin Carpenter[17]

I bought my first house in late October, 1992, a place that would fit my burgeoning life style. The house on the north end of Sheridan was small. It would have fit easily into the garage. It was off the highway with tall shrubbery in front, secluded, yet only an hour from Butte and Peggy. I thought it fortuitous that among the items she left at my house in Sheridan in our first few nights together were a purple bra and panties. There were weekends when, no matter how exciting, fulfilling or fun the time was with Peggy, I rushed home under the pretense of laundry and preparing for work just so I could wear that bra and panties - just so I could be a girl.

What was it, that, which would not leave? The seeds of love had long since blossomed and grown into a beautiful flower that Peggy and I shared without reserve. Yet, there was another seed in me more like a bulb. It had been there longer, buried deeper and only occasionally exposed to light. It was dormant but still alive.

Peggy and I explored one another that fall, in body and heart. In that ephemeral place we each found a mate. As that reality grew, we were increasingly aware that I was still married. I had to tell Joanne.

Once the affair was out on the table, I agreed not to see Peggy anymore so that Joanne and I could try and work it out. We had not been able to communicate to any significant degree in the twelve years we had known each other, so I was skeptical. Nonetheless, I prayed continually for God's will. Though I had sinned for certain, I could no longer force myself to go through the motions of a marriage which, even if it had once blossomed, had died on the vine.

Joanne and I struggled through the summer of 1993. The kids would tromp off to bed around nine in the log cabin out back that had survived numerous attempts at renovation. It locked from the outside, so, I went out with the kids and tucked them in. Meghan would run from her snug bed, turn off the light and run back. I waited to hear her scurry like a mouse back to its nest before grudgingly returning to the house to talk with Joanne.

"Joanne," I said in a curious twist, "You never talk to me."

"I can't read your mind. I want you to tell me how you feel."

Most men might have been happy with that situation; however, I was not most men. I tried to talk to Joanne about us, our relationship and its failings. She said nothing in response. She merely sat in the living room recliner a few feet away from where I sat on the floor. The house was less than 900 square feet and the living room less than a quarter of that. The closeness of the room in the heat of my hard talk on a warm summer night made the space feel even smaller, constricting even the small reserve of determination I had to try and work something out. I wanted to escape as I always had into Montana's vastness, where all I would feel were the wind and sun on my face.

I felt much like the proverbial dentist hard at work trying to extract words that never came. I felt deeply sorry for her on one hand, but on the other her inability to say anything and I do mean anything, sealed our fate.

"Joanne, I need more. I want a healthy relationship – I want to be a whole person," I finally blurted out in frustration.

While I would be blamed for leaving her, for the affair that wrecked our marriage, etc., I knew that the marriage had failed because we could not talk and therefore, did not grow. It has been said that something which is not busy being born is busy dying. Our marriage died, and along with it our youth and the innocence of our children.

I have often wondered how a modern child could grow to adulthood unscathed by the myriad attacks and temptations heaped upon or lying in wait for the unwary to steal their youth and innocence like a "bunch of thyme away."[18] I had grown up in the days when the myth of the Beaver and his Hallmark greeting card family still seemed possible. I knew my childhood family in all its dysfunction was the antithesis of that ideal, but I still believed it was possible. For a while I even believed I could have that idyllic family. I think the rest of my generation thought similarly, while few realized that so many of us were dysfunctional. One might argue that dysfunctional families in this country are the norm, whether it stems from divorce, alcoholism, abandonment or any of the many other things that adults do to children.

On Labor Day weekend, 1993, I flew to Oregon to see Joanne and the kids, which must have seemed strange to Meghan and Shane. They had left Montana only weeks before. On Sunday I asked the kids to gather around the kitchen table for a family meeting.

"Your mother and I have not been getting along," I ventured.

Then, knowing there was no good way to tell it, I simply blurted it out.

"We're going to get divorced."

They both cried, and asked few questions.

Shane later asked,

"Is divorce a four letter word?"

The truth is that after having tried the previous three months to find something to build on and having failed miserably, I was giving up. In March, 1994, Joanne and I divorced.

Peggy and I resumed with all the more vigor and passion to make up for the love lost. I had found something in Peggy that I had long before given up on, even though I was still only in my thirties. I could give and be reciprocated. I could take in that same vain. I could be honest enough to be angry and sincere enough to cry. We could pray together and laugh together.

When I needed a hunting partner, Peggy came along. Peggy was with me as many dawns broke on a Montana mountainside, red streaks across Charlie Russell skies and the cold air filled with the songs of crying coyotes like a wild village crier sounding for the day. When the balloon payment on my house in Sheridan came due in 1995, I sold it in three days and moved in with Peggy at her house in Pipestone, an hour's drive from Virginia City.

Peggy was my lover and my soul mate. I could tell her everything except that one thing that I thought that she would rescue me from and fervently hoped that she would. When I moved in with Peggy, anytime I found myself home alone her wardrobe became my fantasy land. I could not know the ramifications yet, but that bulb buried inside me was exposed to much more sunlight and began to grow. The chrysalis metaphor is common in trans parlance, and try as I had all my life to repress her, the girl continued to morph inside of me.

By 1995, my father had developed more hang-ups than a hat rack. Many things ailed him, and many pills treated him. He had stomach problems and over time basically quit eating. In July of 1995, we all gathered around him as he lay in a coma. My children were there as were their cousins. It was like a family reunion when we were not at the hospital. We downed more than one bottle of wine.

Dad asked once in his delirium,

"Is this heaven?"

It was an almost laughable notion but for the dire circumstances.

Those were the last words I ever heard him utter after all the hurt and unkind words that had passed between us for nearly forty years. If it were not so tragic, we would have fought over that too. Is this heaven, indeed! No Dad, it was your death bed, and I felt far too close to hell.

In early August, 1996, the old friend from Ashland who had hired Joanne in Oregon called me.

"If you don't do something about your children I will," he stated frankly.

Bob did not mince words, a trait I appreciated as I knew exactly how things were and where I stood.

"I already called social services" he said and I knew he meant it.

Having visited in May for Meghan's 8th grade graduation, I had some idea of how things were with Joanne. To say that the house was a mess would lend an air of legitimacy to its dire condition. It was not okay by anyone's standard. Clutter, garbage and long ignored, if not ruined, household belongings dominated the interior landscape. Meghan took me to her room first.

"Come see my room," she said, presenting an oasis of neatness in that desert of chaos. She had gone to great effort to build herself a sanctuary to escape the wreckage outside her door.

Shane no longer had a room, as his place was so cluttered that the door could not be opened. He slept in a bean bag chair in the living room, which undoubtedly pleased him with unfettered access to the TV. When Shane was young he had not quite earned the mantle of "couch potato" though he was well on his way. We called him "tater-tot" instead. Later that summer, after their annual visit to Montana, I cried bitterly all the way home from the airport laden with guilt. I could not escape the crushing feeling that I had deserted my children, and their mother could no longer take care of them.

"Joanne's drinking got way worse after the divorce," Bob said.

"Well, that figures," I replied, duly self-righteous in my indignation, though inside I knew that my daily habit straddled the same alcoholic line that Joanne in her grief and loneliness had slipped over.

I called and spoke to Meghan. Through subtle questions she admitted that things were bad.

"Mom drinks her beers after dinner, and falls asleep in the chair."

It is ironic that I fell into that same daily habit years later.

"I put her to bed and Shane too," Meghan told me.

It is always that first child, the oldest, the one who takes responsibility for all within the lair of dysfunction, who becomes the hero and champion for the more vulnerable. Meghan was more like my sister, Terry, than anyone but me will ever know. It is not likely the role Meghan would have chosen for herself, but it is the one she courageously accepted and performed with aplomb. She was the Mom, Joanne was the child and in the minds of all concerned I was to blame. Meghan hated me for it and has not forgiven me or forgotten.

"The school board did not renew Joanne's teaching contract," Bob confided, although I knew that he was largely responsible for making that recommendation.

We had talked earlier in the spring so I realized it was the right call. But without work she could not pay the rent. I suspect that they were living off the measly child support payment from me, as well as unemployment and whatever other social welfare funds were available to them.

Joanne was too proud to tell me anything about her circumstances or God forbid ask me for money. I had always called her a martyr, and she wore that mantle like Levon and his war wounds. By August she had lost her job and her home and lived with the children in a dilapidated hotel room in Douglas, just off the I-5 corridor in Western Oregon.

I assumed when we got divorced that a custody action would have killed Joanne and that my chances of winning were not great, as the law in the 1990s still favored maternal custody of young children. Thus, I determined, like Springsteen in *Jungle Land*, to "stand back and let it all be."[19] In truth, though people would not detect it in the person presented to them, I had always been passive in responding to my troubles. For a person making his living in the muck of adversarial proceedings, I hated conflict. I avoided it. I fear it still.

I told Bob as much.

"I will not win a custody dispute," I said, but he was fed up.

"I'm worried about those kids, damn it, so you'd better do something," he said with finality.

Even though I dreaded the coming conflict, when pressed by dire circumstances, I somehow acted.

"It may take you a while to make up your mind, but once you do, you jolt into action," Peggy later observed.

Bob's dire warning to take my children galvanized my resolve to step in. I called Joanne.

"I'm taking the kids to New Jersey to live with my mother," she asserted unilaterally.

"You can't unless I agree, and I don't agree," I protested.

It was hollow I knew, even though those were the terms of our settlement agreement and part of the divorce order. I couldn't enforce them from Montana.

"I do not agree and will not allow you to take the kids," I threatened, although I had no clue at the time just how I could stop her.

I asked to talk to the kids to make sure they were okay.

"Are you alright, Meghan?"

"Yea," she replied haltingly.

"Do you want to go to New Jersey?" I asked believing that they had been told it would be for good.

Again, Meghan simply said "Yea."

"Put Shane on," I said next.

"Shane, what do you want to do?"

"I want to live with you," he said.

"I won't let you down, son," I stated emphatically, stopping just short of finishing with "the way I did before."

I went to work the next day at Tucker Law and formulated a plan with my boss. Loren had not been an overtly loving or caring man. He was far too pragmatic, a throw back in a lot of ways. Having grown up as an Iowa farm boy, he lived as a traditional man. He was polite to a fault, especially to women, when in this day and age it may be viewed as condescending. He was strong and handsome and wore his emotions inside. He was Scotch and proud of it. A nickel was a nickel and should not be wasted. Loren was trustworthy and dependable. If someone needed a hand they could count on his.

So it was when I told him of the circumstances with my children. The call had come in the early hours of a Friday morning. By that evening, Loren had helped me prepare a Petition for Modification of Custody, an affidavit that my daughter would deeply resent for many years to come, describing the dire situation, and a temporary custody order for the district judge to sign. I had arranged to fly into Portland the following day where I would intercept Joanne and the kids before their escape to New Jersey. Her flight did not leave until midnight, Saturday. I had lots of time and needed it all, as the judge was hard to find late on a Friday.

We knew, however, that he could be found Saturday mornings talking treason with his comrades in the dim interior of the Dillon hotel. Shortly after they arrived, a light glowed from within that only grew brighter as they attempted to douse it with amber, bubbly brew. It was ten on a Saturday morning, and that bar was plenty lit up as I walked in to find the judge.

Judge Davis had a penchant for drink. He smoked a pipe too, which caused Loren to wonder aloud,

"He must have an iron constitution."

"Yea," I agreed, again playing as if I knew little about such matters.

Judge Davis wore glasses in the aviator style that limply hung over his ears, barely covered by gray, thinning hair. His scraggly salt and pepper beard and mustache were a fitting match. He spoke gruffly as he would sit in chambers, light his pipe with a wooden match, shake it and throw it in the metal trash can without looking to see if it was still lit or not.

A colleague once remarked, "In the Fifth Judicial District, its malpractice if you *don't* ex parte the judge!"

"It's okay," the judge would say. "I asked you."

Once in a hearing, when I indeed had all the law and facts on my side, Judge Davis remarked to opposing counsel after my closing argument,

"You better have something good, 'cause you're going down like the Titanic."

Yes, I always knew where I stood with Frank Davis.

Unlike my weekly visits to his courtroom, the Judge seemed happy to see me.

"Let me buy you a beer," he insisted before we came to the matter that had mysteriously materialized me like Captain Kirk in such a seemingly incongruous setting.

Having swilled a few with the Judge following trials, I fooled only myself with respect to any conclusion that I drank only to get him to sign the order. The truth is that I liked it.

Alcohol had always been like Lays potato chips to me.

"Bet you can't have just one," I often quipped as I fell daily to that temptation for many years.

Later, I would start out with two beers on the way home, pour a couple of 7-7s once home and could not have dinner without a "couple glasses of wine." I did have two beers with the Judge before I presented my documents to him. He scrawled his signature on the order, as I was most assured he would, having properly argued the matter, ex parte, in that most hallowed sanctuary.

I drove madly to Butte and once safely at the airport, had a couple more beers to steel my nerves. I could sleep it off on the plane after all. Once in Oregon, though, my drinking days were done, for a while anyway. Bob and his wife picked me up at the airport and we drove the hour to his house on the coast.

At dinner she asked, "What would you like to drink - tea, water or milk?"

I drank that most disgusting of substances to any self-respecting drunk, and seriously doubt that my bones became any stronger for it. Got milk indeed! Over dinner the rescue was set.

"I'll take you early to the airport. We can wait upstairs and see Joanne and the kids when they get in the ticketing line," Jan said.

"I'll go and stay with the children while you give her the papers," she said as she laid out a plan that sounded pretty tight.

It worked beautifully, although I knew it was not enforceable. I knew, also, that Joanne would not, could not, know as much. I had called the local police and they stood near "just in case." I knew a Montana court order was not effective in a foreign jurisdiction unless domesticated there, but I had no time for technicalities. I knew, too, that service of process was ineffective unless completed by a nonparty. But, that rule really did not apply in an emergency, right? Here I was a servant of the court, some court anyway, even if not in Oregon. I was sworn to follow the law, but I was not even close here, and I knew it. I felt no guilt or remorse though, as I took those children from their mother and all that they knew of home like a Crusader, all in the name of the greater good.

I learned much later that their mother had not told them that the planned hiatus to New Jersey was permanent. Thus, Meghan believed, believes still, that I unjustly tore her from her home and her friends. Of the many things of which I am guilty as a self centered, dishonest and fear driven alcoholic, uprooting my children from their happy home is not among them.

Or was it? I was aware of their mother's vulnerabilities and habits when I divorced her under the guise of seeking emotional health for us all. Her fall was predictable, and I had turned away. I had convinced myself that it was better for my children to see their father having a healthy, giving, responsible adult loving relationship, rather than remain in the pretense of the marriage between Joanne and me. I was the stronger, dominant and more independent personality. I could make it on my own, while Joanne, in the hidden recesses of her heart, had given herself entirely, without ever whispering even a word of it. She had married for the long run, and I had not. I could walk away, and did. She could not let go and move on. She fell.

We left the airport for the hour drive to their home, me with my victory and righteous sense of salvation for my children and they with their meager bags and tattered souls. The next morning we got a Uhaul, drove the couple of hours back to Douglas and packed their worldly belongings, still damp with the ever present coastal Oregon mildew.

When they moved to Oregon five years earlier I had made a vow to God that I would bring them back, albeit as one family unit. In fact, after my first visit to them in Oregon, I had stopped on Lookout Pass to murmur that oath just over the Montana state line and, to commemorate its solemnity, picked a grainy head of some type of grass that, like a grain of wheat I realized must die before its fruits could be realized. I had kept it in a jar during the intervening five years, and as I came back to Montana with the children excruciatingly silent in tow stopped just over the line to honor the fulfillment of my vow and to pee.

The proverbial dentist with the word pliers reigned supreme with the children during most of the two-day drama. I did not push them, but slowly began to cajole them to life. Predictably, Shane, like me, was quick to respond to humor. Meghan wore her disdain sullenly inside out. She hated me then, and I knew it, although could not for the life of me accept responsibility.

I had to live in Madison County by the end of that year when I would take over as County Attorney. Now, with the children, the need to find a place inside the county line was all the more imminent. Peggy still worked in Butte, so, we would need a place in the northwestern corner of the county to be as close to Butte as possible. As fate, karma, God or all the powers would have it, I had seen a place in Silver Star only the week before that we had called about due to its availability. Now, we would take it if we could.

I called the house design "Early American funk." It had been built as a prefab log house, probably something from a Sears and Roebuck catalogue in the 30s. It had gone through a couple of renovations that stuck out at right angles from the original building. The original rooms were tiny, and the add-ons were huge. The walls were adorned with plaster over slats in some places, drywall in some and painted paneling in others. It was heated by no less than four sources, although the main ones were an old-oil burning furnace and a wood stove.

An old barn-like garage stood just off to one side, clinging to the place like the afterthought it was. The yard was large and had once featured a big garden with a homemade drip irrigation system. The rubber tubing had long since rotted, and I unearthed pieces of it every year with the tiller for the five years I gardened there. I began to feel something I had seldom felt before. It was a bit like happiness, although I would not have claimed it for all the contrary emotions that dwelled just below my surface. I started to call it my "big heart" feeling and those were "big heart" days.

In 1997, Brett Favre and the Green Bay Packers won the Super Bowl. I shot an elk the previous fall and had lain in cords of firewood. I had my family about me once again. My children were the joy of my life, and Peggy was its heart and soul. I was the County Attorney, and by Montana standards, I had a pretty decent salary, more than I had ever made before in any event. My life looked good by all measures.

I enrolled the kids at Twin Bridges School that fall, where they met a brother and sister tandem like themselves. Sarah was Meghan's age, and Liam was Shane's. While Sarah and Meghan maintained a rocky friendship through high school, Shane and Liam were the best of friends and as close as two young boys could be. We stayed at a friend's cabin one late summer weekend on Canyon Ferry Lake just east of Helena. Meghan and I both took a picture of Liam and Shane sitting on a dock as the sun set. It was a captivating photo, memorializing both the mood of the day and their friendship as they turned from boys of summer into young men.

Peggy and I did not drink, at least for the first several months of family life.

"They need to see a sober household for a change," I had said to Peggy as if she was the one that needed convincing.

However, by the time the New Year rolled around I was once again drinking.

One of my first activities as the new County Attorney was to go on a hay ride at Sarah and Liam's house in early January. It was a chili feed, potluck and all around rowdy affair. The alcohol flowed freely as it did on numerous occasions over the next ten years.

The man of the house was an old hand with draft horses. He kept them around I suspect because he was sentimental and loved them. He also loved the occasions of their use, such as pulling the hay wagon for the annual event he put on for his friends and neighbors or pulling felled logs down a mountain side.

"Horse logging," he had called it as I watched in amazement while one draft horse made light work of pulling five trees chained together down the mountain to the waiting truck where we bucked and stacked them as firewood.

I had enough to drink to fall off the wagon, both figuratively and literally. I was still trying to prove myself and ever the chameleon, did what everyone else was doing to the best of my ability. I was good at drinking.

Kids in rural schools, mostly Class C in Montana, at a certain grade level almost inevitably become involved in sports and school activities. For some it is no more than relief from boredom. For others it is a chance at recognition amongst their friends. For still others they just have some innate passion for a particular sport or activity.

Shane tried his hand at speech and drama. I admired his originality, passion and willingness to risk and just be himself. If he had perhaps been less so, it would not have been such a bad experience for him. If he had been encouraged more, he may have kept those traits, but he has long since let them go.

Shane and his friend did a Monty Python skit with a jingle that mentioned something about wearing women's clothing called the "Lumberjack Song."[20] It was well done, perfect really, and bold. But, it was rural Montana where he performed on C School stages. There was not much chance that he would be judged on ability, originality and presentation. It was a comedy skit, for Christ's sake, not a moral commentary. He never did win, unless you count my pride in him at that and many other moments throughout his high school years, including the times he sang "The Star Spangled Banner" at the beginning of basketball games while wearing his basketball uniform.

Shane had struggled mightily during his younger years to excel at sports much as I did. He did not get to start until his junior and senior years in basketball. He excelled at point guard, and I took great pride in watching him play. He was smart and basketball savvy. He was a great passer, so was perfect for the position.

He blew out his knee his senior year at the district tournament just after playing the closest to "the perfect game" he ever got. Shane wrote an essay at school that I helped him with about a player for the Boston Celtics (our mutual favorite) that I had gone to college with, Jim Paxson. The Dayton Fliers played Notre Dame every year and mostly lost to the Fighting Irish and their star, Kelly Tripuca, who also went on to the NBA. Paxson was interviewed before the game his senior year at Dayton and talked about how he strove to play the perfect game. He scored thirty two points; Tripuca did not and Dayton won.

I forget what team Shane played that last full game, the district tournament in Hamilton up the Bitterroot in Western Montana. He was sensational, driving the lane for short pull-up jumpers that no one could defend, and making several steals and assists. He scored twelve points and led his team to a lopsided victory. The thing I was most proud of, however, was his unselfishness and compassion when the route was on. He was open on the right wing for a three- pointer at which he was pretty good. He stole a quick glance at the kid belatedly rushing out to check him and passed the ball to a teammate. Shane could have taken that shot and likely would have made it as hot as he was that night. He would have increased his point total, the overall point margin, and given the radio broadcasters something to talk about for the folks back home, but he didn't. He passed the ball and ran the offense.

The next game, it was all over. A week after that, he had knee surgery.

"Stick to soft foods when you start coming around," the anesthesiologist had warned.

As the nurse rolled his gurney back to his room from the recovery room she teased Shane, who was still under the influence, as it were.

"Do you want anything?" she asked.

"A cheeseburger and a shake would be nice," he said, tongue in cheek.

She brought it, and he ate it but paid dearly for it in constipation pain when we got home.

Meghan's passion was volleyball. At 5'4" or so, Meghan is not typical of the high flyers that pounded the ball straight down from the height of volleyball nets, but she was indeed passionate. She had learned the sport in Oregon from her tall best friend's mother, the volleyball coach. She learned well enough to start as a freshman on an annual state championship caliber team and throughout high school. She especially learned to be a defensive specialist. She could get incredibly low to dig up a hit. She was fearless, and she was coachable.

However, I was never as proud of Meghan as I was during her junior year when she blew out her knee, a family tradition it seems, as I had busted up my knee in college. The team had devised a special play for her where the hitter in the front row would fake hitting the ball as Meghan came up behind and hit it. I was in Twin Bridges that night watching Shane, and her volleyball game was in West Yellowstone, a hundred or more miles to the east. I was called away to the phone with my heart in my throat when I learned that Meghan had been hurt.

That was the first time since the kids were born that they had experienced any serious injury, anything other than the usual cuts and bruises all kids get. I was worried for her.

The injury was early in January, but Meghan played the whole season with a knee brace. She limped and winced, but she played. She never complained. The team went to state that year, and though Meghan would be near tears with pain, she played her heart out. Superlatives are tossed out in sports in our culture as mere platitudes, but by anyone's standards, Meghan was indeed courageous. She had surgery the week after the season ended.

She suffered a great deal of pain following the surgery and had an allergic reaction to the pain medication. I stayed up with her, trying to give her some comfort. I read aloud to her as her mother and I had done with her and Shane every night when they were toddlers. I read from *How the Irish Saved Civilization* for some reason. Subconsciously, I may have been hoping that the Irish in her would give her strength and comfort.

The next day we got a prescription for Fenigren, an antinausea medication. The only form available at MacAlear's pharmacy in Twin Bridges was suppository.

To get Meghan used to the idea of a suppository, I reminded her that I had seen her tush before.

"I changed your diapers when you were a baby, so either you do this or I will."

"Alright, I'll do it," she managed between sobs.

She did and soon felt much better.

Peggy and I went to every one of Meghan and Shane's games throughout high school, except when I was laid up after back surgery. They were often on the same night, literally hundreds of miles away one from the other. We could not both attend them all, so split the duty up. I went one way, and Peggy went the other. Some of the other parents had the same dilemma and resolution. It happened that I would see the same woman at every game, while Peggy would cheer right alongside her husband.

"Soon people will begin to talk," I joked with my new date.

Although I did not realize it, the insanity that is alcoholism was beginning to dominate my thinking and publicly reveal itself. I learned later that an alcoholic is driven by a hundred forms of fear that he or she will lose what they have or fail to obtain that which they desire. I was neurotic in my desire for my children's success. I wanted them to excel at sports, to get the boy or the girl and to be liked and popular amongst their peers as badly as if it were me.

Anytime they did not get to play, did not get a date with the popular girls and guys or had some other stumble, I felt bad, which soon turned to resentment. It is certainly considered normal for a parent to feel bad when their child is hurt or disappointed, but at some point my thinking surpassed normalcy. I was angry and would chew for days on my perception that they were not given opportunities that I felt they deserved or were otherwise jilted or treated badly. I would yell at the sports officials in crowded gymnasiums or disparage the coach in no uncertain terms. I would buy a six-pack and try to drown my resentments on the way home. I could usually down one or two beers on the way home and would have a couple of real drinks once I got there and perhaps a few more before going to bed.

Peggy was our family's source.

"She's their rock," Meghan's counselor had said of her in the fall of 1996 and I knew he was right.

When Meghan returned from her Mother's home after that first Silver Star Christmas vacation, she was, frankly, pissed off. Her mother had shared my accusatory affidavit for the temporary custody order. I tried to talk to her about it, but no matter what I said or how I said it, the words came out badly.

"Your mother couldn't take care of you. You had to put her to sleep, and Shane, too. The house was a total mess."

"Stop dissing my mom," she said sternly, as I thought about Don Henley's lyric,

"Offer up your best defense."[21]

It was indeed the end of innocence.

I tried to reason with her, but to no avail. Unfortunately, I had finally learned to "Think like a lawyer," at least when I talked to my children. I think I learned that from my older sister, Terry. Terry could tell you off in such a manner that you could not argue. I tried too many times. Once, when I thought it might be a good idea to use one of Mom's kitchen knives to dig with, she said,

"Don't play with that. You're gonna' cut yourself."

"I don't have to listen to you," I scoffed at her as if I knew better only seconds before running off howling for Mom and holding a bloody finger.

The scar remains nearly forty years later but did not remind me to have a care with Meghan. Pride go-eth before a cut, and some cuts run deep indeed.

In January, 1997, no one admonished me about the cuts from the verbal knife I wielded with my daughter. Discretion is a great gift, particularly when practiced in a fashion which allows me to know when not to speak. Words are a gift too, but they often become a weapon, even when delivered with the best of intentions. I wanted Meghan to understand and process the divorce. That was my intent as I tried to explain.

Or was it? Isn't it true (I was accused often of cross-examination) that I really wanted Meghan to accept, if not approve, of my part in it all? I wanted her to take my side, to still love and respect me. I wanted her to know that it would all be okay. I wanted to hold again the child I had lost five years earlier. Yet, when I presented Meghan with the facts about her parting from Oregon, especially that her mother had planned on taking her to New Jersey for good whether I showed up or not, she resisted hearing it. She met my calm logic first with tears, then with sobs, then with uncontrollable shaking. As her tremors carried on long after the blowout, I decided to take her to the hospital. She continued with her seizure the entire forty minutes into Butte, much like the febrile seizures she had as an infant.

Meghan and Shane both had many ear infections those first few years in Ashland.

"As a baby's fever rises too fast, more rapidly than the infant brain's capacity to handle it, babies sometimes have seizures," the doctor in Hardin explained.

Meghan did with nearly every ear infection and Shane too sometimes.

"Throw her in a snow bank," the nurse at St. Labre suggested with pioneer wisdom.

That seemed a bit barbaric, even by Ashland's standards. So, Joanne would bathe Meghan in cold water in the sink till her shaking stopped. She would be almost comatose, conscious, but not really there, for hours afterward. It was frightening, especially for new parents. The information I was giving her almost fifteen years later seemed too incongruent for her mind to process. It was me. I was the bad guy, the one who had ripped her from her friends and life in Oregon. It made no difference to point out that her mother was not planning on returning there from New Jersey. It did not matter, as she was not really there.

I was an irritable drunk. I soon took issue with just about everyone and everything, particularly when drinking. I was a card carrying Republican in those days, so was angry at the Democrats. I would raise hell on an issue just to bait Peggy (an avowed Democrat) into an argument.

"You don't support me. Either you're with me, or you're against me," I declared angrily.

Often, when I began drinking before Peggy got home from work, I knew that I would verbally assault her on some innocuous point. I was powerless to stop, and it usually resulted in a fight in which we would just stop talking or one or both of us would end up crying.

"What did I do wrong?" Peggy would often say in frustration.

"Nothing," I said, which only made my behavior even more inexplicable.

The simple truth, however, was that she merely had the misfortune to see alcoholic insanity in action.

In 1997 or so, I discovered the internet. As my cross-dressing had increased in frequency and detail I began to wonder about my sexuality and whether I was gay. It seemed that I was interested in men, so, I started to visit gay porn sites. Peculiarly, pictures of gay men did not arouse me.

On one such visual excursion, though, I made a vital discovery about myself that gave a name to what I felt, had felt inside for most of my life. The site referred to "Trannies" and revealed to me for the first time a pre-op male to female transsexual in all her glory. It was late at night, a weekend when everyone was gone, and I was dressed and drunk, a frequent and consuming compulsion for nearly a decade.

I sensed almost as quickly, the hopelessness of my circumstance, married with high school age children, at once enthralled and horrified by the discovery of my burgeoning true self, a transsexual. I also discovered chat rooms, and sought those that featured cross-dressing discussions. Though I felt that there was more to my feelings than merely dressing as a woman, I enjoyed the chat rooms and the "sisters" I met there. There were regulars, and we became a loose association of sorts. For a deeply boxed transsexual, those chat rooms became a place for me to explore who I really was and an outlet to present that person to others, if only electronically.

Alcoholics do not feel as much as they obsess. Feeling is such a normal, inconsequential thing, but obsession - now that is dramatic. As soon as I realized my hopelessness, I became obsessed with it. I discussed it openly in chat rooms and was either ignored or greeted with equal morbidity. Then one night I heard that familiar Compuserve ring and a new name appeared on my screen with a simple greeting. Sylvia had apparently seen some of my comments and offered an ear to listen and shoulder to cry upon.

"Hello." appeared on the screen. "I'm here if you ever need someone to talk to."

Sylvia was a great listener and very compassionate. She was the first person in forty years to whom I could tell the way I felt, and I did. Through the tears and alcoholic stupor I told her of my marriage, my children, my dressing, my confusion about gender and sexuality and often about how I might reconcile it all with God.

"It's hopeless," I had typed out.

"Listening intently," came back across the screen.

Sylvia listened and encouraged me. She gave me links to sites that might help, that would provide resources and information. She gave me friendship. Whenever I hear Elton John's *"Mona Lisa's and Mad Hatt*ers,"[22] I thank the Lord there are people out there like Sylvia. Because of Sylvia, I was able to say good morning to the night on many occasions where I had typed out all my hopelessness the night before. She saved my life.

I had become the Madison County Attorney on January 1, 1997. I was appointed to the post to fill the term of my mentor and friend, Loren, who had recommended me for the job upon his early retirement buyout. It was a post at which I thrived, if never feeling totally comfortable. I spent all my waking hours in one controversy or another. The fishermen wanted river access and the wealthy out-of-state landowners did not want them to have it. The hospital did not like their administrator. The Sheridan School Board hired a superintendent that I had known in Ashland just before I left. I heard he had been driven out after allegations of inappropriate contact with a student. Here he was in Sheridan, calling me just after he groped the home economics teacher in the closet (I later discovered) to ask if I could come over for a beer. Then there were the criminal cases, the motions and hearings, the trials, the cops to please, the victims to console, the budget to keep and the public eye keeping vigilant watch over all.

I had several high profile cases, which usually meant that someone had died under suspicious or outright gruesome circumstances. *State v. Davis* was a potential death penalty case of the gruesome variety. Under Montana law a death penalty charge must be plead a certain way if the death penalty is in the offing, even if later changed.

George Harold Davis was forty-four and single. He picked up work outside of Ennis at the Bar 7 ranch, purportedly owned by the inventor of the center pivot irrigation system. Judging from the number of those apparatuses up and down the country, I would say that he was a wealthy man. Davis read Nietzsche and gun catalogues. He had a summer romance that ended badly after he weirded out on an unsuspecting British woman, a summer visitor to the upper Madison Valley.

It is a beautiful place with rugged high mountains and a world famous trout fishery. I loved that drive throughout the year. Peggy and I made the trip often, especially early on in our relationship, to see her parents who lived just over the Centennial Mountains to the south in Idaho.

Davis took his jilted weirdness to downtown Ennis on a warm June night. He started drinking early before he began hitting on the young girls returning from college to hook up with old friends. Ennis High School was not very large, and the kids were tight. A few of the boys shooed Davis away from the girls without incident, that is, until closing time. Why is it that 2:00 a.m. at any bar anywhere is the witching hour, the moment of truth in which if something is going to happen, it does happen? The answer, no doubt, is the combination of alcohol and testosterone, without which the course of history and human affairs would be decidedly more peaceful.

George went and got a gun and proceeded down Main Street like the avenging angel he may have perceived himself to be, taking his vengeance on the world for all the slights of his miserably lonely life. He walked through a small crowd gathered down the street from the bar. He walked past them, arousing suspicion in at least one boy who managed to turn before taking a bullet just above his groin. Davis continued to fire at kids up and down Main Street, killing one and severely wounding six. They laid out the decedent in the back of a pickup, which, though the quickest mode of transport to the hospital, grotesquely resembled the prize of a typical Montana hunt.

A year or so after Davis pled guilty in order to escape Montana's death penalty in favor of life in prison times seven, "Dr. Death" came to the fore.

Dr. James Bischoff had been in Lame Deer, Montana at the very clinic where my son was born. Thankfully, it was after we left for Missoula. Bischoff was reputed to have some awfully strange mannerisms. For instance, after he was chased out of Lame Deer, he took up his trade at the Madison Valley Hospital where he was reputed to have sat in the hallway in his underwear for all the staff to see.

I had recently had a run-in with him over his hybrid wolf dogs and his neighbor. He was quite agitated with me, and in truth I had been a bit of a jerk. I still had plenty of testosterone coursing through my veins, certainly way more than I wanted. Not that testosterone necessarily makes a man a jerk, but together with my bag of tricky dysfunctions, it certainly did not help.

"Calm down," I said. "We will talk civilly or we won't talk at all."

I acted so tough, but I had adopted a zero tolerance policy for bad behavior in my office. It was small, with only one means of escape, the door across the room with my visitor in between. I did not dare let things get out of control.

The building was ancient, from the days when Virginia City was settled. A plaque from the Register of Historic Landmarks hung on the rock retaining wall out front. The wall was equally old, as it had cracked in several places where different plants emerged from within. Inside, the wood trim had been repainted using a technique that gave it the appearance of light oak wood grain. It was beautiful. The cottonwoods and pines outside had grown as tall as the three story building. Yet, a picture hung on the wall inside featuring a parade in 1890 down Wallace Street (the main Virginia City thoroughfare) right in front of the building; there were no trees!

"If you don't settle down, you have to leave," I said.

"You can't make me leave. It's a public office," Bischoff retorted.

I said, "I can and I will if you can't be civil."

I picked up the phone and said, "I will call the sheriff if you don't stop right now."

He continued to rant until I began to dial the sheriff's dispatch before I gained control.

Bischoff had written a manuscript in which he, as the main character was a woman. It was part biographic and part fantastic, discussing near-death experiences, etc.

Oddly enough, that prompted me to quip to a colleague,

"He does not want to be with women as much as he wants to be a woman."

While it may have been true, it was a little like the kettle calling the pot black, although I was not yet ready to admit it even to myself.

Bischoff could not abide waiting around for elder, terminally ill patients to die. He thought it a better course to hasten the process. After waiting five days for one such patient to die, he administered lethal doses of Fentanol and Versed to the comatose heart attack victim not once, but twice in a fifteen minute interval.

"She's as strong as a horse," he said as he gave her the second shot.

Moments later, he pronounced her dead.

Many people claimed that he and Jack Kevorkian did nothing wrong in hastening the demise of terminally ill patients. Now, if the patient participates in that effort, I might not have quarreled. But this patient had not uttered a word to anyone for the final five days of her life. In Montana, deliberate homicide is defined as purposely or knowingly causing the death of another human being. In my view, death should not be the unilateral choice of an attending physician. I determined to let a jury decide.

The State of Montana charged Bischoff with the crime, which started a wild, unpredictable spree of circumstances, the avalanche of which swept away Mrs. Bischoff and landed Dr. Bischoff in an Idaho jail for bank robbery. Bischoff lost much and suffered greatly. So did the victim's family, and so did the State of Montana.

In an odd twist in that case, Kent Spence, the son of the notorious Wyoming lawyer with the same last name, joined the defense team. He and his co-counsel showed up in Virginia City one law and motion day like the Second Coming and tried to intimidate me. The shine on Spence's new cowboy boots was as pretentious as that of his braggadocio. I was proud to have none of it.

In a bizarre twist in that case, while out on bail, Dr. D., short for Dr. Death, hatched a bold plan to become a fugitive from justice. He might have gotten away with it too but for one small oversight. On a March day in 2005, Bischoff drove to a small town up the Madison Valley, over Reynolds' Pass and into Idaho about fifty miles. He went to the Rexburg bank just as it opened, where he waited just outside with a suit case. He had a duffle bag, a mask and ski jacket and holstered six guns inside. He donned them, took the duffel and left the suitcase behind.

Bischoff entered the bank with the mask over his face and holsters tied down to his leg playing the desperado. He produced a six gun and demanded the cash. He left with nearly $30,000 in small bills, some of which had been randomly marked. He returned to Montana in a borrowed car, evidently satisfied that he did not have enough cash to live happily ever after on a beach in Mexico where, like the boys from Shawshank, he may have found redemption.

However, as fate would have it, the suitcase he left in Idaho still had his soon-to-be ex-wife's name and their home address on a piece of paper in the pocket for that purpose.

At his bail revocation hearing in the Montana murder case, I put on all the evidence of the Idaho bank robbery, and the judge commented on the overwhelming evidence of guilt even though he was not on trial for that offense, but for violating the terms of his bail.

In a dramatic moment much like the OJ trial, the defense lawyer asked the bank teller,

"How do you know the bank robber was my client?"

She answered calmly and firmly, as one might reply from the depths of their gut with no aforethought, and simply said,

"His eyes."

Bischoff's eyes were remarkably blue and clearly visible through the ski mask. Though it really didn't matter, due to the mountain of evidence of guilt, the defense attorney had committed the cardinal cross examination sin; he asked a question to which he did not know the answer. It bit him with a compelling exclamation point to the bail revocation hearing in which Montana proved Bischoff's guilt for an Idaho bank robbery. And, oddly enough, the only prison time Bischoff will actually serve is in the Idaho State penitentiary.

In a peculiar twist in that case, when I got the news of the bank robbery, I was lying in a hammock at a resort in Palm Key, Florida that my friend the public defender, who grew up in Florida, had recommended. Peggy had planned the trip as a vacation to relieve me of all the stressors in my work. Little did she know that so few of the stresses in my life were work-related. I was deep in the throes of alcoholism and lost in my confusion and duality of self. I spent a great deal of that vacation drinking Corona's with a lime twist, but I do remember the seeming electrically charged atmosphere of Key West and the calming effect of ocean waters.

I did not see many of the flaming personalities reputed to live there, but the evidence of their lifestyle was all around, especially in the art and curios in the little shops and outdoor booths. It was colorful, a photographers delight, and funky at the same time. Peggy, a parrot head at heart, took a picture of me with a parrot standing on my head. I loved the place and felt every bit of my feminine self while in Key West.

In a tragic twist in that case, Bischoff's estranged wife was killed in a motor vehicle accident after visiting him at the Madison County jail. I think she had come to give him copies of her divorce pleadings, along with a change of socks and underwear. Among the many charges against Bischoff were several drug related offenses. It seems he had been such a good customer of the pharmaceutical companies, ordering some 40,000 units of dangerous drugs, that they awarded him with a special trip. Later, he could account for only 32,000 units.

Bischoff's drug of choice was Adderal, a more recently popular choice among physicians to treat Attention Deficit Hyperactivity Disorder. Bischoff and his wife may have been responsible for ingesting many of the missing 8,000 units of this and other drugs and giving the rest away, like the candy man to friends and patients. It was likely that Mrs. Bischoff was addicted to alcohol as well, judging from the accounts that surfaced about her during the investigation involving her drinking a bottle of wine at ten in the morning. At any rate, alcohol was involved in the car accident that took her life.

I had a DUI death case years earlier in which a probationer left his friend for dead in the crumpled passenger seat of his pick up after he missed a curve at a high rate of speed and rolled the truck. It is a common scenario. The vehicle rolls, compressing the passenger compartment. A passenger's head would sometimes be pressed against their chest with the neck bending in a way it was never intended to perform. The impact breaks the neck, collapsing the person's esophagus, and they asphyxiate.

Erstwhile rescuers could hear Mrs. Bischoff's labored breathing as she gasped her last cries for help. It saddens me still to think about, along with all the tragic and bitter ironies in that case. It was a twisted case indeed.

A fortuitous circumstance in both of these cases was my association with John Conner, chief of the Prosecution Services Bureau (PSB) of the state's attorney general's office. The PSB mission was to help county attorneys prosecute difficult cases. In that position, John Conner was the single most experienced homicide prosecutor in the state. I had known John for many years through my work with the Montana County Attorneys Association (MCAA), of which I had recently become an officer. But I had never worked closely with him. It was a treat, as I enjoyed his dry wit.

John was nearing the end of his career, and the office was actively pursuing plans for a successor. They appointed an inhouse lawyer as the administrator of the bureau who had been in the law school class of '84 with Peggy and whom I had known for years also through the MCAA. John and his successor would both play significant roles in my coming transition.

Loren Tucker became the District Court judge in the 2000 election. I had helped as much as I could. I hung signs, wrote letters and made appearances on his behalf. I was happy to do it because I believed in him. I knew he was diligent, fair, thoughtful and intelligent. He did not disappoint once elected.

However, the peculiar thing about the legal system in Virginia City is that Judge Tucker is married to Judge Tucker. Loren's wife, Maryanne, is the Justice of the Peace. In Montana the Justice Court has jurisdiction to hear misdemeanors such that all misdemeanors not joined with felonies were handled in the Justice Court.

"Is the State ready," was a question I heard around nine o'clock on most mornings.

"We are, Your Honor," I replied, echoing in the large, airy district courtroom or the cramped Justice Court chambers.

Loren had once told me,

"If you're not prepared, make it look as if you are," though he needn't have.

I was always prepared, out of fear of failure.

The large courtroom in Virginia City is similar to many across the state that were built around the turn of the twentieth century. The landing stood atop a two tiered cement staircase with a black steel railing. Once inside the heavy wooden double doors, a broad rambling staircase circled to the second floor. By the time I reached the second floor, I often marveled at what good condition I was in.

The courtroom itself was cordoned into sections by a low ornate wooden railing erected between court proper and the audience bench seating. The jury box stood to the right as always as I faced the bench. Counsel tables were long, hardwood antiques that stood at right angles, with the prosecution table directly in front of the bench. I am uncertain of the rule or custom that designated it so but usually arrived early to lay stake to my territory.

The tables were large enough for me to spread my gear out in front of me. I usually came to battle with scripted questions for witnesses' direct and cross-examination. I often marveled at how closely the trial followed the script – so much so, that I wondered about my preparation or exercise of prosecutorial discretion if it did not, harking back to Jim Nugent's words,

"The prosecutor should always win."

The bench stood high, and rose off the ground so that I referred to it as "the stony heights," even though it too was crafted of wood. Judge Davis held forth there when I started my career and then handed the gavel over to Loren upon his retirement. Frank Davis was a character. I took a trial practice class at the law school the week after graduation and he was on the faculty. As I introduced myself and my plans to practice in Virginia City, a booming voice came thundering from the back of the room,

"And may God have mercy on your soul."

While it prompted uproarious laughter, it struck my heart with fear and premonition that Judge Davis would not have mercy on me.

In a typical week I would appear all day Monday in front of Mr. Tucker for the law and motion calendar that I routinely dominated with about ten different cases to be heard each week. On Tuesday, Wednesday and Thursday I would appear in front of Mrs. Tucker, who actually went by her maiden name, O'Malley, for Pretrial Hearings, motions hearings and settlements. It was not a stretch to refer to that part of the Fifth Judicial District as "Tucker Law." It had a certain ring of truth, if not drama.

When I lost in court or perceived a slight from other officials, I stewed. I noticeably chewed on such things for days or weeks at a time, depending on the size of the slight.

"It's just not right," went the refrain in my head.

Occasionally, the running diatribe boiled over into my relationships and interactions with the offenders, at least in my warped view, and got me into trouble.

I had a spat once with Mrs. Tucker, where she blurted out with a sort of self-righteous satisfaction,

"I know what's bothering you. You're insecure."

I could not dispute her statement as much as I had wanted to by saying something like "You're crazy," partly because of her position, but mostly because she was not – crazy. Instead, with feigned confidence, I scoffed at the notion and said only,

"You're wrong."

I had the same kind of run-in with Mr. Tucker, where I could not take "No" for an answer, only in the more formal environs of a hearing. I was interrogating a witness perilously close to a violation of some rule of evidence, probably hearsay.

"Objection," said opposing counsel, "Hearsay!"

"Your honor, momentarily, the trustworthiness of the testimony will be perfectly clear if the court will indulge me," I responded, believing that I had made a "straight faced argument," as Loren had suggested to me as the bench-mark.

"Sustained," the judge said.

Chagrined, I pressed further "May I make an offer of proof, your honor?"

"Counsel," came the reply from the "stony heights."

"I understand your argument. It is not persuasive."

Loren had always suggested that each attorney had a pool of credibility capital with the bench from which they must draw on occasion when the question is close. I had just made a withdrawal with nothing to show for it.

It never occurred to me that a direct correlation existed between the perceived size of any slight and that of my ego, just as it never occurred to me that a similar relationship existed between the resentments I nursed and my irritability and growing unhappiness. The more I chewed on the nemesis of the day, the more unhappy I became. I would have full conversations in my head which sometimes went on for hours or even days. So, I drank and I fought, and I fought and I drank.

Chapter Seven

Tolerance for Pain

Captured Angel
Aching to make your break
Your freedom's at stake
You better fly now . . .
Fly now, fly now,

- Dan Fogelberg[23]

I rang in Y2K with Peggy in an airplane somewhere over Minnesota I think. We were supposed to arrive home from our Christmas visit back East before midnight, but our planes were delayed.

"It may be a good thing if the world as we know it is going to end. Perhaps ours might survive as we were suspended above the coming melee," I suggested to Peggy.

"Or maybe it would come sooner as the particles from micro-waves and satellite signals go nuts all around us," she replied.

Of course, I never really believed anything would happen, but, it made for interesting conversation to speculate about what might be. I once had a discussion around the hot tub with Shane about Y2K. Shane relished philosophical discussion.

"Ah, nothing is going to happen," I said, but wondered aloud about it for purposes of discussion.

"But I wonder how it would be if our electronic, throw-away world just stopped?" I began.

"What would we do?" Shane naturally asked.

A friend had once admired my woodpile in Silver Star.

"It's the mark of a wealthy person," Dolly had said.

The many cords I had cut, split and stacked, almost single handedly, were more the mark of an obsessive compulsive personality.

"We have enough wood to stay warm," I said to Shane.

"I have rifles" I continued, "so we can shoot our meat."

I had collected several just because I wanted them, even though I had one that would suffice for hunting. Though I was selfish, I hit what I shot at.

"We have the garden, too. We can grow or kill all the food we need."

We lived in Montana where game was still plentiful, so in my mind the leap to a nonelectronic world was almost welcome, with the sole exception of the computer, that is. The internet was the only link to life for that "other" self hidden from the entire world in a box I brought out only when alone.

My wig was so lifelike that I felt as if I was stowing my true self painfully deeper each time I placed it in its box and put the lid on. When could I come out of my box? When could I live, I often wondered with hopeless demoralization.

"I want so badly to connect," I typed out in the cross-dresser chat room.

"I know what you mean," several of the others replied in unison.

The Goo-goo Dolls, _Iris_[24] came to mind as I typed out,

"I just want someone to know who I really am."

The turning of the millennia also marked the onset of acute back pain. Though I had suffered chronically for many years, all the hard physical activity and stuffed emotions began to take their toll. In 2001, I had an anterior discectomy and lumbar fusion at the notorious L5-S1 level. I had suffered pain down my legs since my twenties and sharp shooting pain in my low back in my late thirties. "Bird back" I had called it, referring to the injury that ended Larry Bird's career. I had given up many activities as a result, including basketball and running, which had been great release activities throughout my life. It just hurt too much, and I realized that all the pounding was probably making the problem worse.

I spent months prior to surgery in physical therapy and in medical tests, some of which were painful by design.

"We want to recreate the pain," the orthopedic surgeon had said about injections with saline solution, "so we know for sure we have the right disc."

It seemed a bit barbaric, and though the room was anesthetized to be certain, it felt barbaric too. I cried, and the attending nurse said to me in sympathetic tones, although it did not give me comfort,

"You do not have much tolerance for pain do you?"

I had been in chronic pain every day for several years and much more acute pain recently, so naturally I was incredulous. She had no idea what kind of pain I endured, both in body and in spirit. I simply said "No," as I continued to cry.

I am continually awed by what a marvelous organism the human body is.

"We are fearfully and wonderfully made," Pastor Wold had quoted many times from Psalm 139.

It was a favorite Bible quote that I often posted on internet profiles. Our ability to cope with disease is remarkable. I was diagnosed with degenerative disc disease and surgically treated and medicated. I had the same problem in my cervical spine a few years later, and the same resolution.

Ironically, both of my initial doctor visits were precipitated by what I refer to as fake heart attacks. I had all the symptoms including pain and numbness on my left side, dizziness, accelerated heart rate and blood pressure, etc. On the first occasion, Peggy and I had gone for a weekend excursion to Red Lodge, a ski resort town in Southern Montana. We had enjoyed our visit there a couple years earlier on our hot springs, gourmet tour-of-Montana honeymoon.

In February, 2001, we returned to celebrate Chinese New Year, as we had done in our courting days at a restaurant in Great Falls several years earlier. I think we both wanted to recreate some of the magic that my drinking had etched away, although no word of the sort had passed between us.

We enjoyed the buffet very much, and I bought expensive white wine to wash it down.

"Would you like some wine?" I asked rhetorically as we always had wine with dinner.

I fancied myself a wine connoisseur. Peggy often paired types of wine with dinner, drawing on her knowledge of such things.

"Let's get a red and a white," she suggested.

"The red will go with the beef, tomato, pepper Chow Yuk," she said.

It was a favorite she often made at home.

"And," she continued, "I think a Gewürztraminer would go well with the sautéed veggies and rice."

I twirled the glass looking for the thickness of the drips as if it really meant something to me. The pungent smell of wine almost makes me nauseous today, but I enjoyed the heady, organic odor then. Yes, I was quite the connoisseur, that is, until the first sip. After that I drank the wine so fast and in such amounts that I could scarcely name a single variety even the next day.

"Let's go work out." Peggy suggested the next morning.

The hotel had an exercise room just off the lobby. I hopped on a stationary bike and began pedaling with nary a thought about what kind of shape I was in or my habits. In my drinking days I featured that an occasional cigar with a glass of brandy was suave and debonair, although, like Tina Turner, I never did anything "nice and easy." Similarly, I must admit that I never did anything I like only occasionally, unless of course, you conclude as I did that every day is a new occasion.

I had once heard that alcoholism is characterized by an inability to stop, which seemed ludicrous to me. I reasoned that if alcoholism was the chronic, progressive and fatal disease that recovery advocates espoused, the principle factor of which was an inability to control the main symptom, then you faced certain death with no hope of a cure once you were afflicted. I could not understand that it was actually an apt description, that I was well on my way and that relief would never come through my own efforts. And I wasn't even looking for relief.

Thus, I reasoned further that if I made a conscious decision to stop drinking every day that I was not an alcoholic. Likewise, I reasoned that as long as I could keep count of my drinks, I was not drunk. I stopped drinking after six or eight drinks every night, usually right before I passed out in the recliner. I shudder to think how lonely that must have been for Peggy and how tormented she was with agonizing doubts about her own behavior when in truth mine was so erratic.

I was an out-of-shape drunk who could not see the truth for all the lies I had told myself. After about ten minutes on the exercise bike, I mentioned to Peggy,

"I'm feeling light headed."

"And my chest hurts."

She asked "Are you alright?"

"I think so," I said.

I felt numbness and pain down my arms, so I gave it up, thinking I was just out of shape and it would soon pass.

"I'm gonn'a go shower," I said.

The pain persisted, as did the dizziness and numbness. All the symptoms remained hours later as we neared Livingston.

"I love all the antique shops and art galleries here," Peggy excitedly suggested as we got off Interstate 90 West.

"I'm not feeling well. Let's go." I said as we sauntered through the third store like a couple on a Viagra commercial, still dizzily in passionate love after years of marriage.

"Still dizzy?" Peggy asked, torn between her concern for me and her doubt that it was anything but a hangover.

As we arrived at the interstate exit on the east side of Bozeman, where a little blue sign with an "H" heralded the presence of a hospital, Peggy looked at me as I at her.

Peggy was driving and asked, "Should we get off here?"

"Yes," I agreed that it might be best.

It was early afternoon at the Bozeman Deaconess Hospital emergency room where I sat at the admission desk.

"Name, address?" the clerk demanded with a lilt at the end of her sentence.

"Do you have an insurance card?" she queried, "I'll have to make a copy of it for our files."

"Be right back," she said as she took the Blue Cross - Blue Shield of Montana card I fished out of my wallet that more resembled a woman's bi-fold check book than it did a man's' typical folding wallet.

"What can we help you with today?" she brightly asked as she returned and handed the card back to me.

"Well," I said, "I'm light headed, short of breath and have pain and numbness going down my left arm. And my chest hurts," I said, describing my symptoms as faithfully as I could.

"I have to find a nurse. I'll be right back," she said.

"Oh, that's how you get action around here. Tell them you're having a heart attack," I whispered to Peggy.

She was not amused. I could see a nurse in the ER scurrying around, not with panic, but calm dispatch and purpose. She pulled back a curtain and announced,

"This one's empty, bring him in here."

"Lay down here," she directed without so much as a "how do you do?" as she pointed to a gurney.

"Let's get a drip going," she said, obviously in charge.

"And Nitro," she asserted as she grabbed my left hand in search of a vein.

"They always have an easier time with the right arm," I said as I knew what was coming.

She quickly found a vein and I felt something cold coursing up my arm.

As she hooked up the electrodes for the EKG, I thought of the fifth grade and failure and tests, that while lavish in their attention, had ultimately betrayed me. They would not expose, nor cure the real problem inside of me then or now. By night-fall the medical team began to discuss an angiogram, even though the EKG did not indicate a heart problem.

"We can't be sure," the nurse said, "But we can't do the angiogram here. You have to go to Missoula."

I thought that was overkill, but Peggy supported their advice. They put me on a life- flight plane to Missoula. At 6:00 a.m. the second day of the Chinese New Year a white haired man wearing a starched, pressed and monogrammed white dress shirt and dark slacks walked into my hospital room at St Pat's in Missoula. Here, obviously, was the heart specialist.

"I'm going to make an incision high on your right leg into your femoral artery and thread a camera through the artery to your heart valves to check for blockage and examine the muscle itself," he explained as I lay in the semi-darkness staring at his monogram, an "R" with ornate olive branches on either side circling the letter.

"There are risks, including death," he went on in a no nonsense fashion.

This guy was all business, but I did not hear death as very likely because he was a heart specialist, and I had always had a sort of blind faith in doctors.

"Do you think it's your heart?" he asked.

If I did not think so upon first checking into the hospital the day before, the treatment since had frightened me to a sufficient degree by the next morning that I believed it was.

"Yes," I said.

The nurse came in to shave me, and though I was anxious about what she would see, I was far too concerned with my present circumstances to be embarrassed by the fact that it had already been done.

"Oh, you're already shaved?" she asked with a mix of bemusement and curiosity in the up-tick of her voice at the end of her sentence.

I simply responded, "Yes," believing that no further explanation was necessary. If only I could have been as confident in my self image and as unconcerned about the impressions of others when I was young, my life might have been different.

I had shaved my genitals for years simply because it looked more feminine in panties, even if I left the hair on my lower legs. Peggy caught me once shaving in her tub before we were married as I hurriedly ducked under the water. She asked with an innocent sort of acknowledgment of the obvious,

"Are you shaving?"

So, I said "Yes," and there was no more said until a few years later when she found a pair of her panties on the floor by my side of the bed, one which we both realized she did not often wear.

"Were you wearing these?"

I did not lie. We were lying on the bed and she quickly felt my legs, as by then I would occasionally shave them completely.

"And you shave your legs, too?" she demanded.

"Yea, I like the feel of it," I mumbled in reply.

"It's some sort of sexual thing, isn't it?" Peggy demanded.

I had wanted to tell her the truth then, but her comment had a chilling effect that would take a couple more years to thaw. I had to be thoroughly beaten down by my secrets and broken-ness to sense that the risk of revealing myself was not nearly as bad as the pain of hiding before I had a chance of becoming honest.

The doctor gave me a local, and I fixated on the monitor as he looked at my heart. When he finished, he said rather disgustedly,

"You've got the heart of a twenty-year-old."

I was amazed and quite frustrated as once the emergency had passed, I was left in my room all day while Peggy and the kids awaited a verdict with me. Although I basically knew the outcome, the delay was much like the jury trials I had done as a prosecutor waiting for those twelve people to return a decision on the fate of a defendant. To me it was more of an indictment on my performance if it was not guilty and recognition of my exemplary skills if it was guilty. I took everything to heart.

The doctor's recommendations here were more likely to be an indictment on my life style choices than any physical malady. I grew so agitated that by evening I pulled the electrodes off and got dressed to leave and would have if the doctor did not arrive and prescribe Lipitor for my high cholesterol and set me free. Peculiarly, during all my medical treatments then and since, no doctor ever inquired about my drinking, nor advised me not to. I told myself hundreds of times that if any doctor had told me to quit drinking that I would have. I would have tried.

My symptoms of pain and numbness did not subside, so my family doctor recommended a series of different tests to identify the problem by ruling out other problems. I had a bone density test, which was cool because I knew it was pretty much of a test for women. If I could not live honestly, I would live vicariously. He recommended another test that is commonly used with women, an ultra-sound. Peggy went with me to see the technician who performed the test. I was glad it was a woman. Secretly I hoped, just as I had when I was young, that she would see what was really wrong with me and have compassion. I strongly hoped and wished that she would find a uterus or something that might explain to the world that I was really a woman.

September 11, 2001, revealed another of my great character defects. I was extremely judgmental. Someone once made the mistake of telling me that I was a good judge of character. Thence-forth, I practiced the art as some sort of divine calling on everyone and everything, usually finding others wanting in some regard. Peggy and I had just moved to a new house, and Meghan was off to college in Missoula. I left for work early that day, listening to NPR on the radio as I drove.

"A small plane has crashed into the World Trade Center in New York," said Carl Castle in his trademark, droll monotone as if it were a mere footnote before commenting on other news and features on Morning Edition. My little Toyota T-100 could not get NPR's signal in the Ruby Valley, so I thought nothing more of it. It was not until I arrived at work forty minutes later that the details of a terrorist attack began to emerge.

As the day wore on, more details emerged. Patty, my secretary, and I became worried, as did all of America and perhaps the world. The images and news began to stream across the computer in a procession that was so shocking that all I could do was stuff it in, as there were simply no words to say.

That night I was angry and after my daily dose, decried and hated all Muslims wherever they may be. Peggy had a gift for seeing the best in people. She seldom said a negative word about someone else, and though it annoyed the hell out of me, I admired that trait of her character. She learned it from her mother, who was equally free of judgments. I could not know it then, but it was that gift in both Peggy and her mother that has allowed me to keep them both as part of my life today.

The more vituperative I became, the more Peggy tried to point out that there were likely as many good persons among Muslims as there were among any other religion.

"Yes, but Islam spawns these terrorists and they have to take responsibility."

"And should the Catholics take responsibility for Hitler?" she replied rhetorically, trying to get me to see how little sense my argument made.

"Yea, but if there are good Muslims, why don't they speak out." I said as a statement, really thinking like a lawyer now, at least in my mind.

You would think I would have had a more intuitive sense of the chilling effect of fear. Peggy was right, of course, but I was drunk and running in front of a full head of the steam of national righteous indignation. We had words. I retreated to the greenhouse and cried bitterly.

"Can we play catch?" Shane asked later, as he looked at me imploringly as if to ask of the world that it spin on its axis as it had before.

It would never again do so, but at least Shane, in his beautiful purity of heart would recognize a simple act of normal life as the best that we could achieve at that moment.

We played catch, as we had on hundreds of occasions previously, as I would give anything to do again. There is something about baseball, for those who love it, which is as essential to life as breath. Perhaps that is why the people of that ilk are wont to say that they "live and breathe the game." I do not know that I was one of them entirely, but I do know this - it was the elixir for my bruised relationship with my father and a strong connection between Shane and me. I wonder now if he waxes wistfully at the thought of it as I do with more than a single tear. I pray that I will have the chance to ask him one day.

They say that alcoholism is a disease of the mind and body. The alcoholic becomes obsessed with "stinking thinking" and craves booze for relief like anti-itch medicine. My insane thinking became an insatiable itch that, though I may scratch it often, never went away. My thinking became the disease and alcohol the cure. I developed patterns of resentment, anger and judgment, reacting to people with whom I took issue. At work, I resented the judges who decided against me on motions and in hearings. I developed grudges for perceived slights from other elected officials and members of the public at large. If the offending party owned some type of business, I would swear to myself that I would never patronize them again. I was running out of local places to shop.

"How do you keep from getting grudges?" I once asked my former mentor, Judge Tucker in an all too rare personal moment in his chambers.

"I avoid them," he confided.

"If there is going to be a grudge, the other guy will have to do all the work," he insisted.

Again, Loren's wisdom was sound and his advice sage. Yet, it did not change my thinking, for I had lost all capacity to control my thoughts. They often went from bad to worse to despair.

Chapter Eight

Be not Afraid

I used to think of myself as a soldier
Holding his own against impossible odds
Badly outnumbered and
caught in a crossfire of devils and Gods

- Dan Fogelberg[25]

I had bitched a lot about what others were or were not doing. One of the people I bitched and moaned about was the Montana Attorney General who was responsible for half my salary. I complained so much that I felt guilty and decided to get involved and showed up at a board meeting of the Montana County Attorney's Association. In a tweak of fate, the Attorney General's successor in the Lewis and Clark County Attorney's office, stationed in the State capital, Helena, nominated me for an at-large position on the board.

The following year, I became the treasurer. The position involved two principle tasks. First I had to give a financial report at two meetings each year, a report that was prepared by the firm we hired to administer our association. The second task, for which I was a natural, was to see to it that the stores in the hospitality room at our annual seminar were well stocked. Oddly enough, I did not drink very much at those meetings. I labored under the guise of responsibility; however, the real reason I tried to stay sober was that I had acted so foolishly in previous years that I did not want to let people see how much of a drunk I really was. As treasurer, I was on the ascendancy schedule to become president of that ignoble organization, a position that my mentor and predecessor, Loren, had occupied years earlier. Thus, I knew what the job entailed and sought that feather to fan my still rising star. I could be grandiose.

One of the good things the association did was lobby the legislature for passage of bills that affected county attorneys and the work we did. Every crime bill fit that category. In 2005, the legislature was contemplating a bill that I was asked to appear and testify on before the Senate Judiciary Committee. I've forgotten what is was about, but I arrived early and signed up as a proponent. I noticed that the hearing following mine involved hate crimes legislation that sought to extend criminal sanctions in violent crimes for those perpetrated against persons based upon their sexual orientation, gender identification and disability. I got in line for my hearing at the appropriate time and introduced myself as the Madison County Attorney before giving my testimony on the bill. When the hearing ended I decided to stay for the hate crimes hearing.

I did not intend to testify, so just sat in the back. However, in a state with small numbers like Montana, it is sometimes hard to escape notice as a county attorney. I should have known better, and I suppose I did, but my curiosity on this topic and my ability to remain hidden in the clothing of a conservative Republican were coming closer and closer to colliding. I was denying vehemently that which I was merely unconscious to.

One of the proponents who testified was the director of Montana's statutorily mandated protection and advocacy program for persons with disabilities. She was beautiful, but it was her testimony that floored me.

"A boy at my son's school began to threaten and harass him because he thought he was gay just because he acts and dances," she began.

I noticed her dark hair and features set against her red wool jacket and gold jewelry. Her quivering voice was all the more endearing as she spoke.

"He is not gay, but that is not what this boy thought. He picked on my son because he perceived him as gay," she said, choking with emotion.

"My children and family were traumatized," she concluded, her voice now a crescendo powered by truth.

Her story was powerfully delivered and left a horribly empty feeling in my gut. When she was done, I wanted to hug and hold her, to console and tell her that I understood and it would be different.

I listened also to the opponents decrying with religious fervor what seemed like a just measure. One reverend, a Bible-toting evangelical preacher, was evidently a proponent of hate inasmuch as he opposed legislation designed to prevent it or provide recriminations for its practice. A representative of the Catholic Diocese took the same position. Oddly enough, both of them spoke in the name of family values. I never understood the connection between "family values" and judgment, condemnation and exclusion. These are not the family values that I was raised with.

The Reverend, Harris Himes of Hamilton, produced a well-worn newspaper clipping from far back in the last century depicting a transsexual in Times Square who was a pedophile. He produced another such sensational article that asserted transsexuals dressed up so that they could venture into the women's restroom and indulge some voyeuristic fantasy. While I concede that I have ventured into the previously mysterious and unknown reaches of that singularly feminine domain, it was merely to relieve myself and of absolutely no prurient interest whatsoever.

Also, while I am most assuredly of the "-holic" variety, I am not a "-phile" of any sort. I must admit too that friends have accused me of being a "shoe whore," a designation that applies with equal conviction to my daughter. I have not yet been able to tell her that a distinct benefit of male-to-female gender transition is that I "get" shoes. The only things a person can see under some stalls in the women's restroom are shoes, and I admit that I peaked, often with jealousy.

Imagine my surprise when one woman in the next stall commented on my shoes.

"I love your shoes, where did you get them?" she said.

"They're *Clarks*," I said of my favorite brand.

"There's just something about red shoes," I concluded about their color.

After the opponents finished spewing vitriol in the name of a loving God, the Senate Judiciary members were allowed to ask questions of witnesses. They could also call informational witnesses to offer clarification on points they thought important. This is what I should have foreseen but did not.

"Mr. Chair, I would like to call Mr. Zenker as an informational witness," said one senator.

"Is Mr. Zenker still here?" the chair inquired as I meekly raised my hand.

"Would you be willing to testify as an informational witness, sir?"

I nervously consented and slowly approached the podium as if approaching God on judgment day.

"Mr. Chair, I have just a couple of questions," said the senator rising to the moment.

"You may proceed," the chairman barked as I marveled at the formality of it all.

"Mr. Zenker," the senator asked, "couldn't people who commit these so-called hate crimes while committing assault be prosecuted under existing law?"

It was logical and I wanted to dodge it, but could not. I was torn because I wanted to support this legislation, and I knew where his question was headed. I wanted to support this legislation for all that I felt inside, for all the pain and trauma that the woman had just described, and I suppose somewhere, deep inside, for all that I might become.

I stalled by recognizing the chair, the quality of the inquiry and the adroitness of the senator asking the question. I stalled until the chair said with a bit of an edge,

"Mr. Zenker, just answer the question."

I said "Yes."

I was crestfallen and for the first time in my life, felt empathy for Judas Iscariot.

As 2005 continued to evolve, I did too. Although I did not realize it at the time, a spiritual shift was beginning in me that would soon become a ground swell. I was deeply and profoundly affected in April as the world watched Pope John Paul II slowly, agonizingly, pass away. I had come across EWTN Catholic Radio on my Sirius Satellite radio long before then. I listened to the Mass and recitation of the rosary on my way to work many times. I tuned in as many across the world waited for the saint to ascend.

I listened intently to EWTN on my way to a turkey hunting trip in Ashland. I encountered a heavy spring snow storm. Since I had driven the better part of a day, I decided to stay and hunt anyways. I sat in a blinding snow storm the first day, ridiculously calling for Tom turkeys as the wind howled all around me. It was just another lovely Montana spring morning. I kept hearing one particular song on EWTN throughout the day as I drove the familiar hills of Custer National Forest by Ashland that I knew like the back of my hand.

"For the sake of his sorrowful passion and the sins of the whole world have mercy on us."[26]

The melody was mournful, and the singing angelic. It became my mantra, as I could not escape the weight of my own sins no matter where I went.

The Pope finally passed after I had been home a few days. I was building a work bench in my green house. I was drinking a beer as I always did when I worked outside, or did just about anything else for that matter. I liked to build things out of recycled wood. My theory was that I could cut down on consumption if I used material already introduced into the stream of commerce. I doubt that Montana's waning wood services industry shared my enthusiasm for conservation, but I did want to do my part.

The wood for my bench came from an old barn on the ranch of one of those notorious out-of-state landowners who happened to own the Winston Rod Company, purveyors of fine fly-fishing rods. I had known many of the people who worked there. Liam and Sarah's Mom, Leslie, worked in the front office, but many of the Twin Bridges inhabitants took on lesser tasks like rod wrapping. The rods were made from bamboo and had to be wrapped, I suppose to hold them together.

Liam and Sarah's Dad, my friend and drinking buddy, was a building contractor who did remodeling work. He knew that I worked with recycled material, so he offered me the wood if I would do the deconstruction work. He got the better of that deal, but I enjoyed the work and wanted the material that would otherwise just be discarded or burned for fire-wood. I have an end table by my bed that I made of oak salvaged from his kindling pile next to the old wood- burning stove in his kitchen. The favorite of Montana's wealthy out-of-state sons, Ted Turner, was a contributor to my growing collection of used wood as well.

The wood for the bench was rough-cut dimension lumber from long ago, so long that the dimensions were true. A 2X6 was actually two inches thick and six inches wide. These days dimension lumber comes a half inch smaller than the stated dimensions. The bench was solid, and the greenhouse became a sanctuary for me during the next year.

I was so moved by John Paul that I bought a book of photographs of the Pope and cut out and framed some of the ones I liked the best. I hung one of him dressed in a beaded rawhide shirt stepping from a teepee in the American West in the bedroom by the computer and in the greenhouse, one with his head bowed and hands folded in prayer like the old man in the painting, *Our Daily Bread*.

I wrote these words:

The death and funeral of Pope John Paul II is profound, if not miraculous. The passing of a single man has only once before focused the entire world on God. Even the media can hardly refrain from evangelizing. The life of this simple, humble, yet brave and strong man who changed the world has now moved the world. Among his first words as Pope were, "Be not afraid." That simple phrase led Lech Walesa to proclaim solidarity in John Paul's homeland. That movement shook communism and its oppressive ways to its very foundation, ultimately resulting in its collapse. But, the Polish Pope did not stop there. He crisscrossed the globe appearing before more people than any other human being ever had before. He proclaimed the gospel by his very life. He held firm to church beliefs and doctrines to the chagrin of many. Yet, he rejected no one. He embraced all of humanity and bridged many of the gaps of the ages.

When he lay on his death bed, he not only blessed and thanked those around him, he reached out to us all saying, "I have looked for you. Now you have come and I thank you." As he spoke those words to us, was his not the voice of Christ saying the same to him and to us all? Now he is gone. Many feel lost. Yet, from the side of God we hear him say, "Be not afraid." God bless Santo John Paul II, the great.

Was I beginning to stir spiritually, or had I just become so spiritually bereft that something had to give? I did not know it at the time, but if I was to survive the coming year, I would need that kind of encouragement and more.

Chapter Nine

Here I am Lord

And there was a new voice
Which you slowly recognized as your own,
That kept you company as you strode deeper and deeper
Into the world, determined to do the only thing you could do
Determined to save the only life you could save.

- Mary Oliver[27]

Montana's wildlife has always captivated me. Whitetail deer and mule deer are everywhere, even inside the cities and towns. I have petted buffalo, shot a bull moose and watched a bobcat sitting on a stump for several minutes not ten yards away. I saw a wolf run across the interstate before they were "reintroduced." I share with many a belief that the wolf was never totally gone from the Montana wilds. This one, however, was just east of Butte on the Continental Divide. Once I sat against a tree stump on the banks of the Jefferson River, and a small bull moose walked up and stood for fifteen minutes within arm's reach. I just sat there spell-bound and even a little nervous about what it might do once it realized I was there. When it appeared that it never would move I spoke to it.

I am not one to personify animals and their actions, but the look on that animal's face when I said hello was priceless. It reminded me of a game I played in college called Sardines. I tended bar at a place called the Shed and shared a two bedroom apartment with a co-worker named Morris. He was a player and often entertained one girl at the bar, while his high school sweetheart waited upstairs as he talked with another on the phone. He asked for help once, but I refused. It was far too entertaining to spoil.

"Sardines" was a bar game of sorts where one person would hide and several would search. When someone found the person hiding they would crawl in with them. As each person discovered the growing secret hiding place, they would pack in like a can of sardines. The Shed had a fireplace several feet wide with a large mantle above where I lay in waiting. Because of the bright light given off from the flames, I could not be seen at all in the darkness above, even by everyone who sat at the table right below me, having given up the search and returned to drinking. I waited a half hour or so until my body began to cramp up before I began talking to them. They jumped in horror in the very same fashion as that moose on the Jefferson.

I have watched hundreds of eagles in flight, and like a spirit animal, they speak to my soul of freedom and strength to be. Like John Denver suggests, I am richer for it. In that same vein, the mountains of Montana are my Rocky Mountain High.

The locals use a term that may seem racist but only in the most complimentary fashion. The term "Indian up" means to sneak within shooting range of an animal. I had learned to walk on well-worn stock trails or fresh snow, so that I have been able to "Indian up" on bedded cow elk a few times. I could not do so with bull elk but have done so with bedded whitetail bucks several times.

Once, in Eastern Montana, I came upon on a bedded whitetail buck by walking around the side of a bare hillside with no dried, dead plants to step on, setting off a crackling alarm sounding far ahead. I got to within several feet and stood stock still. Its eyes were open, but it seemed entranced. It was a warm, lazy October afternoon, and I wondered if deer sleep with their eyes open. He too spooked like hell once I spoke to him, as well as four other nearby bucks.

I went hunting for the first time when I was about twenty three. I am not sure why, but as I look back it seems another of those "guy" things that I did because all the other men did. Also, I had this notion of self-reliance that required a hunter-gatherer mentality. I wanted, no probably needed, to do those sorts of things for my own self image as well as for the sake of appearances. This one, however, I continued to pursue passionately for twenty five years.

My first deer was a mule deer "forky" buck in Eastern Montana. It was a rather ugly kill and probably illegal, as I think it was taken on private property. (The statute of limitations has long since expired.) The people that introduced me to hunting could get pretty crazy about it. They were "road" hunters, which involved driving around till an animal had the misfortune to appear in view. Brakes were slammed as doors swung wide. Would-be assassins piled out of trucks with guns a-blazin' and often the motor still running. I did not like it.

I preferred to still hunt, a method that involves walking very slowly and stopping frequently to spot game. Usually, they would be staring back at me before I spotted them, if I saw them at all before hearing the sound of hoofs on hard ground as they spooked. I love to hunt during a snow fall. Low pressure and falling snow covers the major hunting sins, like walking too fast or stepping on branches broken off in other storms. It brought to mind Psalm 51,

"Wash me and I will be whiter than snow."

That Psalm resonated with greater-than-your-average Catholic guilt and shame. I prayed it often when feeling particularly morose and guilt-ridden over my proclivities. Fortunately, the grace and beauty of a snowy, Montana forest kept me from dwelling long on those thoughts. In the hills, as we called them, it did not matter what my religion or gender was. There I could be closer than anywhere else to what I imagine God sees when God looks at me - a spirit which, although lost and broken, is beloved. "I lift my eyes to the hills from where my strength comes." (Psalm 121)

It is harder for the young to realize that no matter how good or bad things are, they are going to change. People change, or move away, or die. We get better or worse. Our passions cool and our interests change. I had always heard that hunting was about camaraderie, but just about the time I got used to a hunting partner some such inevitable change would occur, and I would end up hunting alone. Over the years though, two such persons stand out, Tony and Peggy's father, Robert.

Tony was Polish and hairy. He could grow a beard in days, while it took me months to grow a scraggly patch that passed for one, barely. I was balding, and Tony had a constant crop of thick, dark hair that no matter how he tried would never quite stay combed. We both loved the film *Jeremiah Johnson*, and could recite nearly every line.

"Watch your top-knot." I would say as we parted,

He would respond in character, "Watch yor'n," as if I had enough hair to be mindful of.

Tony was so effervescent, warm and friendly that when I first met him in the early eighties, I was sure that he was gay, homophobic and attuned to current stereotypes as I was. Yet, Tony engaged the entire world similarly, with a smile and a hug or handshake. Tony came to Ashland as a Jesuit Volunteer a few years after me, and in my typical fashion, I immediately judged him, found him lacking, (in what way I cannot now say) and dismissed him. I have learned since that my first impressions of a person are usually negative and frequently wrong. I have never been so grateful to have had the opportunity to arrive at that conclusion as I am with Tony. He is simply one of the most pure and authentic persons I have ever known. Tony became my friend, and I loved him. I love him still, although we have spoken only once since I came out.

I cannot think of Tony without remembering the time one of the nuns asked me to participate in a church service by walking in the church and intermittently stopping to sing a cappella, "Here I am Lord." I was far too afraid to do it on my own.

"Tony, Sr. Faith wants me to do this song in church – solo. Will you do it with me?" I had pleaded.

He gladly accepted, and we did it together. It was not the last time he helped alleviate my anxieties about life and its attendant circumstances.

Here I am, Lord. Is it I lord?
I have heard you calling in the night.
I will go Lord, if you lead me.
I will hold your people in my heart.[28]

After all the time, miles and changes, I hold Tony there still.

Though I loved him only as a good friend, he once aroused in me something else that I had never experienced. We had gone camping in Yellowstone National Park and decided we needed to wash off some of the grime and campfire smoke. We stripped and dipped in the Lamar River. Tony showed me the Indian trick he had learned from Grandpa Joe of scrubbing with the sand and small gravel from the river bottom. We lay on the bank drying, naked before God and all his people, although none were likely to appear in that secluded spot. I looked at his masculine body, and I wanted him, not as another man would, but as a woman wants a man. If he had made any move towards me, I would likely have reciprocated, but I was far too buried in my gender box to make such a move on my own. The moment passed, and we had a great trip and remained friends for many years.

Tony hunted like I did. Well, he could move a lot slower and actually understood patience. I wish I had learned those lessons when he offered them, but as I was fond of saying after law school,

"If I had wanted patience, I would have been a doctor."

He too liked the snow, and the quiet woods. For Tony, hunting was more spiritual than visceral. The reward was not bagging a quarry, but the doing of the thing. He lives his life in much the same fashion. Tony is a blessed and happy man.

My other hunting partner was Peggy's father, whom I came to love as my own. Robert V. Probasco was a self-made man in the finest sense of that traditional phrase. He was quick witted and ingenious with physical things. There were few things which, after a few moments thought, where you could almost see the blueprint of a solution germinate on his face, he could not fix, fabricate or make work.

Robert was an electrician by trade and a union man. He was the shop steward for the railroad in Utah. He took the men's complaints to the company and got "laid off" for his efforts. He was not popular with the company, but Woody Guthrie would have been proud. In an attempt to be rid of such a scourge, the company called Robert back from across the country in Kentucky, where he had been forced by circumstances to take work. They gave him only forty-eight hours notice, but he foiled their scheme and showed up. The Robert I knew was like that. He took on life like some sort of mechanical problem. He was not worried that a solution did not exist. Rather, it was just a matter of figuring it out with a never-say-die attitude. I was proud of him too.

I had been told that Robert had a drinking problem in the years before I met him and that the family had suffered the attendant consequences. But you would not have known that to see his family about him with children and spouses and their children and spouses and their children. I have seen family pictures with nearly one hundred people gathered around Robert and Peggy's mother, Dorleen. Robert was defined as much as anything else by his close knit family and all the love they shared and good works they performed, even though as Lutherans they did not have to do good works like us Catholics did. Lutherans are fond of saying that it is by grace alone that we are saved, while the Catholics are much more circumspect in their faith. They find it necessary to buttress their faith with all the good deeds they can manage, and if they are anything like I was, they need to perform countless acts of charity and kindness to cover many sins.

Robert also had a problem with cancer. On the occasion of his death, following his third bout with the horrid disease, where for perhaps the only time in eighty-plus years he declined the fight, I wrote these words:

Robert was old when I met him, but hardy, even robust. He was seventy-five years young. He lived and loved the outdoors; his hand built log home in the Northeast Idaho woods a testament. He was beyond his hill-pounding days afoot. But as faithfully as I would drive the logging roads of Idaho and Montana, he would ride along, his old 30.06 at the ready. Although we had little chance of taking anything, his spirit lent new meaning to hope springing eternal. He was genuinely happy, as was I. He spoke in a muted voice, having survived cancer in his neck, of his days in the army, with the railroad and the many hunting camps in between. I had a penchant for driving where no vehicle had before. He never once questioned my judgment, even when I high-centered the truck trying to cross a dry irrigation canal. He sat calmly, even smiling, till we figured it out. That was his way with any problem. He didn't waste his thoughts on worry. He just figured it out.

At 84, Robert drew a moose tag, literally a once in a life time opportunity. I dedicated the fall of 2001 to helping Robert fill that tag. We both knew, although did not say, that the really big boys in that country were miles off the road, back towards the Yellowstone National Park boundaries. Nonetheless, we faithfully went out every weekend I could get away. On a mid-October Saturday we saw a bull on the hillside several hundred yards above us. We knew a road ran across the hillside above him close enough for an ethical shot. Minutes later, Robert sat just below the shoulder of the road, his .06 shouldered, the bull 100 yards below. He was a little bit less robust, and I worried about how steady his aim would be. The first two shots confirmed my fears. The third hit home.

Anyone who has ever hunted moose knows that the shooting is the fun and easy part. The rest is work - hard work. How were a skinny 43-year-old and an 84-year-old man going to pack out this 1200 pound animal? We would get it out whole. Fortunately, I had brought lots of rope. We tied off the bull to the truck and up we pulled. Okay smart guy, now, how do you get it into the truck? Always the problem solver, Robert had a perfect solution, ingenious in its simplicity. With the bull still behind the truck, he suggested I tie the rope off my front bumper and run it over a sturdy tree limb, over the hood to the bull, and back up. Instantly, we had a pulley. What could be easier? The bull's antlers were not that big, and I knew later that Robert was disappointed, perhaps only because his body and age had betrayed his spirit and desire. That would be the way with future hunts.

A couple of years later Robert contracted cancer again. This time, it took a larenectomy, long hospitalization and a few bouts with pneumonia that would have taken a lesser man. Yet he survived again, although it took his voice entirely. During our many visits at the hospital we talked, via a dry erase board, about how fun it would be to shoot a buffalo. By June of 2003, he seemed strong enough. I made all the arrangements with Ted Turner's Flying D ranch in Southwestern Montana for a buffalo hunt for an old man. The outfitters could not have been more accommodating. They would drive us up to within range, where we could take a cow they wished to cull, for a modest price. On the morning of the hunt, we took Robert to the range to make sure the rifle was sighted in. He was still too weak, despite all my best wishes. His shots did not even hit the paper. He handed me the rifle, and sure enough, his .06 was as faithful as ever. Again I knew that his body just could not keep pace with his indomitable spirit.

We went on the hunt anyway, all the while encouraging Robert. I knew it was futile, for he had already pointed at me, meaning he wanted me to take the shot. Robert was not a man to change his mind once set. I did take the buffalo. I was glad he was there. So was he. I have the pictures to recall that hunt.

In 2004, Robert drew an Idaho elk tag. We faithfully went out every weekend. He said this year would be his last hunt. He did not miss the mark by much. We never saw an elk that year. Maybe it was wolves. Maybe it was weather. Yet, we faithfully spent the time together in a place we both loved, doing what we loved.

In 2005, just after learning that he drew another elk tag, Robert also learned the cancer had returned. The risks of radiation or surgery would be too great. He would not fight it. His spirit would finally succumb. We thank God that it was a matter of weeks and not months. A week before he died, we drove the hills looking for elk, the old .06 at the ready. Happy hunting, partner.

During the fourteen years I lived in Madison County, I discovered another vital truth about my hunting, and thus about myself. In my shame, guilt, fear, self-centeredness, dishonesty and secrecy, I had become desperately lonely. Hunting the hills alone had ceased to be a spiritual experience. The passion and the joy of being out amongst God's gracious artwork had ceased. It dawns on me now, like the morning light upon a granite peak exposing every crack and crevice, that I had become spiritually dead. It was impossible for me to see that I could not walk a spiritual path feeling as I did. I had become so sick that I did not know how sick I was. I believed my own rhetoric far more than I could recognize the truth.

I hunted elk, more or less, because I had to, at least I had convinced myself over the past twenty years or so that because this is what men in Montana do, I must too. So, I kept getting up at an ungodly predawn hour and driving into the mountains seeking some elusive prize. Solace had become as elusive as the elk whose tracks I followed. If only I could believe that the footprints behind me were not my own. I felt as if the world might open up and swallow me whole with no one the wiser or even much concerned. I would get so desperately lonely sometimes that I literally ran back to the truck and drove wildly out of the mountains. I would stop, buy a six pack of medicine and go home.

I loved to hunt, however, at a friend's parcel of ground that hugs the banks of the Jefferson River. It is a long, thin grove of cotton-woods, not unlike most Montana river bottoms. Also like most Montana river bottoms, the adjacent fields are irrigated and farmed for alfalfa hay or some other such feed for livestock. Throughout the country whitetail deer call such corridors home. They feed in the hay fields and bed back in the cotton-woods. There was something almost sacred about those woods, where October winds sent yellow leaves aloft with bluster reminiscent of Pooh Corner. With such odd contradictions of body, mind and spirit, I had hunted there almost every year during early season rifle hunts and the regular season. I had taken dozens of deer and annually stocked my freezer with venison.

I grew to where I did not particularly care for beef anymore, which was not something an elected official would admit publicly in Madison County. The purity of a wild protein source somehow seemed much more moral than that which is penned and plugged unawares with a .22 slug placed behind the ear. I have never had qualms about harvesting food from the woods as a hunter.

I agree with Ted Nugent that we are at base a hunter-gatherer species, and though we need not be and could never feed the masses in such a manner, the instinct to kill for food has not evolved out of the human being. My friend's place was only a few miles away, and I did not have the same sense of desperation hunting there that I felt alone in the mountains. I did not feel that fear or desperation while walking in that cotton-wood grove on the Jefferson River.

During the winter of 2004 –2005, I thought a great deal about taking up the bow. The river bottom was the perfect spot. There was even the vestige of an old tree stand where several deer trails intersected in a small clearing. I had shot a nice four-by-four buck there a few years earlier, so I knew it was a good spot to set up with a bow.

I was self-centered with just enough money to be dangerous. I had grown accustomed to purchasing what I wanted, when I wanted it. It was no different with the bow, the targets and other accouterment. I invested several hundred dollars in all, and began to practice in earnest. I shot that bow every day, took the required bow-hunter safety course and got my card in the mail a few weeks later. I was legal, and now all I needed was practice. And practice I did.

My drinking habit at that time usually included a couple of 7-7s as soon as I got home. So, I would pour a drink and go outside and shoot arrows. I got to be pretty good by the end of the summer, hitting the decoy in the vitals regularly from forty yards. I seldom missed the kill zone from thirty yards in. I was ready.

Peggy had been planning a trip back to Nebraska with her folks to visit her sister. They would go in September when the Dr. Death trial was scheduled. Therefore, I would be staying home. I had gotten almost brazen by then in my cross-dressing habits. It seemed that staying home dressed and drunk was no longer enough. I ventured out by driving to Butte a couple of times dressed, and probably under the influence as well. I shudder to think how things would have gone if I had been pulled over. "Madison County Attorney Arrested for DUI Dressed as Woman," the headlines would have read. It would have ruined my career and caused mortal embarrassment for my family.

I had been consistently acquiring more cross-dressing equipment over the previous couple of years, including clothes, shoes, jewelry, make-up and perfume. I kept it all in four boxes I carefully hid in the garage. I had begun to fear getting caught and thought of it with a sense of impending doom. I began to think of it as "the crash." But that was not enough to stop me or change my behavior. I dressed as often as I could, sometimes every day. Peggy was to be the State Bar President in the coming year, so she was frequently gone for overnight trips on bar business. Or she would go to her parents and I would most often have an excuse why I had to stay home. The simple truth was that I treasured that time, so that I could let the girl out of the box.

I had a couple of cheap wigs, but I really did not like them. I had been purchasing things over the internet and having them delivered UPS to my office so that I would be there when they arrived. If my trusted secretary suspected anything, she never said. Besides, I had been getting Peggy presents from Victoria's Secret for several years. I determined to buy a nice wig before Peggy left for Nebraska. She would be gone for a week, and I intended to live as a woman the entire time that I was not at work or hunting. The first week of September was also the first week of bow season, so I would be dressed in full camo then. The wig arrived only two days before Peggy left, and I could not wait 'till she did, so I could wear it, so I could be. And as luck would have it, the Bischoff trial was cancelled upon reaching a plea agreement.

One evening earlier that year, I sat alone in the living room all dressed up with nothing particular on my mind. I was wearing a skirt and heels, one foot dipped precipitously with that leg crossed over the other. A light breeze blew through the open door, and I felt incredibly whole and at peace, like I knew for the first time the freedom to be myself. I began to sense that I was a different person at those times. It was as if there was a voice inside that I had never recognized or heard. I had long since stopped repressing my thoughts. I came to recognize another persona inside of me, and she was definitely feminine.

The girl inside of me lived and breathed. I began to take that sensation and feeling with me to work, even as a man. Often, I would catch myself in court feeling as the woman inside felt. I also began an inward struggle over the duality of the competing personas. There was the man, with all the fear, shame, guilt, anger and depression and the woman, like a cool breeze that only wanted to blow free. She was peaceful, while he was at war. She was alive, and he was dying more every day.

I had also begun taking photographs of myself a couple of years earlier and posting them on-line. There were lots of other similarly situated men, posting pictures and leaning on one another for support and an outlet. Although I had worn women's clothing to one degree or another my entire life and had seen many pictures of drag queens, here were men who really looked like women. Many were as feminine, not flamboyant or garish. The femininity gripped me, as surely as the thoughts of my childhood. It was infectious, and as soon as I allowed myself to bask in the sensation, it consumed me. I felt like a woman, dressed like a woman and even learned to walk in heels as a woman. I had long since discovered Peggy's treasure trove of lingerie and donned every sheer, lacey, skimpy scrap of it. I was exuberant and felt intensely feminine. I had blossomed, although in secret, into a sexy, classy and sensitive woman.

When it finally came time for Peggy's trip, I was so ready. I dressed at night, every night, and hunted for three days that Labor Day weekend. I was horribly conflicted, spiritually dead, as well as physically and mentally ill. Dressing and bow-hunting were the only two things by which I clung to life. That was no small matter, as I had thought often about killing myself. I was in so much pain that I often became overwhelmed. Many nights I went to sleep crying, asking God to just take me. As I have said, no prayer goes unanswered. God took me alright, just not the way I had anticipated.

I had a .41 mag pistol in a holster at the end of the bed. I built that bed by hand years earlier, when the kids first came to live with us in Silver Star. Shane needed a bed, and I had always wanted to make a log bed. So he and I gathered downed logs in the hills and brought them home. I peeled them by hand and did as much of the work by hand as I could. I ended up making him bunk beds with very long legs. It was a lot of work, but I was proud of my woodworking accomplishments over the years. I had made the kids beds when they were little and bookshelves and furniture and wooden boxes for people as gifts. You can scarcely go through a room in my house even now that does not have something I made.

When we moved to Jefferson Acres, I took my chain saw and cut the legs in half to make two log beds. It completed the cabiny western feel to throw the holster over the bed post and provided a morbid sense of safety. I had shot the gun enough to know what it would do, and I thought that it would all be over if I just stuck it in my mouth and pulled the trigger. I have been told since that if I really wanted to kill myself I would have stuck the gun over my heart. I had not thought of that at the time, which is a good thing. The messiness of the thing was one of two thoughts that kept me from doing it. The bullet would make a small hole going in, but a very large one coming out. I knew that someone in my family would find me, or what was left of my head, all over the wall, and I just did not want that to happen. Besides, maybe they really needed me. The other thought that grew stronger and stronger was the awareness that killing me would kill the woman inside too. I had long since reached the point where I did not want to live, but now I could not kill her who had not yet had the chance to live.

It amazes me that a person can feel these things right up to the gates of hell without notice, without the touch of another to intervene. Three or four other Montana lawyers took their own lives in 2005, and I had very nearly joined them. Though I have come to see that suicide would have been the pinnacle of selfishness, my heart goes out to them and their families still.

I cannot say that no one noticed that something was wrong though, as I had steadily been losing weight. In fact, a glorious weekend spent drunk and dressed usually involved very little in the way of sustenance. At some point in my burgeoning femininity, I bought into the same ethic that so many other women, especially the young, believe. Skinny is the picture of feminine beauty. Many people at work asked if I was alright. I learned later that some suspected I was very ill and may be dying. They never knew how close they were to the mark.

Alcoholism and weight control do not mix. Something has got to give, either food or the empty calories of booze. I had determined to stay on a less than 2,000-calorie-a-day diet, and if I was drinking 600 to 1000 calories a day, then I could not eat a whole lot. Sometimes when Peggy was away, I ate next to nothing. One morning, after a particularly hard night of drinking, I was so weak that I could hardly get out of bed. I did not have the strength and suddenly realized with horror that I had scarcely eaten a thing in days. I stumbled to the kitchen so I could nibble on a piece of cheese. Peggy had once suggested that I was getting anorexic, and she may have been right. She did not know it, but I had a goal for my forty-eighth birthday to weigh the same as I did when I graduated from high school - 136 pounds. I made it.

In September, 2005, I was well on my way to insanity. I was depressed, alcoholic, anorexic and a transsexual in a box about to explode. Yet, I found some peace in a ground blind on the Jefferson River in the early September sun. I still recall that sleepy, hazy feeling of the leaves in the wind and the dappled light falling on brown grass. While I may have cursed God in my hopelessness the night before, I could still appreciate the beauty of God's creation all around me. I wrote this piece.

CONFESSIONS OF A FIRST TIME BOWHUNTER

On September 3, 2005, I sat in ground blind on the Jefferson River that I had placed the week before. The set-up was perfect. My friend's eight acres formed a narrow travel route along the river, where whitetail deer made pathways like stock trails from irrigated alfalfa fields to their bedding areas. The blind stood amongst some brush fifteen yards from the river. A southwest wind blew in my face. At 5:30 a.m. it was cold. I had not dressed warmly enough to sit for hours in forty- five degree temperatures.

As daylight broke, a bobcat came in downwind and sat on a stump not ten yards away. He milled about for several minutes and then scampered away. His unperturbed presence was foretelling. Twenty two deer passed the blind between 7:00 and 8:30. Only three small bucks came in by 9:30. I was too cold, and the lure of coffee at my friend's house too great.

The next morning, bolstered by wool socks and vest, watching the dawn was much more comfortable. Fifteen deer passed the blind by 8:30. Guess I left too early, as I saw fifteen more on the way out. No bucks, though, so no big deal.

On day three, like clockwork, the deer began to go by just after 7:00 a.m. I cherish this place. I have taken many deer here over the years with my .270, with a couple of nice mounts on the wall to show for it. I could not have guessed twenty-five years ago when I left Ohio, a city boy born and bred, that I would be sitting in a ground blind in Waterloo, Montana hunting deer with a bow and arrow. But here I sat. I heard, not the sounds of cars, horns honking and sirens blaring, but a cacophony of natural sound. Against the backdrop of constant rippling water, sandhill cranes greeted each other and the day. A large gathering of Canada geese flew overhead, honking of a different kind. Then, all is quiet.

There is movement amongst the shadowy cottonwood tree trunks in the half light before sunrise. They move as apparitions, at once present where they had not been a moment before. It is a doe with two fawns. Nearly all the does this year have twins. Sixteen deer streamed past. Their tan color is striking in the morning sun. A single doe browses slowly, not ten yards away. She is completely unaware of my presence. The bucks seem to have a different sensory system, though. The seven I see are much more cautious. Back in the shadows I catch a glimpse of instantly recognizable horns. They are large and covered in velvet. The buck approaches straight on to fifteen yards. He is a large 4 X 4. His horns are high and heavy. I wonder if he hears my heart pounding as he stops, looks up at the blind and calmly turns and walks away. I watch him go, thrilled, as the doe just outside my window continues with her breakfast.

Two bucks wander in. They stop at twenty five yards, and study the blind for several minutes. They turn and mill about. Then, one follows the route of the big buck. Where is the other one? Just when I think I have lost him, I watch this 5 X 5 with long, thin tines walk into view. He is thirty yards out and closing. As I begin to draw I realize I am too close to the opening in the blind. My broadhead is sticking out and shaking. My muscles are stiff from sitting so long in the cold. I have trouble with the draw. The bow string makes a sound. I hear a whistle and know instantly where the other buck is. He is fifteen yards away, still studying the blind, standing not five yards away from where I first saw him. The 5 X 5 crouches and both spook. I am busted, but smarter. I must be able to come to full draw inside the blind.

I got to see two more bucks of modest size. It was a good morning. It beats the best day working. The bucks I spooked did not spook badly. The others, including the big one, never knew I was there. The temperature was supposed to remain cool instead of the near nineties of the previous week. I would return that evening.

At 3:00 p.m. I was back in the blind. I sat, wrote in my journal and thought a lot. The late afternoon sun streamed through the trees. A breeze blew. It was calm and peaceful, almost ethereal. I sat quietly, completely at ease, in stark contrast to my work as a prosecutor. My nerves were still defraying from recently settling a homicide case I had been working on for over a year. I tried to sleep and watch simultaneously. A couple of fawns played in the sun, like polka dot puppies. Their mothers retrieved them. They bedded within fifty yards of the blind. It was 7:00 p.m. before I caught a glimpse of points, several of them, out of the corner of my eye. I tilted my head ever so slightly to confirm the vision. The buck jerked upright on high alert. I didn't even breathe as he turned and trotted off, slightly spooked, but at what, he did not know.

As I exhaled I began to wonder at how unforgiving the blind was. I second- guessed my decision to purchase it instead of a tree stand set-up at roughly the same cost. I had taken deer here from the ground many times. With that in mind, I bought the blind because it is safer and more versatile, if still unforgiving. I had just read an article about the importance of persistence in hunting. I had been at it too long today already eight hours total to give up.

He returned. I knew instantly it was the same buck I spooked not an hour earlier. He was walking in a straight line along a trail running parallel to the blind I had ranged earlier at thirty yards, just within my effective shooting range. His head was down, as if on a mission. I realized the angle from my chair to where he would present a shot in the clearing was not right. I must move. I stealthily found my way to one knee. I knew then I would have a shot. It was a moment of truth, devoid of all pretenses, unlike much of my workaday world. It was as significant in my life as the upcoming guilty plea in my homicide case. The parallels were uncanny. If there was higher drama I do not know.

He moved. The moment was here. I came fluidly to full draw. It felt as smooth and easy as the thousands of practice shots I took during the summer. Would they pay off? He advanced ten yards, still broadside. My second pin, tuned religiously from the fence post where I stood at practice to the 3D target thirty yards away, now rested upon this buck. My heart jumped. It was now or never. The release was anchored as always just behind my ear. The tip of my nose touched the string. I stretched across my chest, shoulder blades back. I breathed. I pulled my index finger back like a hook. The trigger released, my thumb coming back to my shoulder. I realized intuitively that there was some kind of art in glimpsing an arrow in flight, unlike a bullet you cannot see. I heard a sound I had never heard before. It was not like the sound of my field tips hitting a tree early on. I realized in that moment it was the clean hit of a true arrow.

As high as the stakes in my life had been, I was elated. I don't believe I cried, but only because I didn't think of it. I know I smiled, breathed and laughed out loud. Now I understand that the guys on TV do not laugh because there is anything funny about killing a great and graceful animal. They laugh as the natural release of emotional energy and the unfettered joy of their craft. For me, the moment was nothing short of spiritual.

I thought back to the bow-hunter's education class in May. I had to wait thirty minutes in case he was not dead. It was punishing. I busied myself putting gear away and closing up the blind. Okay, that took five minutes. I sat on the river bank and thanked God for the pink and purple Charlie Russell sky. A doe appeared on the opposite bank and took a drink. A bald eagle flew overhead as the natural world remained undisturbed by my presence and dramatic encounter.

I could hold out only twenty minutes. I rationalized it would be better to find a blood trail before dark. It was not necessary, as I saw him piled up just over thirty five yards away. I was ecstatic, not just because of the quality of the 4 X 5 point buck. I worked hard to accomplish a goal. I proclaimed to myself with pride, "I am a bow hunter."

The stakes in my life were indeed high. I was so many things, or I was nothing at all. I just did not know. I truly did not know whether I was a man or a woman. I was demoralized, that is to say, without morale, without God, without spirituality. I had a spiritual disease, indeed spiritual death. I had become so incomprehensively sick of spirit, with body not far behind, that I would surely go crazy or die very soon. I knew that I could not live this way.

All I knew was that there was this tiny female life inside, some part of me waking up and wanting to be born. She was rousing me out of years of somnambulance, and something had to be done with her.[29]

While Sue Monk Kidd was writing about the awakening of her feminine soul, no other words could better describe my life that fall of 2005.

Reaching for Mom's purse. Should've known.

First Communion

Jr. High

Watterson High School

Senior Picture

Proud Papa

The Man

Madison County Attorney

Starting Transition

My Subterranean Refuge

Peggy & Me at the Butte Recue Mission - Thanksgiving 2006

Mom & Me in Trinidad

Kynni & Me - MT Transgender Day of Remebrance 2008

Blake Edwards & Me on KGVO Conservative Talk Radio - 2010

Standing in the Pacific - 2010

Christmas 2010 in Cardwell, MT

Fashion Show at Holter Museum – 2010

Bozeman Mayor, Jeff Krause & Me

Dani, Me & Kynni at Carroll College in Helena

Soaring above the Clark Fork Basin

PART TWO: THE GIRL

Chapter Ten

I'm an Angel

And I don't want the world to see me
'cuz I don't think that they'd understand
When everything's meant to be broken
I just want you to know who I am.

- Goo Goo Dolls[30]

On February 14, 2006, I drove into the mountains west of Silver Star, a place off Pipestone Pass called Fish Creek. I had been there often over the previous ten years to hunt and gather fire wood. Peggy and I celebrated our engagement there seven years earlier, sharing a bottle of Chianti as we watched the fading sun lighting upon the Tobacco Roots, pink and gold. I had planned to go for days as I just wanted to be out as a woman in the light of day, in the world.

I felt like the world, my life, was closing in ever nearer to the crash. I had just lost a two day child sexual abuse trial, one that I should of course won, or had the judgment not to take to trial. A man reputed to have a chicken fetish was charged with sexually molesting his teenage stepdaughter and his four-year-old baby girl. Advocates have come a long way in refining forensic interview techniques for such situations. The four-year-old's interview video was compelling. I had determined to take the case to a jury, even though I had no intent of putting a four-year-old on the stand.

Defense counsel decidedly erred by admitting a police report into evidence that referenced the allegations regarding the four-year-old. I knew it, but said nothing. The attorney's paralegal, however, adroitly informed the lawyer of his error, and defense counsel asked to be able to redact the information. Of course, I opposed his request; however, the judge was not persuaded. I drank for three days after the acquittal, chewing on that moment all the while. I was near to breaking.

In big cities cross-dressers go out en masse to clubs that cater to them. It is an outlet for them, a place to be themselves in a supportive environment and to enjoy their feminine persona. We had no such place in Silver Star, Montana. For a cross-dressing alcoholic public official in Southwest Montana the mountains would have to do.

It was cold, so I dressed in a rose colored turtle-neck sweater with a matching scarf made of a fringy kind of yarn and my red ski jacket. I wore a pair of jeans and hiking boots. I drove up Fish Creek Road to the crest and immediately got stuck in the snow. I was petrified, not that I could not get out, for I had gotten unstuck in the mountains numerous times. I was afraid that I would get caught before I could dig my way out.

I took off my wig and make-up and as many of the female articles of clothing I could without being exposed to the elements. I feverishly put the tire chains on that were in the tool box, where it seems they stay until after one is stuck. It's the Montana code. I had a shovel in the box too. I dug and drove, and drove and dug, until I got extricated from the deep snow.

The rest of the outing was exhilarating, and I took several self-portraits amongst the rocks and trees of the Great Divide. I sat atop a huge rock with my head tilted back, my long hair shining in the sun, with the lyrics of Don Henley ringing in my brain: "After the boys of summer have gone."[31]

The air was cool and the sun warm on my face. I was out, if only to the sun. The world, however, was not long away.

Two days later, February 16, 2006, the crash was upon me and though I did not fully realize what it meant, I was reborn. The girl in me would live. Bob had survived long enough to bring her into the sunlight. I would not return to the darkness of my box. It would take many months, however, to overcome the fear, self doubt and insecurity, the guilt and ambiguity of self that I had built up for nearly half a century. I knew I needed help.

I had seen the contact information of Monique Mandali, gender thera-pist, months before on a Montana Gay website, and the day after the "crash" I called her number. I got an answering machine and said,

"My name is Bob Zenker, and my number is 406-684-5629. I need help with some gender issues."

Her office was on the second floor of an old building in Helena, for-merly a nunnery or some such thing. I had to wind my way through a maze of hallways and stairways to get there. I was nearly unnerved by the time I found it. It was a small office, minimalist in appearance. Her sparsely fur-nished surroundings, with a small writing desk, full book shelves bearing titles like *Transgender Warriors* and a couple of chairs, told of her personality. She was not a complicated person and had long abandoned the frills, pre-tense and conveniences of mainstream Western culture. The chair I chose, which would be the same for many months to come, was a Papasan, a large, round wicker affair with a thin cushion. I was incredibly uncomfortable, and the chair offered no reprieve.

Monique was my therapist, my coach and self-titled "midwife." She talked about gender transition very much as a birth, so the moniker fit. Monique was tall, thin and athletic, with a short crop of silver hair. She spoke with an accent that I later learned was Dutch. From the moment I entered her office on February 23, 2006, I knew what the ultimate outcome would be. I would become a woman.

A few days later I heard Van Morrison's "Tupelo Honey" on the radio. *"She's as sweet as Tupelo Honey. She's an angel of the first degree, yes she is."*[32] From somewhere inside came the refrain,

"Yes I am. I am an angel of the first degree," I said out load as I drove to Virginia City.

For the first time in my life, I claimed myself out loud. I was willing to let myself be female. So too I claimed my true self. I said out loud, like Dorothy in her ruby slippers, as if saying so could finally make it all real,

"I am a transsexual, I am a transsexual, I am a transsexual."

In that moment of realization and acceptance, I knew that my life as a man was over.

I had known of the Serenity Prayer since I was young. Catholics relied on it, so, of course, I did not think much of it. Now, I prayed with fervor to accept the things I could not change. I was a mystery, a conundrum even to myself. Born and baptized Robert, I had been male, mostly, for 48 years. All the while another voice sprang from my soul. All along, whether a whisper, a tear or a shout, she cried out,

"I am."

Patiently, yet inexorably, she rose singing, crying,

"Let me be, let me live."

Monique was dubious of me at the outset, as I was of her. We tiptoed around the general concepts of gender dysphoria and the transgender continuum from cross-dressers to transsexuals. I presented as a man in dress and speech, so she did not have anything to go on except what I told her. On our third or fourth visit I brought copies of self portraits I had taken over the years, a sort of top ten. I could almost see the light go on for Monique as she looked at those photos and exclaimed,

"This is a woman."

The comfort I felt at that instant has continued to grow in me as something I had never before known, the only word for which is joy. It is a sacred kind of happiness punctuated by a deep and abiding peace.

In first grade I learned a song called *"Joy is Like the Rain,"* about how joy is tried by storm. I loved that song, as I love the rain today, for we have so little of it in Montana. Sr. Edward Ann was my first grade teacher. She, in marked contrast to Sr. Archangela, was sweet, good and kind, lots of sugar and spice. I was happy when I was in her class singing that song, and I suppose that is why I remember it forty-some years later.

Monique was not like Sr. Edward Ann, but she aroused in me that same comfort and happiness that I had not felt since I was young. It was as if she was awakening me from a long, long sleep. I felt somehow like that first grader. I was not immature, but somehow pure and authentic, and in her skillful care, I regained a measure of innocence lost.

Monique helped me claim myself and give myself a name. In her calm, yet assertive way, she took my fears and brushed them aside to open the door to experience and truth. She called me a woman, a description I had never before heard in reference to me that fell around me as soft as a silent November snow. And, her name is Bobbie.

I did not think of Monique as a "mid wife," because I was not giving birth in the sense of a genetic woman, passing a too large child through a too small passage. I would most definitely be reborn, however, in body, mind and spirit, which Monique emphasized from the first. The awakening would be painful.

"I am an alcoholic," I told her as she took my medical history that first visit.

It was the first time those words had ever crossed my lips, and I lost interest in drinking almost magically at that very moment.

"I cannot work with you if you are not sober," she plainly told me, a first from the medical profession.

"I want you to make a plan for how you are going to cut down. What can you replace alcohol with? I want you to tell me your plan at our next meeting. Let's see, how about next Tuesday?"

"Yea, I can do that."

I was thrilled and filled with fear simultaneously.

"Yeah, I get to be a girl," I thought to myself as I walked down the stairs from Monique's office.

At the same moment I began to think about life without alcohol. It never occurred to me that I could not do it. I just did not know how. I reasoned that I had spent half my life drinking and that I could spend the rest of it not drinking. Here was the plan I wrote out as a list:

Plan - drink less - do more (fill the void)
Read about what I am trying to find
Remodel Bathroom & Greenhouse (Plant)
Wait till 4 - forego 1 (Beer, wine, or whiskey)
Quit whiskey
Make them last longer
Go longer in between
First 4, then 2, then 0
Pray
Pray again
Talk to people in recovery
Do yoga w/Peggy
Soak outside, not in
Eat well
Spend $ on counseling not booze
Lo-cal flavored water (like last time)
Chew gum

As I began to look at myself in therapy and recovery, I questioned everything. I questioned every conclusion, judgment and belief I had built up over the decades and found that many were remarkably hollow and insincere. I had to confront my own biases. The journey required of me that I determine what values were real and worth keeping, as opposed to those that had been contrived as part of the role, the cloak and image I wore. Sue Monk Kidd calls it "initiation."

> Initiation is a sacred disintegration. Despite its pain, we carry the conviction (often only faintly) that even though we don't know where we'll end up, we're following a soulpath of immense richness, that we're supposed to be on this path, that it's required of us somehow. We move in a sense of rightness of lure, of following a flute that pipes irresistible music . . . . I carried the sense of belonging on this path, but I knew nothing of the intensity I was about to enter. I only knew I had waked and was entering a place where the old meanings, concepts and values no longer fit. The vista of the Great Transition.[33]

I called my journey "transition" from the start, and it was indeed "great" as I beheld the sweep of the vista I proposed. I had no clue where I would end up, but I knew deep down in my core that it was the right thing for me to do. I was wide awake, perhaps for the first time in my life. I was sober and willing to be the real me without fear.

It is ironic that among the first biases I had to cast aside in my "initiation" was my former judgments as a homophobic right-wing conservative Republican. Two of my most ardent supporters were gay men. They showed me nothing but unconditional acceptance. They had passed through their own fires and clung to no pretense. I had adopted so many roles to fit in as a man in rural Montana that did not reflect my values. I began to cast them aside with abandon that felt more like freedom.

In June, 2006, I voted my first entirely Democratic ballot in more than thirty years. I had detested Hillary Clinton and swore that if she ever became president I would move to Canada. I did not care much for all Democrats for most of the Clinton years and both Bush presidencies, father and son. Yet I found that many of my friends were Democrats. What was it about them that made me like them? What was it in me that resonated so strong and clear with them?

I decided to read Hillary Clinton's book, "It Takes a Village." I was impressed by the work she did worldwide for women and children, and just how politically savvy she really was. I became a convert and voted for her in the 2008 presidential primary. I hoped that I would have the opportunity to eat my words about moving to Canada.

The truth, that I epitomized Shakespeare's notion of protest, was beginning to dawn like the light on the darkness of my addled beliefs. I was homophobic for fear of who I was. I thought of the oft used metaphor of the onion layers in relation to the multiple layers of fear, resentment and self pity I began to unravel. Uncontrollable tears fell freely as I started to strip the layers away. It was especially ironic that the onion layers I peeled away to reach my soul represented the religious right. I was amazed at the revelations that came with even a small measure of openness and honesty.

Yet, it all seemed so endless and overwhelming. I wondered if I had hit bottom. Though I had written down the plan outlining the steps I would take to stop drinking, I knew it was not enough. I would need the help of some kind of a recovery program as I sensed innately that I could not quit on my own. I had no idea what recovery looked like, but I now had a mandate. Finally, after more than ten years of frequent contact with the medical profession, someone among them suggested that I stop drinking. I was relieved, and determined to use this opportunity to heal.

When I worked at St. Labre, I participated in training regarding the disease of alcoholism. I had my doubts about that concept. It did not make sense to me that someone could recover from a chronic, progressive and fatal disease when they were powerless to control its main symptom. Much of the evidence I had witnessed as a prosecutor confirmed my doubts. I did not believe it possible until, it seems, I was a very sick person. I could not see that I was powerless to recover on my own, but that through unity with others and reliance on a power outside myself recovery from a chronic and fatal sickness was possible.

I knew other persons who would readily admit that they had suffered from this disease. They were getting better. One was my friend and drinking partner from law school. I would love to wax clever here, but the pathetic truth is that practicing alcoholics seek one another out. A fundamental truth was lost on me; misery loves company. I had been losing for a long time. I often wondered why I could not get any breaks.

In our drinking days I had my friend, though, and he had me. We did manage to do a few things together that were not limited to drinking, but alcohol was always present. We hunted, and packed along a bottle of Ten High.

"It's for medicinal purposes," he said.

"A-huh, a-huh," I coughed and cleared my throat.

"Here, have some medicine," he said with mock severity as he handed me the bottle.

We faked a cough every time we returned to the truck, so that with each return we could take a shot for medicinal purposes. Our returns to the truck became more frequent until the last time we set up hunting camp, and our cough had gotten so bad that we never left camp.

I carried on that way for years, even after my friend found recovery in rather dramatic fashion. In 2001, a couple of weeks after my first back surgery, my friend wrecked his truck on the interstate. He left Rhino's in a huff after demanding that his girlfriend return the keys to his truck. If hell hath no fury like that of a woman scorned, then heaven has no righteousness like that of a pissed off drunk. If you do not trust this just tell a practicing alcoholic "no." My friend got his keys and took off on the interstate east towards his home. He wound up sliding down the west-bound lane, the truck on its side with his head playing basketball with the pavement outside his window. He broke his neck in a few places and dented and scarred his face in a few more.

I caught up with him at St. Pat's in Missoula, the same place where a year earlier I had been for my "fake" heart attack.

"I have been here for five days they say, but I don't remember a damn thing," he told me.

A comrade of his, another regular at Rhino's, had passed away during the interim. He had missed the funeral but felt compelled to pay his respects in some fashion. He had also grown tired of hospital food and thought that Double Front chicken in the store would be a great idea. He begged, pleaded and argued with the nurses until they agreed to a reprieve that would not be against medical advice, which would allow him to leave the hospital for a few hours.

"I'd like to pay my respects to Doug," he told me in confidence.

His idea was to go and commiserate about his dead comrade with the other regular patrons at Rhino's, unbeknownst to the nurses, and then go for roasted chicken, the official reason for the reprieve. He seemed anxious to me. I too was nervous as hell as I entered Rhino's with my Frankenfriend. We sat down at the bar and ordered sodas. I was relieved.

He tried to talk with a few of the folks about their dear departed associate but spent most of the half hour or so we were there fielding inquiries about his dire condition.

"I got in a wreck a week ago, broke a few vertebrae and got some scrapes," he said, vastly understating the injuries the neck brace and gaping wounds on his face belied.

I hesitate to say that no one cared about the decedent, but life at Rhino's went on, regardless of the respective death and dramatic accident of two of its best patrons. My friend agreed with me that these friends of his were not really as close as he thought. I think some light dawned upon us both. A drunk loves company only for so long as the company is drinking. Alcohol is just a beverage to most, but to the drunk, it is a relentless river whose flow never stops, even when the drunk has stepped from the stream, and the flow is all too ready to become a torrent to wash the unwary away. My friend got wary fast following his second DUI and brush with death. The next day we went to meet with an alcohol counselor, and he soon got hooked up with the recovery community. I knew whom to call when I at last could admit that alcohol was kicking my patootee too.

I began recovery in earnest. I joined a recovery group in Butte, forty miles away. The group met weekday mornings at 7 a.m., so that I had to drive forty miles one way for the meeting, another forty miles home and another forty before arriving at work. I drove 160 miles nearly every day for the next six months. In this particular group, we read certain recovery literature to begin every meeting. After a few months, I was asked to read certain of the materials at meetings. As I did, I began to practice speaking in a higher pitch. I do not know if anyone noticed or cared or perhaps put it together later when my gender transition became common knowledge, but the seeds of transition had germinated.

I began to notice that they celebrated what they called sobriety birthdays by giving out coins that commemorated certain intervals of sobriety, like three, six and nine months, a year and annually thereafter. They would pass the coin around for whatever intentions, mojo or karma the others could muster. On the back of each coin was Shakespeare's famous line, *"To thine own self be true."* I wondered a great deal about that as I continued in therapy and began to make the connection between sobriety and transition. I knew that I must do both.

"Do you think you can give up your place at the top of the food chain?" Monique asked during one early session.

"I never thought about male privilege and care about it less," I told her.

"Yes, of course," I concluded with a quizzical look on my face.

"Gender transition is the most difficult thing a person in our culture can do," she said. Similarly, sobriety is difficult to obtain and even harder to keep.

"If you think a sobriety birthday is easy, try and get one," they had said.

I began to feel as if the same were true of gender transition. They say too, amongst the recovery community, that to drink is to die. I realized early on that my useful life as a man was over, and thus for me it was transition or die. The risk of failure truly seemed like a double death sentence hanging over my head.

My first several months of sobriety and therapy were incredibly anxious for me. As I started to unravel the mistakes and mysteries of my life, I would readily lapse back into hopelessness, depression and suicide ideation. I was easily overwhelmed, as if the submarine I was in, still searching for the surface, had screens instead of hatches. I vainly tried on my own to batten them down against the flood of emotions whose tide I could not stem. Sue Monk Kidd's words resonate now with my experience, but at the time, I had no awareness of the tearing down I must endure.

> My experience was teaching me the truth of Nelle Morton's words that there is an 'awful abyss that occurs after the shattering, and before the new reality appears.' 'But first, before the reshaping, the recreation, there is the blank, stunned space of feeling stripped and peeled. We are not who we used to be and not who we will become. We are in the terrain of 'unmeaning.' And we are alone in it.[34]

I was alone, crushingly so. I am convinced that this abyss is what sends many newly sober people back to drinking. It is a terribly lonely, dark space. We are soulless, desperate, and our old means of coping have been stripped. When so demoralized, fearful and hopeless, many alcoholics simply give up the fight. I felt many times like giving up.

"I am so anxious and depressed most of the time," I told Monique.

"Have you thought about anti-depressants?" she asked.

I had not, and until that point, would not. I would not have admitted it, but it looked like weakness, and I had believed for so long that I was in control, that I could fix myself. I had believed the lies that I told myself to feel okay.

"You tell your doctor you would like anti-depressants," she told me.

So I did, although, I was afraid to ask him because I didn't want to tell him what was going on with me.

"I am an alcoholic," I told him, revealing only half my problem.

He took me very seriously and asked,

"Have you thought about hurting yourself?"

"Yes, many times but I won't do so now," I told him wondering suddenly whether through sobriety and transition I might find a way to be happy with myself.

Antidepressants helped.

They often spoke of sponsors in the recovery group. I knew that I needed one but was still too afraid to expose "mine own self." Except for Peggy and my therapist, I was still terribly alone with my turmoil. Sometimes, when happy hour rolled around, I thought about how calming a 7-7 would be. I thought of the saying I had learned,

"Don't drink. And go to meetings. Don't drink even if your ass falls off. Just pick it up and go to a meeting."

Because of that saying, my ass never has fallen off completely. I knew intuitively that once I had a sponsor I would have to be honest about everything, and I was still far too fearful to allow myself to be so exposed and vulnerable. I had begun to realize too the value of a higher power. They said that power could be anything, a light bulb or door knob for instance. Somehow, I just could not turn my will and life over to the care of a light bulb, even if it did represent a better idea.

In the first week or two of sobriety, I was driving into Butte to get to an early morning meeting and thinking about selecting a higher power that was not inanimate. I had always had a God in my life and became a drunk anyway. It reminds me now of the character in *Major League* (the movie featuring Charlie Sheen as the "wild thing") named Cerano saying to the clubhouse evangelist in a thick Hispanic brogue,

"Ah Jesus, I like him very much, but he no help me hit curve ball."

I had always believed in God and asked almost daily for his will, but at the end of the day, I was still drunk. Though I would continue to believe in and pray to God, I figured that a new perspective might be useful. The Beatles' "Let it Be" came on the radio, and I knew instantly who my higher power would be.

"When I find myself in times of trouble, Mother Mary comes to me, speaking words of wisdom, let it be."35

Those words of powerlessness, surrender and humility were perhaps the wisest I had uttered in many years. At those times when I obsessed over the happy-hour blues, wandering in that "terrain of unmeaning," that desert of alcoholic insanity, searching for the oasis that might fill the void, I prayed. Where so many prayed the serenity prayer when tempted, agitated or doubtful, I said Hail Mary's.

Chapter Eleven

Girls are Better

How long have I been sleeping?
How long have I been drifting on through the night?
How long have I been dreaming I could make it right,
If I close my eyes and try with all my might?

- Jackson Browne[36]

Montana has many mountain vistas, backdrops against which our entire lives play out. As dramatic as our lives may become, the mountains look unchanging, stoic and distant, dramatic in their own way. As I daily returned to Silver Star from my meeting in Butte, I looked to the western slope of the Tobacco Root Mountains. There were two slopes to the north that I thought resembled the profiled left breast and stomach of a pregnant woman lying down. To the south was Man Face Mountain, which resembled the face of a man in repose looking up at the sky. The juxtaposition of the two in my mind's eye served as a metaphor for the duality I felt. It was a daily reminder of the journey I proposed to undertake. There I was both the man face and the fetus daughter.

I felt as if I straddled madness like a wounded soldier grasping for the remnants of my emasculated soul. I kept thinking that I had missed so much by denying, repressing and ignoring who I was that now that I had found acceptance, I did not want to lose even a second more. I just wanted to get to the end of the tunnel, burst into the light and live my life as a whole person instead of two halves. I wanted to run through the door screaming to the world, "I am! I am! I am!"

With the insights and decisions I had already made, the duality seemed more a lie than ever. I felt as if I could see a brand new cloak across the room. It was hard to justify not casting the old cloak away that never fit particularly well, walking across the room and donning the new one and turning around with a swish to check its fit and style before walking the cat-walk of public scrutiny. In the end I could expect no more of the destination than I gave to the journey. I was happy with me. I was okay, even good. I allowed myself to be without regret, guilt, shame, fear or uncertainty. I was forty-eight years old, and determined to undergo sex reassignment surgery before I was fifty. I had so far to go, yet I believed that I would get there. I had hope.

I no longer had to be anyone or anything for anyone else. I needn't adopt any roles that were not real. I was Bobbie, a sweet, thoughtful, caring and happy woman on the way to being whole and wise. That summer, as I began the physical transition in earnest with hormones, laser hair removal, voice lessons and follicular hair transplant surgery, I also made some decisions about where I would live and work and how I would be known. I felt as if I was awakening from a very long and deep sleep. Rip Van Wrinkle had nothing on me. My eyes were open, and I felt right inside. I could be honest or least start to be. I started to lose my fear of allowing people to know me as I truly was. I was becoming a woman and in so doing, a complete person.

A colleague wrote these words to me:

I believe that you should keep your last name. That name is part of who you are; there is something sacred about family names and one should be slow to change them. I also think you have much to offer the Montana legal profession and therefore encourage you to attempt to maintain your engagement in our profession. Consider the excellent work you have done as a lawyer; that experience will not change simply because you have decided to respond to that voice at the deepest part of your being which is calling you to be the person you were created to be.

Much of the grief that we experience in our lives is a function of our awareness of the unlived life, i.e. the life we know we were called to lead but have been too fearful to embrace. You were called to be Bobbie Zenker - an intelligent and compassionate human being and wonderful lawyer. You have fully accepted that call and the courage to live it. Yes there will be people who are narrow in their thinking who will belittle you. The truth, however, is that their narrowness of perspective is largely a function of their own fear of life and their basic ignorance. You must never allow those people to dictate the direction of your life. Your fundamental calling as a unique creation is God's calling and ultimately being true to the creation you were meant to be is all that counts.

Bobbie, I am proud of you for the courage and faith you are demonstrating in taking the steps to reclaim your life. Be strong!

I do not know whether his was the voice of experience but the advice was as sage as could be found. *Here I am Lord. I will go Lord if you lead me.* I will get up every day and do what I have to do. With that resolve I kept going, as my mother had often said when I was a child, like the little engine that could.

"I think I can, I think I can, I think I can, I can!"

I went to the Pride Celebration in Helena in mid-June.

"Will you go as Bobbie?" Monique asked.

"I don't know," I said, still feeling very uncomfortable and afraid in public.

I had been presenting as a woman for months in Monique's office and at home, but the streets of the state capital were another question.

"But that is who I am and I just feel so much better as Bobbie."

Also, if I was ever to present successfully as a woman to the world, I would need lots of practice. I had to overcome fear, self consciousness and doubt. I had always believed that action was the best antidote for anxiety.

"There's nothing to it but to do it," I had always said.

I had to get out there, and Helena was as safe a place as any.

On a bright, sunny mid-June evening, I checked into the Hampton Inn in Helena, and used my American Express Card bearing the name "Robert R. Zenker" to pay for the room. When I got the card in 1986, it was my first credit card, and I felt proud, as if I had become someone. I stepped from the room an hour later as Bobbie, an attractive woman in jeans, heels and a cotton pullover blouse with an open v-neck and a collar. It was one I had advised Peggy to buy as we strolled through Herberger's in the Butte Plaza Mall a year earlier. What attracted me most to the blouse was the way the open laces hung lightly, exposing enough skin underneath to look sexy. I had suggested it for me, not for her, although she had no idea at the time. I had worn it many times since, so naturally selected it for my first night on the town.

I had picked up a purse at the Goodwill in Butte as Monique had suggested.

"Shop at Goodwill till you know your style," she said. "It's much cheaper, and you won't lose much when you decide you don't like things."

She was right, and I developed a habit then which has stayed with me. It's the least expensive form of shopping therapy, and I often find real bargains on clothes with the tags still on them. I let the strap of my purse slide off my shoulder as I climbed into the driver's seat of my 2004 GMC Sierra pick-up with the heated leather seats. I tossed the purse on the other seat and drove across town to the Myrna Loy Center for the evening's 2006 Montana Pride activities.

As I climbed the cement steps to the restored building, I grasped the handrail as if I clung to life itself. I was afraid. I felt conspicuous, looking just like a man in woman's clothing with too much make-up to cover the ravages wreaked upon my face by years of testosterone and over exposure to the sun and the elements.

As I approached the ticket table, I looked down upon a young person seated there dressed in a formal evening gown, an obvious wig and no make-up needed, as his face was still pure and clear.

"Can I write a check?" I asked.

"Sure. Just make it out to Montana Pride Network," he said as he smiled up at me.

"Here you go," I said nervously after writing the check and handing it to him.

"Are you related to the Madison County Attorney?" he asked as he looked at the name.

"I am the Madison County Attorney," I said, "and I wish you would let this be our little secret."

"I went to school with your children in Twin Bridges," he confided, "and I won't tell anyone." I have no reason to suspect he ever did.

Being my authentic self amongst the LGBT community was an incredible experience. I found unconditional acceptance and support and fairly floated through the first day, highlighted by a parade in which I marched through downtown Helena wearing a rainbow serape. I even sensed a certain protective instinct from those around me. They had my back, even though they need not have, as there were no incidents.

On the downside, the lesbian community perceived me more as a guy in drag - kind of a straight drag - but not as a woman. I really hadn't learned bathroom etiquette yet, so I knocked a few times and went right on in to a small crowd of women waiting, of course, for an open stall. No troughs or urinals for the girls, thank you very much. One well meaning women said,

"He has to make himself look pretty."

It did not bother me at the time. I just sat down in the next free stall and did what I came for. But at the end of the day it left me wondering if they really got it. I thought,

"Jeez! If they don't get it, who will?"

At about the same time, it occurred to me that I had missed much in the life of a girl and young woman. I resented it. I completely missed being a girl and was never completely a boy. I acted one way to fit in, yet even as I did, I desired to be someone else entirely. That dichotomy describes gender incongruence as much as anything. In many ways my sisters exacerbated that schism as I would watch them and want to be like them and do what they were doing, yet intuitively knew that I would never be accepted under those circumstances at home, school or with friends.

I came out to both my sisters. They were very supportive and encouraging. To cheer me my sister Kathy reminded me of some of her unpleasant girlhood experiences.

"We hated our school uniforms," she said.

"We'd take up the hems, and Mom would let them down again."

She understood how I felt, however, as she said,

"There is no sense trying to move forward while dwelling on missed things of the past." What might have been, perhaps even should have been, like the road not taken, leads nowhere.

I called my brother Mike in early July. He was having a tough time with his back and work, so my timing was bad. The conversation was hard for us both, but he listened and asked a lot of questions.

"Mike," I said, "I don't quite know the best way to tell you this, so I'll come straight out with it. I am the proverbial woman trapped in a man's body. It's always been that way."

"I don't know what to say," he replied. "I love you."

"Let me send you the letter that I sent to some others. Terry and Kathy know, and maybe you can talk with them about it. I'd like to send some pictures too, so you see the real me," I said.

"Okay," Mike responded haltingly and without much heart.

"I know it's hard to understand, but I need your support," I said imploringly as we hung up the phone.

He has not spoken to me since.

He was shocked and already grieving the loss of his brother, but he had said that he loved me. I sent him the promised "letter" and some pictures but did not hear back from him. I knew he needed time to get his thoughts around this but feared that his Bible Belt Baptist wife filled in the gaps of his ambivalence with not so flattering religious rhetoric. I was sure that he would have my back as I had his countless times before, and remain crestfallen and bewildered at his lack of tolerance.

One of my colleagues suggested that if I intended to stay in the Montana legal profession, I should start telling other lawyers about my transition and garner such support as could be had. The brain trust agreed.

"We will see if Montana is ready for a transgender lawyer," I concluded.

So, in late July, I arranged to meet with ten or more of my colleagues to deliver the news, which I realized would likely mean coming out to the world. I went as Bob, but I took along pictures to show them Bobbie. These were the same photos that Monique had commented on months earlier, and to my delight and surprise, some of my friends had the very same remark.

"This is a lovely woman," said Karen.

Karen was my friend and colleague from Ennis, a few miles to the East of Virginia City. We had confided with each other on many occasions over the years. She was a kind, considerate and compassionate soul, having walked through more than her own share of personal suffering. I was confident that she would at least not run away screaming in horror at my news. She was the first colleague to whom I came out.

"I have gender issues. I'm switching," I said.

It was awkward, as you might guess. It was not the usual thing that a man in Ennis, Montana says. But the words I chose to say were not nearly as important to me as just getting it past my lips and out into the light of day. Not one iota of Karen's good countenance changed, and I loved her for it. She got right up and hugged me.

Stephanie, the public defender in Sheridan just the other side of the Tobacco Roots Mountains, was next. She was a friend and colleague with whom I had confided much and listened as well. She could be assertive almost to the point of aggression. She was smart, confident and savvy. She was conscientious and an excellent trial lawyer. She kept me honest as a prosecutor and made me work harder than anyone else. She could advocate for the guiltiest of clients even in the face of criticism, and I respected her immensely.

"It's gender. I'm becoming your girlfriend," I told her.

She knew my meaning instantly, smiled and gave me a big hug.

"You got it going on," she said, as she looked through the pictures.

Though I do not see her often, we remain friends today. I knew that she and Karen too were just being nice and encouraging to their friend. However, it was still incredibly affirming to hear such kind things in light of all I had imagined over the course of my lifetime. I wanted to come out to the world.

"Can we just, like, have a girl's world?" I said to Monique when I saw her next.

My sisters echoed that sentiment when they later revealed to me that they had called each other to discuss the news. When we were young, my siblings and I competed along gender lines.

"Girls are better than boys," or "boys are better than girls," each of us insisted.

With three girls and three boys we were hopelessly deadlocked. Terry and Kathy's discussion included a congratulatory "Yeaaaaaaa," now that the deadlock had been broken. And, if nothing else, my transition afforded me a unique perspective on that age old question to which I may definitively answer,

"Girls are better."

I had needed my own lawyer for the previous few years to defend against a malicious prosecution suit brought by a lasting nemesis, Reid Rosenthal, a real estate developer in Sheridan, Montana, whom I had prosecuted unsuccessfully for violation of Montana's Stream Bed Preservation Act. That law requires a developer to obtain a "310" permit prior to starting a development project that would disturb the bed or bank of a stream. I had consulted with lawyers who practiced in this field, including the chief legal counsel for the Department of Natural Resources and Conservation, that administers the "310" program. We all agreed that a telephone pole anchored above the stream on what appeared to be the bank, with electric conduit stretched across, required a permit. Rosenthal had not obtained one.

Rosenthal had filed no less than sixty lawsuits in the previous ten years, and had been feuding with a colleague and good friend over a land deal and appurtenant rights in a subdivision he was developing. He had made and lost millions in the Silverado Bank scandal that had rocked the Denver financial world years earlier and escaped to the relative calm of Sheridan to pursue his dreams and schemes.

I would be changing my legal name, residence, job and gender during the pendency of this lawsuit and thought my lawyer may want to know. Paul was very accepting and supportive. He never missed the proper pronouns from that day forward. He performed magnificently, and of course, we ultimately won at the Supreme Court, even after the plaintiff made a motion to change the caption of the suit from *"Rosenthal v. Robert R. Zenker"* to *"Rosenthal v. Roberta R. Zenker, f/k/a Robert R. Zenker."*

It is axiomatic in the least to say that his lawsuits were vexatious, but I must concede that this last legal joust was an unanticipated victory for Rosenthal, even though I ultimately won the war. That Supreme Court caption, with both the male and female nomenclature, would be the first hit every time you would "Google" my name, so that anyone who bothered would know about my transition. I could never prove it, but I think it did have some impact on employment opportunities.

For instance, later on, in the fall of 2007, I got a part time job as a legal instructor at the local community college. It was an introductory paralegal course in which, among other things, I taught the students to conduct online legal research. One student brought in a copy of the Supreme Court opinion granting me summary judgment in the Rosenthal case, and there were both names on the cover like a beacon announcing to the class that their instructor was transgender. Nothing was said, although I gladly would have explained as by then I felt I had nothing to hide. The student asked for a reference at the end of the term, and I did not feel that she had done all that well. I could not in good conscience recommend employment as a paralegal with a law firm and found some way to let her down easy. I suspect she "outed" me to the administration in her resentment because they did not invite me back the next term. Instead, they readvertised the position and did not even return my phone calls and emails inquiring about the job as they had the year before.

Another outcome of telling my lawyer about my transition was a little chain reaction that took my news to the governor's office. I had forgotten that even though my lawyer was a good attorney in his own right; he did work for the State. He was responsible to a bureaucratic hierarchy and felt compelled to apprise his boss of the new twist in the Rosenthal case. His boss, Bill, whom I knew from my first year internship at Tort Claims, wanted me to tell my story to his boss, the Director of the Department of Administration and a representative from the governor's office.

"I might as well take out a full page ad in the Independent Record," I complained to another trans woman I knew in Helena.

"Trans Ladies of the world unite; break free of the tightywhities that bind you," I went on sarcastically as if quoting from a Transgender Manifesto.

I was afraid that if I disclosed my secrets altogether, they would indeed become a matter of public record, as Montanans enjoy a fundamental constitutional right to know everything that goes on behind the closed doors of government. I would waive all confidentiality, and word would get back to the Madison county commissioners before I got home. I was at a loss, as I did not see how such disclosure would advance my position in the litigation. I was afraid it might also result in Helena exposure that I did not want, at least not in that fashion. I felt more than a little consternation and anxiety.

I decided not to consent to release of my confidential information, but Bill wanted to talk to me anyway. I was sure that my interests were not his intentions but rather he was concerned about covering his own butt. At about this same time, the city manager in Largo Florida, Steve Stanton, made national headlines and a CNN feature as he announced that he would be transitioning. I did not want to become Montana's version of the media circus that dogged Steve. I understood the argument that since I had already openly told so many people that it was bound to surface, but I did not want to invite it. We went round and round. I finally agreed to speak with the governor's chief legal counsel, Ann, whom I had also known from my Tort Claims days.

Ann and I spoke often that summer of 1990, and I thought of her as left of left. I trusted that Ann would get it and be okay with the gender transition concept. However, I was afraid that Rosenthal would get a hold of it and try to exploit the information against me somehow. I was afraid too that word would get back to Madison County, and people might make it uncomfortable for me. Somewhere in all of this, I feared for my personal safety, although there had been no threats.

The meeting with Ann was anticlimactic. Once she got over her mild shock, we had a nice conversation about gender transition.

"My reading group just read a book about that, *The Danish Girl*."

"Really, what's it about?" I asked, keenly interested then in every bit of trans literature I could find.

"It's the story of a transgender woman in Denmark in the 1920s," she said.

"Really," I remarked warming to the story.

"Did she have gender reassignment surgery?" I asked.

"Yea, she did," Ann apprised me, "but she died in the end."

She was as curious personally with the transition process as she was confused as to why she was the recipient of such personal information.

"Why are you telling me all this?" she wanted to know as she shrugged her shoulders.

"I really don't need to know."

"Well, Bill thought you should know, and I really don't mind. I'd like to promote as much understanding as possible."

Though she blithely tossed off some references to my party affiliation, she informed me with just as much tongue in cheek flair that the administration had greater things to worry about. She did feel a need to apprise the chief of staff but assured me that it would take only two minutes, and she would not use any personal identifiers.

Most of the people I confided in, though shocked, were very supportive, much to my surprise and everlasting relief. Some colleagues really stepped up. Jack did my name change, charging me for his expenses only. As I mentioned earlier, John figured prominently into my transition. When I revealed myself to him, he accepted it warmly and supportively.

He even suggested that I speak with his wife about employment with the newly created State Office of Public Defender. That would be a switch for a career prosecutor, but as I had been questioning everything I thought,

"Why not?"

It would not be the only switch I would make.

John's wife, Randi, a highly successful and well thought of criminal defense trial lawyer, had been appointed as the inaugural director of the new state agency. I called her and met with her within a week. She talked to me about a position with the appellate defender's bureau.

I met with the bureau chief, Jim, the following week. I had known Jim for years. He is an amazing man, who retired as a District Court Judge in Western Montana to become a lawyer with Montana Legal Services just off the Fort Peck Indian Reservation in the far northeastern part of the state. I knew no one who could make such an adjustment and much less be willing or interested in doing so. He had worked for several years more recently in the prosecution's appellate division of the Attorney General's office. We had even served on a Governor's advisory task force together about ten years prior. I knew Jim, and he knew me, sort of.

Jim was, and is, a different kind of character. He is a liberal to be certain, intelligent and a polished legal writer. But his social and administrative skills left much to be desired. He knows this and cares little about the conclusions others might draw of him. He is very much a self-directed person, if not merely self-interested and eccentric. But he loves chocolate and offered me a job.

Jim, Randi and John had conspired to some degree to allow me to work there while I transitioned. It was more or less a place to hide out while I did so that provided me with a pay check and health insurance. Jim knew what I was doing and he simply did not care, so long as I did the work. That weekend I found a place to live in Helena, where my new job was located. I had given my will and my life over to the care of God. I had trusted God, and a path opened before me.

There would be a way up that mountain, where it had seemed impossible. I thought of the scene in *The Call of The Wild,* where John Thornton begins his trek up the Chilcoot Pass on his way to Dawson.[37] For me the mountain's shadowy distance had become clearer and much closer. Now I stood high upon its slope, not yet to the top, but well on my way. I put one step in front of another without staring hopelessly off into the distance. I had gotten up every day and done what I had to do.

I put in my resignation to the Madison County Commissioners, effective September 11, 2006, the same day that we would sentence Bischoff. I had a lot to do before then, like pack up and move the last ten years of my life, separate with my best friend and soul mate, close out all my county and criminal files, tell my mom and children that I was a transsexual in gender transition and start my new life as a woman.

As impossible as it all seemed, it felt wonderful to allow people to know the real me. Their acceptance and support was a gleeful surprise and I cried many happy tears. It was something I had never known, and I was overwhelmed. However, this time it was not sadness, but the first glimpses of gratitude. It was hard for me to grasp why God had been so good to me when much of the world at that moment seemed a bit lost. I had felt for a very long time that there was so much wrong with me that I did not deserve to be happy. I was wrong. I was good, and it was okay to be happy. The drive to be the real me became so strong I felt like a prisoner just before the jailer opens the door the final time.

I now relied on faith instead of dogma. Accordingly, I believed that God was with me through every step of my transition, holding my hand, carrying me at times, but always loving and accepting. I emailed a friend that I had felt a lot of religious guilt and shame right up until I began transition. Yet once I accepted myself, so many good things began to happen that I saw the hand of God at work, accepting and loving me long before I could do so myself. And God loves me still and blesses every step I take.

God wanted me to be happy and loved the woman I was becoming, even though some others cling to rules and scriptures of supposed axioms rather than inspiration. It begs the question: to whom do we attribute greater faith, the one who reads the rules and then follows them or the one who prays and then acts? The question is rhetorical, not to criticize one or the other, for both are valid in my view, if only to show that each person's path to spirituality, life and God need not ascribe to a group doctrine. Is it enough for me to pray for God's will and then sit and wait for it to happen to me, for God to act upon me? I may sit for a very long time. Or, must I offer myself and my will to the care of God, and then take action? I have yet to be thunderstruck, so, in the end, I believe that I must act. And, to the intolerant I ask,

"What is it about women that you do not like?"

When they can answer that question, I will tell them what they do not like about me.

Peggy and I went to Missoula in mid-August to visit with Meghan and Shane. They had gone off to college in 2000 and 2002 respectively, and though neither completed their degrees, they both remained in Missoula. They both worked at the mall and naturally became "mall rats." We had lunch at some Mexican place there.

When I met Peggy, I could barely tolerate anything spicy. The first time she made me dinner, she made Thai Hot and Sour Soup with shrimp. As I tried a few tentative sips, my face flushed and I began to sweat.

"Would it be okay if I just ate the shrimp?" I asked.

"Oh sure," Peggy said, "You don't like spicy food?"

"Well, not this spicy."

I have grown more accustomed to spicy food, even crave it from time to time. However, I will not attempt Thai Hot and Sour Soup. Fourteen years later, I had come to love a lot of spicy foods, especially Peggy's Thai peanut sauce and noodles. Even though my initial experience with Mexican food in an Alpine, Texas jail had been miserable, Mexican food became a staple. I still make Peggy's Green Chili Enchiladas.

I had hoped to come out to my kids for months. They had gotten the same recovery letter that everyone else had and knew that I was recovering from alcoholism.

"Do you want to make your amends to us?" Meghan teased (or so I thought) when I told her after lunch that I needed to talk to them.

Although I did need to make my amends to them, I was not near far enough along in my program to even think about how to accomplish it. Meghan had been resisting the chat I requested for months, finding one or another thing that would make it impossible to get together, as if I was an unwanted suitor that she put off with excuses. We would not have the opportunity to talk that weekend in early August because she had to go to work.

Somehow the lunch conversation turned to me getting my ears pierced. I knew I had to do this, and looked excitedly forward to it. Meghan worked at Claire's, a chain boutique at a lot of malls that caters to young, fashion minded girls, offering costume jewelry, hair accessories and other assorted accouterments. They also did ear piercing, and Meghan almost challenged me to do it. I had wanted badly for my children to be involved and supportive in my transition, so badly it seems that I let wishful thinking take advantage of Meghan's offer.

I took her up on it, and on August 12, 2006, Meggie pierced my ears. I felt bad for the false pretenses but thought that she would not hold it against me as she knew I had been wanting to talk to her for a couple of months. I could not have been more wrong, as it is clear now that Meghan had anticipated expressions of my selfishness at divorcing her mother and abandoning her, and what she got was more self-centered, if not necessary, verbiage.

The need to talk to Meghan and Shane became critical when I got the job in Helena and had an actual moving date of September 12, 2006. It was clear by now, after all the resistance, that Meghan knew it was something ominous, and if Meghan knew, so did Shane. Joanne and I had conditioned them in that regard by something we had called "family meetings" when they were young, which indicated that something very serious was to follow, like moving to another town across the state or getting divorced, for instance. I should have known that I was dragging up all that unresolved anger and resentment in Meghan when I told them I needed to talk to them, but I did not consider it, so urgent was I in my need to transition.

It was with that same single minded self-centered ignorance that I optimistically agreed with Meghan to send her a letter setting out what I needed to tell her, and she could respond. All my other landings as I stepped off the cliffs of uncertainty had been soft, padded with confidence and affirmation from the encouragement offered by my colleagues. I naively hoped it would be the same with the kids. Not too long after my visit to Missoula, before the holes from my ear piercing were even healed, I pierced their world in a way that would not heal. I sent Meghan and Shane the same academic form letter on August 18, announcing my gender transition save a few personal remarks about my love for them and some mumblings about discovering something about love and family.

I was not far from the mark on that last little bit when I received a written response a couple of weeks later addressed to "Residents." It was not the discovery I hoped to make, however. It was hurtful, mean spirited, angry and hateful, written in Meghan's hand and asserting that Shane agreed. I later called him to find out.

"Shane, did you agree with all that Meghan wrote?" I asked.

"Yea, pretty much," he said, lacking any real conviction.

"Stay warm and let me know if you need anything," were the last words my son spoke to me.

The letter did not spare Peggy from its vitriol either. We went for a walk and talked and intellectualized about children. We rationalized that it must be hard on them. I went out to pack a few more things in the garage and broke down. Just as I began to sob, Peggy was there to hold me. It hurt as much as I had ever hurt, and my crying sobs seemed to match. I could not imagine any worse result than my kids intentionally hurting me just because I was trying to be genuine and honest, no matter what had passed under the bridge before. There were no words of love or family, no questions or any willingness or interest to even talk about their thoughts and feelings. Even though all my friends and supporters said they would come around, they have not. Neither of them have spoken or attempted to communicate with me in any way in the five-plus years since.

I kept the letter and pull it out every now and then, like a thorn in my heart. That Meghan is angry and hurt is plain, but at what is not quite so clear. Is it because I left her mother? I had thought at the time that it would be good for them to witness a healthy, loving parental relationship. Was it abandonment? Probably, but that does not explain it all. While she misapprehends the facts of her leaving Oregon, her mother's alcoholism and mine, she hit a few things right on the head. She repeatedly referred to me as selfish. She wrote,

"This is the definition of a midlife crisis." It was that at least, although more of a whole life crisis in my mind. She rightly pointed out that I selfishly thought they would stand by me. This expectation was as foolish and naïve as my belief that Peggy would save me. I really did think they would be okay with this once they got past the shock. I thought that after the thirteen years since I had divorced their mother and the ten years since they had left Oregon that they were past the drama and ill will. I was wrong, dead wrong as it turned out to be. Her parting words in the letter were,

"My Dad and stepmother are dead . . . ."

I was being selfish, I knew, of course. Survival is like that.

In a certain way I am dead. While I shall always be their father, the persona that they knew is no longer here. I am a new person in so many ways unknown to them.

"God does not give you two lives," Meghan had written.

"We have many lives," Monique responded when I told her.

I am dead, yet I live. The Gospel message seems to be very much about new life. I am a grain of wheat that has fallen to the ground and died so that I may have new life.

People who know me tell me that the kids will come back. They want to comfort and encourage me. I appreciate it. But they do not know Meghan and her brother's allegiance. They do not know that little girl who said, "Don't bother me either." I am afraid that if her stubbornness doesn't lock her into her position, her pride will. I must take some responsibility for both of those traits, so I will not bother her. Yet, I am grieving the loss of my children. I have to let go and pray that they will someday return.

But if not I still must live. My approach when I came out was to offer my soul in as honest and gentle a manner as possible to those who would take it, but if not, to shake their dust from my sandals. I could not stop or be dragged down by those who would not go with me, even where family was concerned. I could not afford to dwell on my losses, given as I was to morbid preoccupation. Depression and alcoholism are often a lethal combination, just as therapy and recovery had been so vital. I could not have turned back even if I wanted to. As for Meghan and Shane, the door will always be open, just as it was with my father and my God.

I wrote to Kathy:

I realize that you are afraid that my stuff will break up the family. I will regret that if it happens, but I can do nothing to stop it except present myself in as honest and gentle a manner as possible. I have done so, blaming no one and asking only for support. If that is not to be had, I hope you understand that I cannot do anything else about it. I learned that with Mike. As soon as I start to think about how much rejection hurts, I get depressed and want to drink. If I ever do that I just cannot trust myself. I greatly fear the result. So, I quickly put it out of my head, give it up to God and move on. I do not mean to be hard hearted, but this is really the only way I can do this.

I sent my Mom the "letter" too, just a few days after sending the kids theirs. Mom's response, for as much as Terry, Kathy and I had fretted about it for months, couldn't have been more different than the kids' response.

I called her just after receiving the letter from my kids and greatly feared another horrid rejection.

"I was up all night thinking about you," she said, when I called the following Saturday.

"I am sorry," I humbly offered as I knew it was not the first time on my behalf.

"I was worried for your everlasting soul," she said, "but I must tell you."

"I spoke with the priest at church," Mom continued, "and he said he worked with a couple of transgender women in Nashville."

"The Church does not have anything to say about this," she finally reported from her discussion with the priest.

She was relieved, but shocked, bewildered and in great turmoil. She shared the same obstacle as my brother, Mike.

"There was no warning. I did not have a clue." Mom said.

There were clues, but apparently so subtle as to escape notice or commitment to memory. I had wanted it that way. Evidently I had been most successful.

"It doesn't matter whether you are male or female. We are all the same in God's eyes," Mom said, paraphrasing the gospel.

"You are my child."

I wept silently.

Mom was relieved to learn that it was nothing she did or did not do. Most significantly, there was no moralizing or judgments.

"It takes a lot of courage to do what you are doing. It is a hard path you have chosen."

Mom got it. She did not miss a beat. She was concerned about my depression though.

"Depression runs in the family," she said, though I knew it was yet another trait I got from my father.

I called her that Saturday morning, just as I had been doing for years, and it could have been just another conversation, except that I knew that she still loved me.

Mom wanted some pictures, and when she saw them said,

"You make a good looking woman."

After that, I was heartened. I was encouraged also to learn about the Nashville Catholic diocese's positive treatment of trans women. There seemed to be at least some tolerance, if not acceptance, somewhere within the Catholic Church. Although, that hope has been recently dashed as Pope Benedict proclaimed to the world about those who change their gender,

"We do not condone discrimination. But we must distinguish between people."I looked up discriminate and distinguish, and they are all but synonyms. Mom offered to send me some of her clothes and jewelry, a magnanimous gesture in my eyes that quickly became filled with happy tears.

Chapter Twelve

Right Sized

Rowing in Eden!
Aha! The sea!
Might I but moor tonight in thee!

- Emily Dickinson[38]

It was not a flash of white light, my spiritual awakening. It was more like awakening slowly from a long nap. I realized that God had always been there when my mind was sufficiently clear to allow me to see that the prints behind me were not my own after all. What I could not figure out though was why God did not seem to be present in the first few months of my real life test. "Real life test" is a therapeutic phrase for trans people in an early stage of transition. We take the gender of identification for a test run before surgery. I was incredibly excited to begin mine on September 12, 2006 when I would be in Helena lock, stock and wig box. There were many times I wanted to get away - far away, like a beach somewhere.

Yet, I had to make a stand somewhere, and I chose Montana. First though, we had to move Peggy to Butte. She found a craftsman style house on the west side by St. James Hospital, another of my "fake heart attack" haunts. I had been having dizzy spells as the result of my drinking and had again the same mimicking symptoms as before, mostly numbness and pain down my left arm and shortness of breath. This event was not nearly as dramatic as the first, as Butte had its own heart specialist by then. It did, however, result in neck surgery and a multi-level fusion in September of 2003.

I helped Peggy pack the furniture I had made and much of the accouterment of the life we shared. It was bittersweet as I thought about reducing our marriage to bath towels and tea cups, yet I felt comforted that we survived. We remained people who loved one another, and I often reminded myself that there were no rules in this game.

September 11 was my last day as the Madison County Attorney. My last official act was the Bischoff sentencing. The story had been front page news, and on the 12th, the *Montana Standard* and *Bozeman Chronicle* were no exception. Bischoff had pled guilty to the reduced charge of negligent homicide, which meant in essence that while he may have been terribly negligent in the victim's death, he did not intend to kill her. It did not make sense to me, but I was outvoted by the prosecution team. We had decided at the beginning that a jury should decide whether the doctor's conduct was criminal, but at some point along the line that objective changed.

The change was not formal or dramatic, but like so many things, you look up one day and things are differenet. We had gotten beaten up in a deposition of one of their experts, and our doctor was just no match for theirs. At some point too I had gotten into a personal tiff with one of the defense lawyers. I had impugned his integrity as he mine. Of course, that was before I got sober and began to recover. I had no tools by which to see my part, even if I had wanted to. It was preferable, as a young friend of mine says, to "marinate in my misery." In my pickled judgment, I wanted to try the case. Fortunately, I at least had enough good judgment to defer to the majority of the prosecution team, which included my friend, John, who, as I mentioned, was the single most experienced murder prosecutor in the state. He was also the most successful.

John had prosecuted the Duffy murders in Boulder a few years earlier with, as Judge Davis once recounted to me from the bench, only a week's preparation. John had also litigated the prison riot cases. On September 23, 1991, maximum security prisoners took over the Montana State Prison in a grisly riot in which five inmates were brutally murdered. John was assigned the task of prosecuting the main perpetrators some of whom were already in prison for other gruesome murders. Two of them committed suicide while awaiting their appeals and one died of other, unnatural causes, like lethal injection. John displayed his quick wit and rather dry, if not dark, sense of humor.

"Jeez, all the State need do to win a homicide appeal is appoint me," he quipped, knowing that if you could not laugh in this business you would not survive.

It was true in any event.

Like many seasoned prosecutors with any higher moral sense, John did not believe in the death penalty personally. Neither did I. It seemed incongruous, if not disingenuous. I understand that some crimes are so far beyond the pale that the perpetrator can no longer be allowed to live in society. However, taking that person's life seems barbaric as the crime and little better than the murderous conduct identified as criminal.

I was utterly convinced that Bischoff purposely ended his victim's life, even if she was already dying. She had survived for five days without life support. She indeed had the constitution of a horse, and who knows what that strength and the grace of God could have done for her? Bischoff did not know any more than I did. But he did not rise to the level of the heinous murderers that John was used to, and Bischoff had suffered greatly already. He was going to serve ten years in prison in Idaho for the bank robbery, so we agreed that he would serve his Montana sentence concurrently. He would never do prison time in Montana.

I was glad to be done with the case in any event, as I would be starting my new life the very next day. That made the papers too. I had made several moving trips to Helena, carefully nesting in each room of my new place as I went. I also had a storage unit in East Helena, or should I say that Bob did. I legally changed my name to Roberta R. Zenker on August 23, 2006. A colleague offered to help when I told him of my transition. He had clerked for one of the judges and knew the statutory short-cuts to expedite a name change procedure available when the petitioner is at risk, as in domestic violence cases. I was very fortunate to have been a lawyer and cultivated friends and a good reputation. I drew upon all my credibility capital then.

The storage unit had the feel of a mausoleum, sort of a memorial unit for Bob. All his tools from the shop, gardening supplies and hunting gear and clothes were carefully stuffed into a 10 X 20 box. I thought it ironic, if not fitting, that Bob was tucked neatly into a box as Bobbie had been for so long. Monique thought it odd that I kept the guy stuff so readily available.

I did not think of it as a safety net. I just wanted to get some value for some of my things, like $400 Italian wool suits. I had two, together with a wool overcoat worth just as much that Peggy bought me the previous Christmas. I was afraid that selling it only added to her still festering sense of betrayal. Between eBay, consignment and Goodwill I managed to get rid of all the boy clothes in a year or so. I kept the shop, gardening and hunting stuff though, as I hoped to make those things part of my new life.

On the morning of September 12, 2006, Peggy went to work as usual. I cannot imagine what must have gone through her mind and heart as her life dismantled before her eyes under its own momentum. I thanked God for the previous six months that allowed us to slowly unravel our marriage and life together, yet remain good friends. Although we took to sleeping in different rooms very early on, we began living as girlfriends almost as quickly. We often talked into the night as we sat on her bed in our jammas. The thing we came to find about love, I mean real love, is that it can grow and change right along with those who are fortunate enough to share it. That we love each other still is testament to the power of love and the true union of our souls. Though our relationship has changed, I believe that we are joined there still.

On the day I left though, my emotions were jumbled. I was apprehensive and excited about beginning my new life. I was sad and resentful about much of what I had to leave behind. I was certain that Madison County rejected me, as word about my transition had slipped out. Yet, I never gave the place or its people the chance to accept me. Instead, I ran. It had been easier all my life to run rather than face my fears.

Judge Tucker called me a month later, as I had only sent him a card in a futile attempt to explain my reasons for leaving.

"I can understand you lacking the courage to speak to me in person," he said.

I struggled for words, but none came. It was like trying to describe to children of the light what it is like to walk into the sunshine after a life in darkness. No matter what words are used, children of the light cannot understand life in the darkness. Loren's judgment of me was harsh and hurt all the more because it was true.

I wore sandals the day I left, merely so I could shake the dust from them as I crossed the county line. Whether that was a final act of defiance or a first step beyond convention, I cannot say, but it did mark much more than the start of a therapeutic stage. I turned my world insideout and upsidedown. One day I sat atop the social order. I was married with children, had a home, a car and a truck, a shop, greenhouse and garden. I was an elected official earning $75,000 a year. The next day I gave it all away. I was as much as a little girl alone just starting out in the world, and I loved it.

I had my own place, a subterranean refuge known as a daylight basement apartment. I shared a garage with my landlord who lived upstairs. I made it my sanctuary, my porch to escape the coming storms. *Mother Mary comes to me, speaking words of wisdom, let it be.39* I had a seldom-used front entrance to the street. The base boosters in the cars commandeered down 11th Avenue by youthful drivers shook the foundations of the house from thirty feet away. The rear entrance into the garage gave the place a "bat cave" feel. I traded my vehicles for a little blue Subaru with tinted windows and looked like a "G" girl. The garage had an automatic door opener, and the car had an electronic remote starter. I could open the door and start my car from inside the apartment. Playing super hero on those cold winter mornings was simply irresistible. After meetings I would often wait for a few minutes until the guys had gathered outside the door to smoke. I sometimes parked there, and when I would hit that remote starter from inside the building, they much resembled that moose on the Jefferson River.

The apartment was safe, warm and inviting. I took pains to feminize each room as I moved in, my buffalo hide and firewood sculpture notwithstanding. The hide rested on my recliner, as I had nowhere else to put it. It was Robert's, and I held it as sacred.

"It looks like the king's throne," Monique said, and I did not miss the masculine reference. I later gave the robe to my friend, Barb, as she understood how important it was to me and would hold it sacred too. The sculpture rested on a small stand constructed for that purpose. It was fashioned in the likeness of a pregnant trans woman of three logs in various stages of cutting and splitting. I enjoyed the irony, as well as the symbolism. It might not be the kind of decor a middle-aged woman would feature in her living room, Monique suggested. I threw it away as I had so many other vestiges from my past, ghosts really, of the man who used to be.

My landlord gave me flowers, and I set them in the west window to catch the evening sunlight, as other flowers did throughout the winter for comfort. All the walls were painted a soft white which I liked. I preferred to decorate with photographs and dried flowers and such. I put a lavender and yellow pastel throw on the little futon love-seat Peggy had given me. It was small, but I did not have room for a full size couch anyway.

My pass-through bedroom was scarcely large enough for my queen size bed and dresser. There was not even enough room to fully open the closet door, so I took it off its hinges and threw on an over-the-door shoe rack to better accommodate my growing collection of shoes. The bedroom walls shared red accents with black and white photos and one blue print from an etching of the refurbished railroad train engine now running in Virginia City. I had gotten Peggy and myself on the occasion of her birthday the previous August, a framed print from a local artist who had passed away from a brain aneurism. It was called *Sleeping Beneath the Window*. We both loved Dolly's work, so it too was a fitting vestige of my past. I would add mementos I collected throughout my new journey. The room was mostly underground and had no windows, thus repeating the cave theme. But it was warm and cozy, and I felt safe as I burrowed deeper within the same comforter I had taken refuge under the preceding six months at our home in Silver Star, often on the couch, as I listened to the spring rains give way to a soft summer.

The bathroom was long and narrow, just wide enough to allow for a large claw foot tub that was long and deep enough so that I could lie submerged up to my neck and still have my knees under water. I had not previously been one for baths, preferring instead a pounding hot shower. However, I had known since the days of Calgon taking women away, that women enjoyed baths. It was not long before I came to appreciate their calming, restorative powers. I would think of myself as in the womb of the Mother of Earth and Mother of all Children, a higher power of sorts that I clung to with hope for my children. I did not wish to deny or contest my understanding of God. However, in my eight months since coming to believe in a power greater than myself, I could still not trust the God whom I feared had abandoned me.

The wounds of separation from family and friends were still fresh. Though some cuts never heal, I could not even get these to stop bleeding. Any time the topic of kids or family would come up; I resented it and could barely contain my tears. Once, just as soon as I arrived home, I fell to the floor bawling, sobbing and moaning, a blathering mess. Open went the hatch on the submarine. God grant me the grace to overcome self pity. Since I could no longer be part of my children's lives I turned them over to the Mother of all Children with a prayer that she would watch over and care for them. She gave me a measure of solace until I learned to ask God to remove my self-pity, talk to another alcoholic, and find someone to serve.

I used to write letters to my son during his first few years away from home. I enjoyed the exchange and tried to impart my knowledge of life and its ways in words, since I had failed to do so in deed. Among the things I suggested were the words from an old tune the name of which I cannot recall,

"You got to get in to get out."

My spin was that I had to get into something or someone else in order to get out of my-self. If only I had been able to do it when I was much younger, I may have avoided much pain and actually been present to those around me. The seeds of service, however, had been planted in me since my days at St. Michael's. I knew I did not do well on my own, and I feared being alone through the winter. I determined when I moved to Helena to be involved in a church community and service.

"I'm looking for a church," I said to Monique prior to my move, "an inclusive spiritual community."

"St. Paul's," she said without hesitation, not even knowing the denomination.

It was and is United Methodist. St. Paul's became my home away from home.

"Open hearts and doors," I heard the pastor proclaim the first day I attended.

They had just moved into their new church, a grand architectural structure. It needed to be grand, as it stood in the shadow of the formidable façade of St. Helena Cathedral, the seat of majesty for the Roman Catholic Church, Diocese of Western Montana. My friend from law school had first shown me the Cathedral at great personal risk of lightning strike. I was duly impressed, both with its magnificence and at my friend's risk of being suddenly struck a believer.

I attended services at St. Paul's my first Sunday in Helena, September 17, 2006. It was called Welcome Home Sunday, fittingly, I thought, as that is precisely how I felt. I chose a pew by one of the pillars holding up the balcony. It was my fifth day presenting full time as a woman, still new enough for every experience to be another first. I was afraid that everyone was looking at me and could see right through me. Instead of seeing the girl in the boy as I used to fear, I feared the flip side of the same coin, that they would see the boy in the girl.

I was comforted as I read the bulletin and came across a familiar name, Pastor Marianne. As I looked up and saw her, I simultaneously recognized the Methodist Pastor as "Sister Marianne," a Catholic nun at St. Labre nearly thirty years earlier. In that same moment I realized that she had gone through her own metamorphosis, a life-changing transition that was bold and coura-geous in its own right. I continued to sit in the same seat for the next couple of years so that Marianne and I joked that I was holding up the pillar that was holding up the church. That first Sunday, however, Marianne spoke of coming home.

"No matter who or what you are, you are welcome here," she said, and that is still precisely how I feel.

In my fear, heartache and timidity then, however, I nearly cried.

Here I am Lord . . . .

It was short lived, however. I got up to go to the restroom just as Marianne announced some sort of children's presentation. As I walked into the foyer I almost ran into a former colleague from Prosecution Services Bureau. She and John had been in my office in Virginia City not two weeks earlier to discuss my still open criminal cases. She was all business then, and no friendlier as I greeted her at St. Paul's. Perhaps she did not recog-nize me. Later, when I went back to my seat to hold up the church, she was there, ostensibly watching her child.

"Hey, you stole my seat," I whispered to her jokingly.

She literally ran away from me. It hurt, and the rejection stuck.

I felt much better though after the service when a woman named Barb came up and gave me a big, warm welcoming hug. She was the female in-carnation of my old friend, Tony, effervescent, full of life and love for all. She introduced her partner and her two girls. Barbara is a dear friend and was my sponsor on a religious retreat known as Walk to Emmaus. She has a beauti-ful, clear soprano singing voice that I try to emulate when we do the music for the retreat group. Barb is a woman of faith, always seeming up and on, despite her difficulties. She always has a smile, hug and encouraging words for a friend or anyone who might need comfort or care. She sends inspir-ing emails to our retreat follow-up group known as a Fourth Day group. We have become so close and reliant on each other's love and support that we call each other Rocks - Sista' Rocks. They have buoyed me many more times than I can ever repay. The old saying about not knowing how we touch the lives of others, perhaps when most needed, was never truer than it is with the Rocks. But Barb, my sponsor, has been a confidant with whom I trust the big stuff, like whether gender transition is really God's will for me.

The day after "Welcome Home Sunday," when my computer was hooked up in the new house and I was electric once again, I emailed my friend Sylvia.

"You cannot imagine how whole and beautiful I feel in this woman's world. Everyone I have met has embraced Bobbie as the woman she is. Yes, I'm good. Man, I love being a woman."

I thank the Lord there's people out there like Marianne, Barb and the Rocks too. Because of them, and their friendship and support, I was able to avoid resenting those who rejected me - well, for the most part, at least enough to keep me from stewing and obsessing over them.

Word in a small community travels faster than I could, even when Montana had no posted speed limit. If I bought underwear in Butte, I swear they knew the size back in Madison County before I drove the forty miles home. It was sort of funny when I came out to colleagues in Helena that one lawyer told another, who told his client in Twin Bridges, who was on the school board, who told the school superintendent, who told the guy who used to work down the hall from me, and so on and so forth. My size is six for any who may have been away and did not hear. Peggy and I were going to have a garage sale at the end of September for what was left of the stuff of our life together in Silver Star, and though I did not care what people thought, I did worry for my safety. I needn't have, though, as I was not, nor have I ever been, physically threatened or harassed in any way. Many trans women, have been, however, and some murdered just for being who they are.

"Yes, but they put themselves in that position too," Monique had told me with grave caution.

As heinous and awful as the murders were, she may have been right. Many victims put themselves in a position to be hurt. I took the lesson to heart and avoided such circumstances for the most part. For the parts where I was foolish, I credit my safety to Montana's spirit, good fortune, and God's grace.

As September came to a close, I sensed that things were going well, better than I could have or did imagine. I had some down days, but they were mostly up. The most amazing and wonderful thing was my awareness that by God's grace I was beginning to make it as a woman, even though I would have a few more down days on that score. I was perceived as a woman almost always and treated as such everywhere I went. And I went everywhere a woman just starting out in a new city would go - stores, post office, church, work, gas station, etc. It felt so good to be living in my own skin, that is to say, living as I believed I should without fear, shame or guilt. I was beginning to feel this certain overwhelming contentment that I would refer to later as inexplicable happiness.

In early October, I met with Marianne at her office. I wanted to reveal myself to her, learn of her transition and seek her aid as I continued to reconcile the faith I had been raised in and feared held no place for me with the faith I would find in my new life. I left a few telephone messages to pique her interest.

"I knew you in another life," I said after the beep. By the time we met, she was indeed intrigued and could not put it together even as I sat before her.

"So, how is it I know you?" she asked after the usual small talk and greetings.

She honestly did not know, and I could see no point in prolonging the mystery.

"You knew me as Bob," I said, just like that.

"Oh, Ohhhhhhhhhhhhh," came the reply.

It was cute and funny but belied far greater acceptance and support than I could have hoped for, as that was all she said about the concept of gender transition.

She had kept in touch with one of the priests from St. Labre, Fr. Dan. I had known Fr. Dan from my start in Montana twenty six years earlier. He was tall and had looked very monkish in the brown robe the Capuchin's wore, with the braided rope tied around the waist. His face was narrow and his nose sharp, so that he bore a hawkish appearance, except that his top feathers had long since fallen away. I had always liked Dan, although we were not close as I had become with Br. Paul, a Capuchin monk with whom I spent a great deal of time chatting and drinking beer. Paul was French and had a great sense of humor, so we just clicked. Dan, on the other hand, was a bit on the serious side, and I never could get past that to really know him.

Fr. Dan came to St. Paul's that fall as part of its lecture series. He would be talking about St. Francis, as he was well versed in all things Francis. His lecture was titled "Radical Heart: St. Francis for Modern Times." I was excited about the topic and seeing the speaker again. I thought it might be a good opportunity to get his thoughts about my transition and my faith. I met with Dan after Sunday services at which he offered the homily. I had always enjoyed his homilies, as they felt real, and offered a more humane glimpse of the Deity. It was still Catholic, but it was a brand, in the words of Louis L'amour, that I could ride for.

After church that late October weekend, Dan and I went to Applebee's to talk. I was heartened and encouraged by his understanding and lack of judgments and moralizing.

"God is more concerned with what lies on the inside rather than the outside," Fr. Dan said, and I loved him more in that moment than ever before. He sent me an email a few days later in which he thanked me for sharing my journey with him and assured that there was nothing wrong with me. He blessed me, writing,

"May the Lord comfort you with peace, strength and hope."

God said yes to that prayer.

As October passed, I took a few of her lessons with me to "nod down their heads" as Dan Fogelberg sings in Old Tennessee, "to the winter."[40] It was coming and I still feared its long lonely nights and cold gray days. I suppose I experience Sunshine Affective Disorder in the winter, so I have since experimented with vitamin D. It seems to help. The learning curve was steep, not just for me but also for the few around me who used to know Bob. I went to my friend, Pam's house a few blocks away to borrow a cup of milk (really) for a pie I was making. She had to reintroduce me to her husband whom I had met a few times as Bob. He was a federal probation officer, and our paths crossed in a couple of criminal cases. I was sorry that I went, as I felt so awkward, like I did not pass very well. Perhaps I did, and the awkwardness was due only to my lack of experience in impromptu social settings. But when a car full of kids laughed and pointed at me on the way home, I knew I had been read.

In keeping with my unreasonable expectations, I thought I would just show up in Helena and be a woman, and everyone would love me. The learning curve was steep indeed and painful as I discovered just how dishonest and unrealistic my expectations could be. Through that pain, I concluded that beauty was worth learning from the inside out, and that no matter how difficult it was, I had an obligation to life itself to live out this journey. To help, I started a notebook with three columns headed by the words, "Grace, Beauty, and Truth." Before going to bed every night, I wrote down the way in which I experienced God in my life - people, places or things that moved me with their beauty, and truths that occurred to me about who and what I was. It kept me positive and helped me to learn gratitude.

Then, there was work. I began my career as an appellate defender on September 14, 2006. As a prosecutor, I had referred to criminal defense work as the "dark side of the force." My office was on the 5th floor of the Park Avenue Building, an old federal building where the notorious "Unabomber" was housed during trial. It was particularly ironic that the bureau chief's office occupied the very spot that had been Ted Kaczynski's cell. I started out in a small room with a window for my meager plants. I had geraniums that bloomed year round, and I looked forward to their color in the dead of the winter to come. I had a Norfolk Pine that was almost 5 feet tall. I bought it as a seedling when Shane was born, as I had with Meghan. Her mother took hers to New Jersey.

The office staff included four to five other lawyers, including the division chief, a receptionist, a legal assistant and a paralegal that did it all. She was the office manager, editor and fiscal person. She was short and very Italian. Sarah was in charge. She was diligent and strong spirited. To her credit, she wanted to produce a top quality product, and we did, in no small part because of her efforts.

Sarah and I clashed from the start. I did not have appellate experience when I started, although I was adept at legal research and could write well. That was not sufficient. I had grown quite lax at citation form at the district court level, as the judges there are more interested in content, likely due to the many other functions a district court judge must serve. I wanted to do things one way and did not understand that Sarah was looking for uniformity. I had become accustomed to calling my own shots and really didn't play that well with anyone else who wanted to do so.

It took a while, but Sarah finally got me trained and broke me of many bad legal writing habits and counterproductive ways of thinking. I am grateful now. But back then I felt as if I must exert my authority. I thought that there should be some sort of pecking order, where the lawyers were sort of more important than the support staff. After all, who was it that they were there for? I ended up feeling angry and resentful, often to the point of tears. That led to self-pity, and back into the misery marinade I would go.

Ultimately, I learned to ask God to remove the resentment, called my sponsor and asked God to teach me love and tolerance. Sometimes I wonder if God does not have a speech impediment or some other disability that deprives God of speech. Would life not be easier if God would just tell us stuff? If God would just tell me what I am doing wrong and gently point out some alternatives, I am certain that I would soon learn. But no! God works in other, much more mysterious ways. The way I learn is through pain and discomfort, by admitting my flaws and having other people make suggestions. I suppose those others have seen the same defects in themselves and have been able to overcome them in much the same way, thus reinforcing their own growth and changes by talking about their own experience to me. Humanity is such a bulky, awkward thing.

Sarah, for her part, tried. She has a good heart. She became a Body Shop representative shortly after I began working there. I was very excited and gratified to be invited to my first "party" of the sort where they model use of the product and you feel compelled to buy at least the cheapest item in the catalogue. My sister, Terry, calls them "vagina" parties, as it seems you have to have one to gain admittance to such events. I went and passed, even through the makeover. I bought some sort of tea tree oil to hide the appearance of pores. My facial pores are huge, and the wrinkles are ever increasing. I have tried every product to "reduce the appearance" of pores and wrinkles, as they each claim they will do as no other product can. None seem to work much.

As soon as Sarah and I returned to work, we squared off over one issue or another. We went on that way, up and down for months. She even arranged to have me move to a window-less office down the hall. Jim had just fired one attorney for, among other things, her troubles with Sarah. I was certain that I was next. Jim's unabashed view was that the lawyers who did the research and authored the briefs, the sum and substance of appellate work in Montana, were expendable. At least, he let me know that I was. Sarah, however, due to considerable skill in formatting the briefs, a task that could take days for the lawyers to do, was sacrosanct. I had few choices but to stay even as I grew miserable and hated going to work. It was not as if the legal community in Montana was eager to embrace the first and only transsexual lawyer in Montana history.

Gender transition complicates the workplace, to say the least, and I was no exception. I was the highest maintenance employee in our shop, and I knew it. I was not happy about it, and neither was Jim. I needed time for doctor's appointments, blood tests, therapy sessions and electrolysis in a town sixty miles away. I think Jim had his fill long before surgery, but to his credit, he honored his commitment to employ me throughout the process.

My saving grace in that office was Jocelyn, a young attorney there. Jocelyn was a Butte girl, possessed of an inner toughness such as is only bred in Butte. But after that, Jocelyn was all sugar and spice, well, a little lace too. She was petite, thin and pretty. She was smart and diligent. Her most endearing quality, however, was her capacity to care and ability to do so without getting all mushy. She let me know in little ways that I was one of the girls, inviting me to lunch with her girlfriend and to her "vagina party." I think it was the kitchen stuff. I got a glass mixing bowl with marked measurements, a handle, spout and lid and a bottle opener with an ergonomic handle for Peggy's Mom and a melon baller.

Life at the Appellate Defender's Office was complicated by the fact that it was a state agency. Jim observed, shall we say, high standards of stewardship of the public dole, while I perhaps might have preferred a less diligent course. I consistently, albeit unintentionally, skated a fine line of violating those standards but felt like I had very little choice. The whole purpose in my coming there, by mutual understanding was to allow me a low profile job during transition and to fill a need they had in the office for another attorney. So we were both getting something, Jim and I, but I did not want to abuse the kindness shown to me. It was the right place for me to be, and though it was painful, as most growth is, I learned a great deal about appellate work and myself.

I was often offended because I thought that I was right, even if no one else did, and that I had to stick up for myself because no one else would. I learned two crucial virtues in the process. First, as I prayed for patience I got adversity and learned humility by letting go of my pride. As my late friend and wise woman, Nancy T., would say, I learned to be "right size," deluding myself with neither grandiosity nor self-pity.

"It is better to be happy than to be right," my sponsor would say, "Cuz' you can't be both."

She told me, "Go to work every day with a smile on your face and say good morning."

I did, even though I was often met with little more than a grumble or no response at all. Work improved, and I even won some cases. I came to see what some said,

"Adversity is just another fucking growth opportunity."

And so it was, even though it felt like mere survival, like my head was just above the water level as it flowed through the screen door in my submarine. I learned a great deal from Jim, Jos and Sarah, much more than I can repay them for. I learned gratitude.

Chapter Thirteen

Let it Be

And when the night is cloudy
There is still a light that shines on me
Shine until tomorrow let it be
I wake up to the sound of music
Mother Mary comes to me
Speaking words of wisdom let it be.

- The Beatles[41]

What is it in the caterpillar that gives the butterfly her wings? What tells her how and when to fly, which flowers to light upon and where to escape the storm? The girl in me had always been there, more or less, and she was glad to be alive. I did have to learn to speak like a woman, though. I went to see a local speech therapist, another provider on Monique's list. I had a voice deep inside that now must speak.

But first I had to learn how. I had to learn to speak, as if anew, with a different timbre, tone, cadence and pitch. The therapist tape-recorded me reading from a newspaper and asked colleagues to identify whether the voice was male or female, and young or old.

"The good news is that most of my colleagues think you are a woman," she said.

"The bad news is that you sound like an old lady."

I bought my own micro recorder and practiced as I drove the ninety miles to Helena for services those first few months. My hero after all these years, my sister, Terry, gave me my voice in a very real way. I had always admired the things she said, and she always seemed so right, so certain. I wanted that, so naturally pictured her speaking in my mind's ear, as it were. I tried to emulate what I heard in my mind as her voice, repeating: "One, one, one. One, one, one."

"A women's speech is 'sing-songy,'" Monique suggested.

"It goes up at the ends of sentences, and even in between."

"Yo-u me-an li-ke th-i-s?"

Eventually, my voice improved and became feminine, although, the "boy voice" still lingered deep within and even surfaced on occasions when I was anxious or angry.

Most trans people will tell you that transition is about "passing" in the gender of identification. I would like to say that it is not so, as it should be about self identity, expression and congruence. Transition is that, but we must still exist within the larger world. We must find our place with the herd. Our human herd simply has little or no tolerance for in-between or dual-gendered members. Thus, to belong, you must pass in one of the two genders accepted by the majority, or live on the fringe. This concept is not new. Feinberg points out that it arose in medieval Western Europe with the departure from matriarchal culture and customs and the rise of patriarchal class divisions.

With the pressure of needing acceptance and affirmation, I began my outer transformation from male to female. Presentation for a trans person in transition is all about how they appear to others when they first appear, literally only skin deep. I have surmised since that we are conditioned from earliest childhood, during the socialization process we all go through to identify another's gender instantaneously when we first see them. In a National Public Radio interview about his new book, *The Hidden Brain*, author, Washington Post columnist and new NPR commentator, Shankar Vedantam reports that scientific studies confirm these phenomena in children as early as three years old.[42] While the interview unfortunately focused only on race, it seems to me to be just as true with gender. As adults, we make immediate subconscious decisions about people we see. As we process the visual verbal cues, we see people as conforming to one gender or the other. We think no more about it. But if something is amiss in that initial presentation, in dress, voice, movements or gestures, we investigate further. Is that a woman or a man? We also learn gender specific roles and behaviors, such that if they are different from what we know, we investigate further. It is in that millisecond that a trans person fails or succeeds, is "read" or is "passing."

Getting read is very discouraging, depressing and often painful, if not dangerous, depending on the reaction you get when read. Chrissy Polis, a twenty-two year old Baltimore transwoman, was severely beaten at McDonald's as bystanders and even employees looked on and laughed. For me, the dangers lurked inside my own mind in the form of fear and self-pity.

One of my transition challenges has been whiskers. Many of my early cross-dressing photos revealed a five o'clock shadow in ridiculous relief set against the rest of my feminine presentation. I hated whiskers then and truly wonder about their current evolutionary purpose. Haven't we outgrown them yet? One of the gross injustices of humanity is the ravages that hormones wreak upon us all as we age. It is no mistake or accident that when men are of child siring age they are physically virile, handsome and, as a friend used to say,

"Young, dumb and full of cum."

At the same age, women are generally receptive, thin and fine skinned. They are usually, at least by current social standards, as physically attractive as they will ever be. However, in my view, gray hair gives a woman style, grace and elegance unknown by those who are young.

With age, men lose their high levels of testosterone and produce greater levels of estrogen, as the opposite takes place in women. Both bear the physical consequences, the cruelest of which involves hair. Men lose it where they want it, and women get it where they don't.

Women grow whiskers as they age. It is a crime of nature that I must surely question God about if ever I have the chance. It seems to me that whiskers long ago outgrew, so to speak, their purpose. They do not even look good. I was a woman with whiskers upon which I waged war daily. Among my weapons were the low-tech razor and tweezers, electrolysis with increasing technology and the big guns - laser hair removal.

I had only once been under the big guns when I moved to Helena, so I still had to shave twice daily. Besides, laser warfare is effective only on the dark hairs, and I had a whole crop of light pigmented facial hair. It was not until after I had five laser blasts by September of 2007 that the tide of the war begun to turn. However, as with every war, it is never completely won. I had to endure two and half years of driving to Butte for weekly or biweekly electrolysis. It was the most painful part of the war, and I would gird myself with Tylenol III and the numbing agent, EMLA. I had to wrap my face with plastic wrap to keep the stuff from evaporating.

"Plastic girl," Peggy teasingly announced one day when I came to visit her before my session, as if I were a superhero.

"Duh-dahhhh," I sang with my arms spread out like wings.

Peggy made that first year of electrolysis bearable. She was always a caretaker, and when I was wounded, she comforted me, both as a spouse and as my friend. I would go to her house after my electrolysis sessions, where I would eat a hearty meal she prepared, take a bath and go to bed. I was happy to be relieved of the sixty mile drive back to Helena, often in the dark through two winding mountain passes in the snow, both ways. Well, you get the picture - it was bad.

My electrolysis operator in Butte seemed a bit unlikely to me. Before we started, I had envisioned someone with large tattoos and scant clothing. But Jawana was a modest, beautiful woman just trying to earn some extra income. She was tall with gorgeous long hair. She was married to the man who had worked on several of our cars over the years at Baker Auto in Butte. They had a daughter who often called to check in while we were in session. I marveled at how Jawana could hold the cell phone between her ear and shoulder and still work.

"Love you too," Jawana said at the end of every conversation.

I was more than a little jealous of the closeness of her family, as mine had all but broken apart.

Electrolysis involves repeated needle injections to your face for an hour or so. But it is not the injection itself that causes pain as much as it is the hot electrode that burns the follicle. It produced in me a mild form of shock that left me shivering and often in tears, overwhelmed by painful physical and emotional circumstances.

In recovery we have an acronym, "HALT." It suggests that we stop when we are hungry, angry, lonely or tired and attend to such needs. I changed it for my electrolysis sessions to "HELP," which meant that when I was H-ungry after E-lectrolysis, L-onely and in P-ain, I needed to go to

Peggy's house. Again, in her selfless demonstrations of the power of love, Peggy was there.

During my early battles in the whisker war, I got read once in Safeway by a woman and a young girl who appeared to be her daughter. My five o'clock shadow was visible beneath my makeup, despite all my concealer camouflage. It was a Friday after work, and I wanted to grab a few things at the store before heading home. I hadn't yet gone home to shave and re-apply my makeup before going to an evening meeting as I usually did. In my first year of recovery, I went to 2-3 meetings a day to steal me against the loneliness as much as any recovery issue, which unbeknownst to me, was neither unique nor unexpected, as it often *is* a recovery issue.

As I stood in line at the Safeway store, the woman turned to me and executed a perfect double take. I was read, which was shameful enough in my early transition, but what followed really hurt. The woman nudged her daughter and whispered something in her ear. The girl, who appeared to be about nine years old, did not perform the double take quite as well as her mother, but her thinking was plain as they both began laughing. I was philosophic in my initial response, reflecting on my penance for my own sins of prejudice. Two stand out in my memory forty-some years later.

When I was a boy, a Jewish family moved in across the street. They had two children, a boy about my age named, John, and his sister who much resembled Carole King in my mind, revealing at least some initial stereo-typing. At first, John and I played together. At some point that changed. I cannot remember the reason or precipitating event, so I would like to say that I do not know why our budding association took a turn. However, I do not think that is so.

People it seems, and not just children, have a remarkable ability to zero in on their differences, which become exacerbated by conflict. What if we had to get a long? What if resolution, no matter our differences, was the only acceptable outcome, for children, adults and countries? Hell – fami-lies too for that matter. John appeared different, and I could not see our commonness as people.

We relish sameness because our need to belong is so great, no matter how boring it would be if we were entirely so. Differences threaten our as-sociation with the herd. John was such a one, a dark horse unlike the rest of the kids in our Irish Catholic neighborhood. We, the neighborhood boys and I, called him "Ratty" in a word play on his very Jewish last name. I can see even now the occasional look in his eye, masking the hurt but still looking rather lost.

So strong is the human need for acceptance, affirmation and love that, like a lost kitten, no matter how cruel we were, John kept coming back. I was wrong and fear that I shall never be able to make amends. On that day at Safeway I was like John, the lost kitten so freely abused. I did not fit and it hurt. I knew not where I belonged.

On another occasion, a young black boy came to our completely white neighborhood with his father, who looked like a painter. He wore paint stained white coveralls and had a truck full of buckets and stuff. The young boy was excited to be out in the world on a new adventure. It reminds me now of the time I went to work with my grandfather, a "druggist," as pharmacists were once known. It was a rainy summer day, and I suppose my mother was hoping to foist her noisy, complaining and quarrelsome son off on someone else if even just for the day. I was excited and hopeful, filled with youthful anticipation.

My brother and I began to play with this black boy, likely some military type adventure that involved throwing things like sticks and dirt clods and making repeated gun shooting sounds. We got on famously that is until we did not. Disagreements between children at play are essentially the same as those that big people have and at base no different than those between countries at war.

Someone else, whom we cannot control, takes a different view of things, which we deem important. We voice our dissent, again focused on differences and imposing our beliefs rather than similarity and compromise. We lack tolerance and good will in the most important of our values and beliefs. The differences between this black boy and me, although in reality no more than pigment deep, became greater, and I declared war.

Perhaps he was not a nice kid, but that is not what I thought. I thought we disagreed because he was black and I was white. Thus, although I would not have stated it as such, our differences were perceived as fundamental, and I was then justified in releasing a verbal onslaught of despicable names, including the "n" word. It is hard for me to fathom the distinction between this conduct and the dynamics of hate and war, but for the age of the combatants and the choice of weapons. I was wrong and fear that I shall never be able to make amends.

Montana State University, Billings Professor Jeff Sanders, who is Jewish, tells his students,

"We all misunderstand things. All of us are human and misunderstand things, but not one of us mis-experiences things. If we've experienced it, we know it."

As those sins came back to visit me that evening after I left Safeway, I did not cry, but I did experience the sting of prejudice. I *knew* it. Today, I am glad of it, for I know empathy for others who suffer prejudice and discrimination. I judge far less than I used to.

A great defect of my character has been that very inclination to judge. I would judge everyone and usually found them lacking in some important quality, which I undoubtedly possessed in spades. I pray today that I am less judgmental than I was yesterday. I ask God each morning in prayer and meditation for patience, tolerance, kindliness and love just as soon my eyes open.

I did not feel as gracious, however, on October 10, 2006, once I arrived home from Safeway still feeling the sting of that girl and her mother's laughter at my expense. We have a couple of sayings in recovery that suggest that we keep our heads where our hands are and keep our own house clean. Sometimes the best way to accomplish both is by literally cleaning house. Our own minds can become our worst enemies, especially when we start believing our own rhetoric. We cannot see the true for the false that we have come to believe about ourselves, others and the world around us. We spend a lot of time lost inside our own thinking, our own heads.

My sponsor said, "Don't go in alone; it is dark in there."

Today, I call someone when my head needs inspection, but back then, I did not have a sponsor and was too afraid of disclosure to get one. I made it through Friday, but I could clean house for only so long.

On Saturday I was read yet again, this time by a car-load of teenagers who hooted and jeered at me as they drove past. I began to think that if I could not make it in the world as a woman that I could not make it at all. I knew that my life as a man was over. As I obsessed over that thought, it became dark indeed inside my head. I began to feel the insanity that drives us to drink, or worse.

When we are like this, and until we accept that drinking and dying are not options, it would be better for us to drink. I "white knuckled" it as I began to contemplate the "worse" option with all the attendant hopelessness and desperation of a year earlier, in the box, dispirited and demoralized. My weeping became fall on the floor sobbing, sniveling and moaning.

I put myself in a dangerous position, an exemplary manifestation of all the reasons they tell us not to make significant life changes in our first year of sobriety. As my friend from law school told me when I came out to him, "You are fucking nuts right now."

I was not drinking, but I had none of the tools of sobriety to help me cope with all the loss and changes in my life. I was desperate and devastated with almost nowhere to turn, at least that I was willing to risk. I bitterly sobbed with the submarine hatches wide open as I sank in an ocean of emotion. It did not occur to me to pick up the phone and call another alcoholic as they suggested. It amazes me that I might have taken my own life rather than risk revealing myself to another person. It defies belief that a person would forfeit life for pride. I turned to Mother Mary, clinging to my grandfather's rosary beads.

My grandfather passed away in 1981, my first year in Montana. My family decided not to tell me until after the funeral, as they concluded that I had enough on my plate already.

Mom called on an October Saturday.

"Your Grandpa passed away," she said sadly and meekly.

"When?" I asked, as all people do.

"Two weeks ago," she said as I listened, suddenly stunned into silence.

"How come nobody told me?" I finally blurted out.

"Because we did not want to disturb your mission work and knew you could not make it home for the funeral."

I was incredulous but decided that Mom was probably right even though I wasn't really a missionary in the truest sense. I was mildly perturbed, but more grateful for grandpa's life and influence. He was born in 1890, when wagons were the principal mode of transportation. He once told us a story of the time he rode a freight wagon from Columbus ten miles north to the old Worthington Inn to stay overnight and return the next day. It was one of the very rare occasions that he spoke of, for he was a quiet, modest man. The Worthington Inn in the 1960s and 1970s was a restaurant with a wonderful smorgasbord that we all loved. We sometimes went there as a family on holidays and special occasions like Mother's Day, so no one who could cook had to cook.

Getting a table for ten, the six kids and four adults, was always difficult. We often had to wait, but it was well worth it. The buffet at the Worthington Inn was fabulous. I have vivid memories of my mom painstakingly savoring her second cup of coffee as six anxious children clamored for release after already finishing their meals.

"C'mon Mom, let's go," one or the other of us would beg.

"I haven't had my second cup of coffee yet," she would insist indignantly.

She ate very slowly to begin with, enjoying every bite of a meal that she did not have to prepare. When she finished, she sat in blissful oblivion and enjoyed one of her extremely rare selfish delights - a second cup of coffee while still seated at the dinner table.

Grandpa had lived through much of the advance and technological boom of the twentieth century. He watched the automobile become a household necessity, watched the world light up with electricity and saw television as it first broadcast to the world. He saw it all come into being, including the "giant step for mankind." His life encompassed world wars and military engagements around the globe, not to mention the rapid acceleration of social experimentation and change, including the first successful sex reassignment surgery patient, Christine Jorgenson, in 1956, the year before I was born. This incredible scope of social, scientific and medical advance was unprecedented in any previous ninety-year period, and will not likely be repeated, the advance of electronics notwithstanding.

Pappy, as my parents called him, was a quiet and gentle person. He was not my father's father. Rudolph senior had died of breathing problems developed from gas in World War I when my dad was seven years old. Dad had uncles whom we never met and never did know why, as no one ever talked about that great family rift.

Pappy told few stories of his life and times. I regret that almost as much as I do my own shyness to ask for them. He was a man of prayer, too. Grandma and Grandpa were members of a civilian Catholic group called the Third Order Franciscans. I suppose they sent them money and got things in the mail in return, like newsletters or bookmarks or other holy insignia. They had a prayer book from which they together read daily devotions, morning and night. Despite their beliefs, or anyone else's for that matter, there is a certain grace and beauty in an elderly couple fully aware of their own mortality, sitting down together to begin and end each day in recognition of their own higher power. Pappy was an inspiration to me.

After his passing my mother sent me a few of his things including a monogrammed key chain with the letter "R" for Ralph, his first name and my middle name, (Although now I use Ralphelle.) and a decade of the Rosary on a key chain. The "Rosary" is a type of prayer and meditation that Catholics of a bygone era fervently prayed. It involved devotion to the Triune God and Mary. To keep their place in a string of Our Fathers, Hail Mary's and Glory Bes, Catholics would count each prayer in turn on a string of beads with a crucifix that went by the same nomenclature, the Rosary.

A great many Catholics would be surprised to learn that one of their most venerated traditions was borrowed from the Hindu and Buddhists tradition of *japa malas* beads brought back to Europe during the Crusades. A decade was an abbreviated version that involved only ten beads for Catholics on the go.

After those two incidents of getting read and laughed at, in my despair, I grabbed Pappy's beads. I prayed Hail Marys as I sobbed holding the ring of the key chain Rosary around my index finger in a clenched fist. I was afraid that I might take my own life and asked God to save me from myself.

When I awoke the next morning I did not hear music, but I was still clutching the Rosary. I had found my porch to safely whether the storm of self-pity, doubt and fear. I had made it through the night, and I was not drunk or dead. The rest is *gratis*. As I ventured from the bat cave that morning after a long bath and prayer to the Mother of All Children, it was with a certain lightness and gratitude. I went to Starbucks. I deserved it.

I took my latte to a nearby park, known as the Women's Park. I did not know its history, but it seemed like the place for me to be. It was a brisk, yet sunny and bright fall Sunday morning in Montana, a strikingly beautiful place and time. I wore a skirt, heels, nylons and a dress blouse. I needed to feel pretty and feminine. The sun shone brightly and lightly filtered through colored leaves as I sat at a cement picnic table.

I watched a woman walking down the sidewalk toward me. She was a local street character whom I had seen before. Her hair was graying, short with no particular style. Her teeth were crooked, and her face blemished and red. She had white whiskers, wore no makeup, and one eye drooped. She was overweight, which surprised me inasmuch as I always saw her walking. She did not appear developmentally disabled as from birth, and I wondered what calamity left her in such a state.

To my surprise she walked right up to my table

In a voice as soft as angel feathers she asked, "Can I talk with you?"

"Yea, sure," I responded somewhat reluctantly, as I was not sure what she really wanted.

"May I sit down?" she said as haltingly.

I waved my hand and said, "Please do."

"You look so beautiful sitting here, like a model," she confided.

I could have kissed her and almost started crying all over again.

"Thank you," I said, more from politeness than from the sense of goodness welling up inside me.

As she told me of the accident and resulting brain injury that stole her youthful beauty and promise, I knew that I would make it in the world as a woman and that real beauty lies within.

"Life is beautiful and short," she said.

I realized that this was my second chance and that I must get up and grab it every day. It reminds me now of an Afghanistan War veteran I heard on the radio a few years after her legs were blown off as she piloted a helicopter.

"I want to be worthy of the second chance at life given to me," she proclaimed to the world.

God always answers prayer. Sometimes the answer is yes, or, "you'll be okay. Just trust me."

Chapter Fourteen

One Helena Woman

Oh divine master, grant that I might seek
Not so much to be consoled as to console
To be understood as to understand
To be loved as to love another

For it is in giving that we receive
And it is in dying that we are born again.

- St. Francis[43]

In 1889, Montana became the 41st State in the Union, but it was far from settled. It was still very much the frontier, although less so in the capital city, Helena. Still, the streets were likely muddy or caked and dried. The town was lit by candlelight and had few of the comforts of its contemporary Eastern counterparts. It was hardly refined, and few self-respecting Montanans would assert sophistication or aristocracy, even now. Yet, it was here that a young woman arrived from New England a year earlier to teach school and rise to the rank of principle. Twenty-nine year-old Ella Knowles "spurned the security of this position and decided to resume her legal studies in the office of Helena lawyer, Joseph W. Kinsley."[44]

At that time, women were excluded from the law, as well as just about every other profession. (Now, women are merely underpaid.) "Exclusion of women from the law was a very ancient rule that was founded on both Roman tradition and English common law,"[45] as are most of America's legal precepts.

The resistance to women in the law, insofar as it had any rational basis, rested on widespread notions of physical and mental differences between men and women, differences that supposedly unsuited the latter professionally. The woman was not regarded as the man's equal in body and mind, and as such it was believed that she lacked the physical stamina required by the burdens of a law practice as well as the essential mental attributes of discretion and aggressiveness. Common opinion held that a woman's mental makeup was also emotional rather that rational and therefore more suited to aesthetic expression than the pursuit of legal hard truth.

Finally, the demands of the profession were viewed as incompatible with the woman's traditional and proper role as wife and mother. This is reflected in the language of Justice Joseph P. Bradley of the U.S. Supreme Court in a well known opinion. 'The natural and proper timidity and delicacy which belongs to the female sex,' he wrote 'unfits it for many of the occupations of civil life. The constitution of the family organization, which is founded in the divine ordinance, as well as in the nature of things, indicates the domestic sphere as that which properly belongs to the dominion and functions of womanhood . . . . The paramount destiny and mission of women are to fulfill the noble and benign offices of wife and mother. This is the law of the Creator.[46]

It is peculiar how the laws of the Creator become clearer over time. However, in 1889, Montana State law limited admission to the State bar to men only. Ella suffered prejudice and professional ostracism, as she not only had to pass the bar exam, but also had to get the law changed to allow her to practice. She succeeded on both counts.

The bill to change the law was not unlike anti-discrimination laws of today, except that it was limited to sex. Legislative councilman Walter M. Bickford, a Missoula lawyer, introduced the bill as "Council Bill No. 4 to amend the law to read that individuals otherwise qualified should be allowed to practice as attorneys without regard to sex ...."[47] Legislative commentary within the "flood of eloquence" here is worthy of note:

In the House, Samuel Murray, a Missoula lawyer, took the position that passage of the bill was an issue larger than the ambitions of one Helena woman. To him the question was one of justice, of a step forward or backward. In the past, Murray lectured his colleagues, men had regarded women as slaves or playthings, and some men still regarded them as graceful ornaments limited to domestic life. But, he reminded, the only relevant question was their mental capacity; if theirs is the equal of men, they should be admitted to the practice of law.[48]

The media twist, including that reported in the *Madisonian*, the Virginia City newspaper went like this:

I will not attempt to describe the airy flights of eloquence with which the debates on this bill were embellished, nor the spicandspan style in which the honorable legislatorssome of whom one would suppose were too old to be affected by such frivolitieshad gotten themselves up to pass muster under the eyes of the fair ones who were expected to enliven the house with their presence during the racket.[49]

The verdict on Ella was as follows: "Both in and out of court her reputation as a capable lawyer was soon established, and those who at first scoffed at her now concede her marked ability."[50] The Montana Historical Society, in a 1982 article about Ella, attributed her success at "crashing the gender line" at least in part to Montana's progressiveness and "the Western spirit of liberality."[51]

I discovered the *Montana Magazine* article during my transition, following an article from Montana's former US District Attorney, Sherry Scheel Matteucci, in the *Montana Lawyer*, the State Bar of Montana's journal. I was taken with the resonance between Ella's story and mine.

She was Montana's first woman lawyer and crossed a societal gender line and I was Montana's first transgender lawyer crossing the same sort of line a little over a century later. I was struck that a person of courage and vision would challenge convention at a time and in a place where the prevailing spirit would accommodate her. I do not claim to possess the same attributes, but I do put my faith in Montana's progressiveness and that certain Western spirit which may or may not be so liberal, as it is individual.

Too, I am impressed that Ella was a woodworker, and a women's rights advocate, as was Montana's first and greatest suffragette, Helen Rankin. It brings to mind Gandhi's sage advice to "be the change you wish to see in the world."[52] They were, and the world is better for it.

Many Montanans appreciate a person not so much for what or who they are but by what they may accomplish while the sun still shines. People such as these have less time and inclination toward social causes and culture than they will stand ready to assist a neighbor in need. They are less likely to "go with the flow." There is often little which flows by their door. Historically, Montanans are known as individualists, both rugged and thoughtful. Montanans might rather be of their own mind than of one mind. It is sometimes more difficult to reach consensus in such a social climate, except where necessity is concerned. We are a pragmatic lot. I think Montanans as a whole are still more tolerant and less judgmental than much of the rest of the country as a whole.

It is a shame that Councilman Bickford did not have greater vision when he introduced Council Bill No. 4, which is, at the very least, an anti-sex discrimination law. If the bill were geared more to all professions, as Samuel Murray had intimated, and did not attach a specific classification of persons, vis-à-vis sex, we would perhaps not need an Employment Non-discrimination Act today. However, if the bill was geared at anything other than the fortunes of only a single "Helena woman," it would not likely have passed, even in those progressive and liberal times.

Just think, though, what Montana would be like today if it had been illegal for the last one hundred years to discriminate on the basis of anything but skill, knowledge, work experience, training, formal education and aptitude for the job. Notably, these characteristics are all objectively measurable, and would-be employers could actually give a specific reason for rejecting a candidate. We would not need civil rights law, the ADA and local and state antidiscrimination laws, at least where employment is concerned. However, far be it from me to decry or impugn a century of legislative wisdom and jurisprudential brilliance.

While I love a twist of phrase as much as anyone, the media reports of the bill were as patronizing as could be. And, how about that jurisprudential gem from Justice Bradley?! It is always the God card that they play when their arguments defy common sense. It is especially ironic to me now when I hear the same kind of ridiculous God rhetoric about LGBT people.

I am the only out transsexual ever elected to public office in Montana, a dubious distinction perhaps. However, the distinction is probably worthy of note if you are an elected official in Montana who undertakes something as unconventional and seemingly beyond the pale as gender transition. The papers thought so anyways, as articles involving some of my cases after I left would state things like: "*Roberta R. Zenker, formerly known as Robert R. Zenker*, the former Madison County Attorney." I cannot say why such a distinction was worthy of note. Two newspapers even asked for interviews. It was tempting on one hand because after living so long in secret, I felt an overwhelming compunction to be known. However, on the other hand, I had enjoyed early success at passing as a woman, and many people that I came to know and share mutual affection with knew me as nothing else.

I was concerned, as I am today, that some may feel that their trust was betrayed. Thus, I chose anonymity over notoriety. As Sue Monk Kidd wrote, "But secluding my experience during that early period was both cowardly and wise. Some things are too fragile, too vulnerable to bring into the public eye. Tender things with tiny roots tend to wither in the glare of public scrutiny."[53] I was indeed fragile and vulnerable with roots so tiny they had not yet taken hold of solid ground. Public scrutiny might well have destroyed them.

Elected officials in Montana have to file for public office in order to keep their jobs, even if unopposed, by the end of March in an election year. My second full four-year term was ending in 2006, so that it was necessary for me to file if I wanted to stay. At that time I was scarcely a month into therapy and did not fully understand gender transition, when I would start, what it would entail and how it would impact my marriage, family, job, home, etc., in other words, everything. It was a time of ambivalence to say the very least. I thought that I might stay another year before beginning transition in earnest. That would give me the chance to pay down some debt and perhaps save some money. So, I reluctantly paid the fee of $300 plus and filed on the very last day. In a position where salary had nearly always been a sore subject, this added insult to injury.

However, as changes often do, mine took on a life of their own when things began to happen in August. As I resigned as county attorney and moved to Helena, the least of my concerns was whether my name was still on the ballot. I just assumed that it would be removed automatically. However, in government little happens automatically. Indeed, I found out in November that by the time I resigned in August, the period within which to remove my name from the ballot had already expired.

Robert R. Zenker was on the ballot for Madison County Attorney in the November, 2006 election, even though he no longer existed as a legal entity. I had legally changed my name almost as soon as I got the job offer in Helena, courtesy of one of the first colleagues I came out to who was concerned about bank accounts and such things. The judge who signed the order changing my name turned out to be a neighbor of the woman who later became my sponsor. Montana is as small a world as could be. The degrees of separation are merely incremental. I was grateful to both the judge and my friend, although I have not talked to either since.

By Election Day I was knee deep in my new life, which I had just begun trying on for size and was having trouble making fit. My replacement as county attorney had already assumed office and had a couple months under his belt. He ran a write-in campaign. One County Commissioner posted a notice in the *Madisonian* explaining the circumstances and suggesting that voters write in the new county attorney's name and **REMEMBER TO FILL IN THE OVAL**.

I had never run opposed before.

"If you don't like me, vote for the other guy," I had quipped with jocularity and feigned braggadocio.

Now that I truly did not care, there actually was another guy. Still, I won by a 3-1 margin. I assumed that it was merely due to name recognition and the general ignorance of the electorate of my life circumstances. My name had been in the papers routinely, and I had been on TV many times in the previous ten years, as I had never avoided publicity against the day that I might be opposed. I believed as they said,

"For a politician, the only bad press is no press."

Now I wonder about the Madison County electorate as I have with so many others with whom I had not discussed my transition. Had I sold them short by not allowing them the opportunity to accept me? Is it possible that I achieved some good things while in office and that people liked me as Loren used to say, "anti-dis-ir-regardless?" I had worked hard, and perhaps did have a good name still. Is it possible that, like many Montanans, they were more concerned with my performance than they were with my person?

Many Montanans are less concerned with what or who you are than they are with what you accomplish. Rural Montanans are mostly ranchers or farmers, or from that stock, and are often pragmatic at their core. They rise early, work long and often have little time or inclination to concern themselves with others' personal lives. A person's business is their own, and Montanans have a live and let live attitude towards many socially controversial matters. As long as you show up and do the work, many Montanans really don't care what you do when the sun goes down, even if they lean politically, socially and religiously to the right. Well, I had done the work for ten years.

Just after Election Day, 2006, the Madison County Election Administrator, a former colleague, called.

"Hello is Bob there?" the Madison County Clerk and Recorder asked.

"This is Bobbie," I responded, affirming my new identity.

"Oh. Well, I called to tell you that you won the election and to ask if you will be declining," she stated assertively as a statement, not a question.

"Yes," I replied. "What do I have to do?"

I gladly and quickly relinquished the election. However, the affidavit she sent to accomplish the chore was not sufficient. I had a conundrum. The name on the ballot was Robert, but my legal name now was Roberta. The affidavit stated "Robert," whose name I could no longer legally sign. I did not feel that it was proper, if not even binding, to sign legal documents with a name that was not legally mine. I singed as Roberta, such that I wonder even now whether it was legally effective.

Chapter Fifteen

Which Way

Be careful how you bend me
Be careful where you send me
Be careful how you end me
Be careful with me

- Patty Griffin[54]

Montana is not a wealthy state. It never has been, at least for the common person. It has, however, produced fortunes for those lucky enough to reap its riches. I was neither fortunate, nor lucky when it came to finances. I did not realize it at the time, but my transition would cost me dearly. A more patient, thoughtful and reserved person would have worked another year or two before starting such a journey, if for no other reason than to save up some cash. I, however, was desperate and did not care to wait a single moment longer than I had to. I was willing to take a very significant cut in salary with almost no cash reserves.

$75,000 is a good salary by Montana standards. I had lived like I earned a good salary, which is to say that I spent a lot of money on toys and my own amusement. Peggy and I had traveled a bit. We went to San Antonio for a conference of hers while I just goofed off and took a ton of colorful photographs and to Key West, where my gender confusion was simply electrified. More recently we went to Scottsdale for the

Fiesta Bowl in which Ohio State beat Notre Dame, showcasing the talent of Ohio State's linebacker who was dating the Notre Dame quarterback's sister. It was the last vacation for Bob, and it was memorable, if for no other reason than that daily living had become such a struggle with depression, alcoholism, borderline anorexia and my gender confusion.

I had built up somewhere in the neighborhood of $30,000 in revolving debt, including school loans from law school and the first few years of college for the kids, as well as loans on two cars. I was getting in pretty deep, but with a sordid sense of self-indulgent pride I paid my monthly bills. However, when I took the job in Helena, I started at only $47,500. My budget was reduced to beer levels while I was ensconced in champagne tastes.

Nonetheless, I plunged ahead, believing that I would return easily to a higher income bracket once my transition was complete. My goal was to be back in the game, so to speak no later than January, 2008. I reasoned that it might take three months to find a new job once I started looking, and I was free to go anywhere and do anything. I was badly mistaken as it turned out but had made no interim financial plans for daily living expenses and payment of my outstanding debts. I traded off my truck with its $400-a-month payment, and my car, for a blue Subaru. I still needed a part time job, almost from the start.

I went to Starbucks on Sunday mornings beginning in October so I could, among other things, like seeing and being seen and indulging my current vice, to scour the want- ads in the paper. Safeway was my local grocery store because Peggy had convinced me of the gas savings value of the Safeway "card." I had noticed a Help Wanted display on a sign board out front one day and went in to apply. Too, I was hoping for an employee discount on food.

Safeway had an application kiosk which, as I passed, I decided to try. I put my bags and purse down and started filling out an online application. I was stumped for a moment by the question about other names that I had been known by. Despite the realization that it was probably a veiled attempt to ferret out married women who might become pregnant and require time off, rather than an attempt to expose the unsuspecting trans applicant, I decided in favor of disclosure. I believed I had nothing to hide. I wrote down "Robert."

I was called for an interview about a week later. When I arrived, freshly shaved and showered, I was left waiting for several minutes for a supervisor who, when she finally appeared, said,

"The interview is cancelled."

Without so much as a word of explanation or rescheduling, the interview was simply cancelled. I called back a week later and learned that the position had been filled.

I was angry and hurt. I was resentful and stewed again in the marinade of my own self-pitying juices. Was it discrimination? I do not know, but how does a person ever know for sure? The Montana Supreme Court has written that evidence of discrimination is rarely direct. It is not like an employer will come out and say that they will not hire you because of your gender identification, even had they known that it was not a protected class under antidiscrimination law. I let it go. I did not want the attention anyhow

I went to a job fair about a week later. A young woman from Macy's had a display table there with applications. She was nearly as tall as me, and like me, she too looked like a misplaced California girl with her long blonde hair. She was warm and professional with an inviting smile as I walked up and introduced myself. It was late in the day, and I had rushed home to shave, learning from my earlier experiences. My makeup was fresh, and I always could smile, although I had some problem teeth up front. One was darkened by a root canal I had years earlier, one was just stained and another had a calcium deposit. I sometimes smiled in more of a smirk as I tried to hide the dark tooth. Also, late in the day, my voice is sometimes strained and slips into the "boy voice." I was worried that it might.

I walked right up nonetheless, held out my hand and said,

"Hi, I'm Bobbie Zenker. I'm looking for part time work."

I brightly smiled, feeling confident, yet not nearly as happy as I appeared.

"We have openings for seasonal help over the upcoming holidays. You should apply."

I filled out an application as we stood and chatted. I liked her and sensed that she liked me too. I was called to an interview in early November with three women, including the blonde I met before, another supervisor and the HR person. I was poised and confident as I sat with them, woman to woman.

"Women like to shop at places like Macy's to feel better about themselves," I said, as much from the experiences of my recent past as any wealth of knowledge I tried to portray.

I told them about what my father had told me when the world and our lives beat us down.

"When I'm feeling down, I buy a new shirt."

Only for me it was (and is) shoes. I followed that advice often especially in those early days of RLT when my wardrobe was so meager, and I was so down. I believed in "shopping therapy," as I had come by it honestly. I justified the expense along with credit card expenditures, because I needed the clothes. I had to experiment with the various elements of a wardrobe including, color, size, fashion and style, until I found my own.

I started at Macy's at 9:00 a.m. on "Black Friday" 2006. The madness of holiday shopping was already in full swing, and clothes were tossed everywhere, stacked on carts and littering the changing rooms. My first job was to restock the shelves. That's all I did for eight hours. I had more glamorous tasks later, like selling lingerie and jewelry and working the register. I liked that best because I got to interact with more people that way. I remembered the lesson I learned from Peggy's Mom and tried to say something nice to each.

"You have such pretty hair," I might say to one customer or "That's a great outfit you picked out."

They would inevitably smile and say "thanks." It made them feel good, which in turn made me feel good. Feeling good is like that.

I loved Macy's, and still do. Not only did they hire me, but they never so much as referred to my being transgender. I learned in orientation that their nondiscrimination policy extended explicitly to gender identification, as do the policies of many Fortune 500 companies, an important talking point in later attempts to secure legislation to the same effect. I loved everything about Macy's, management, coworkers and products alike. There was a palpable feeling there that people really did like the place, and even though they could have been paid better, they cared about each other.

As I got to know the women that I worked with as a woman, I observed what seems to be a fundamental truth about our culture of which many men are still largely, albeit blissfully, unaware. American society is still deeply male dominated and driven. Women make great sacrifices for the men in their lives. I was dumbfounded by the number of women that I worked with who worked retail while holding professional degrees in fields like engineering and social work.

"I came here because my husband got his dream job," the engineer told me one day.

Not only are women paid less than their male counterparts, it seems that many take lesser jobs for men's sake as well.

I started to notice also that I was being treated as a woman in most circumstances, even by people that knew of my former life. In each of the communities I was involved with - church, recovery and work - I began to cherish the relationships I developed with women as a woman. In particular, as I contemplated disclosure with friends I became close to, I decided I needed to come out to a few of them.

One woman in particular, who was about my age, became my very best friend in recovery. We were both new to the program and needed each other more than either one of us could say. As that winter came and went, we went to many meetings together, sometimes three in a day. We went shopping at thrift stores, watched movies and generally discovered life without alcohol. I called her on the phone and she called me. We both called each other's bullshit.

Like so many things in God's world, Macy's was what I needed when I needed it. It was another "yes" answer to prayer. I knew the Christmas holidays would be hard for me, and Macy's helped me through in ways greater than mere finances. I had never been alone at Christmas. Peggy was traveling, and the kids were not even speaking with me. Just thinking about it often brought me to tears, and I hoped for a Christmas miracle of reconciliation. I was becoming aware, vaguely, that my unmet expectations formed many of my disappointments, which often led to resentment and self-pity. I had not yet figured out just how unrealistic those expectations were. So, I determined to minimize my Christmas expectations. I would not celebrate Christmas, 2006.

Rather than be a Grinch, however, I decided that I would try to help others celebrate the season. I would be present to the people I met and those around me to help them with their Christmas Spirit. I worked at Macy's almost every day from early December through New Year's and the annual inventory season for most retail stores in January. I earned enough money to pay the rent, buy food and what few presents I would buy that year. Working thirteen to fourteen hours a day left little time for anything else but meetings and sleep. I went to a meeting at noon every day, except weekends when I was working. The rest of the time, I kept my head where my hands were.

I was happy to be at work. I was busy, worked hard and spent all my time talking to other people. There was no time for self-pity. I did not have to think about not having Christmas with Peggy and my children. I had spent every Christmas Eve with Peggy for the previous thirteen years and had some sort of Christmas with the children their whole lives. To think about them and not having Christmas with them, or anyone else for that matter, was too overwhelming, like a whole fleet of screen door submarines. I would surely drown.

As I focused on being present, I learned one of the great lessons of recovery - service. It had actually started in October when I signed up at St. Paul's to be a hospital visitor. I went to meet with Jan, who coordinated the program as a member of St. Paul's and as a hospital employee. She worked with the hospital's palliative care program. The Bischoff case had taught me that such programs were for terminally ill patients to help them and their families prepare and go forward with the process of dying. Palliative medicine requires something extra in a person, so I knew that Jan was special. She was not much older than I, and we had talked some about cross-country skiing. She was in great shape. I had at least some trust and confidence in her when I arranged to have lunch with her at the hospital cafeteria to talk about the volunteer visitor thing.

I had arranged for a meeting more as a guise so I could talk to her about my transition. I was not sure how I was perceived, and I did not want to offend people who were already having a hard time in the hospital.

Jan and I met to talk about the visitor program. We went through small talk and chatted about what was expected of a visitor. The program was the kind of thing I had decided before moving to Helena that I should get involved in to ward off loneliness. As the conversation dwindled, I knew it was time for the transition issue. I was not sure how to broach such topics with a near stranger, so I just launched into it by asking,

"Are you familiar with the term, transgender?"

Monique and I had spoken some about this, and she advised me to prepare some kind of nomenclature that I was comfortable with and a story to go along with it. I did not like "transsexual" because it sounded like it was all about sex, and there were many trans women feeding the stereotypes by making ends meet in the sex industry. I did not want to be associated with the kinds of negative images that might conjure up. I thought about the term "gender blessed," as I felt I was fortunate to see the world and life from the perspective of both genders.

However, a friend and colleague whom I was out to, told me in rather pragmatic fashion,

"That sounds hokey."

It was just a bit California for Helena.

I have since learned that the French have a much more elegant word, *transexuelle*, but "transgender" was the term I defaulted to.

"I am in gender transition, and I just wondered if I would offend any of the patients or staff," I ventured quizzically.

She responded with a question that melted me with great relief.

"Which way?" she asked. "I don't have a clue."

I could have kissed her right then and there. The fact that she truly did not know whether I was a man or a woman was actually a compliment and a great confidence booster for me after only a couple months of living as a woman full time. However, of greater import was that she simply passed it off as a minor detail. I volunteered at the hospital when I had time between work and meetings. I found that attempts to comfort others comforted me. Happiness is like that too.

At Thanksgiving, Peggy and I volunteered to help serve the festive meal at the Butte rescue mission. I had always wanted to do that, and this was the perfect opportunity as neither Peggy nor I had anyone else to be with that year. We had always gone to Idaho to be with Peggy's folks, but since Robert had passed away, Dorleen went to Florida to be with her sister.

We went to the mission in the morning, and Peggy prepared our feast with her usual aplomb in the afternoon. I enjoyed my time at the mission, especially because I found no reason to fear the people. They were unpretentious, their pride and ego surrendering to their need. They were grateful and told wondrous stories of their lives on the road. For a person as self-centered as I presence to others relieved me of that burden.

St. Paul's had been the doorway through which I walked out of myself and into the lives of those around me. I became a member there on December 10, 2006, having completed the classes introducing me to Wesleyan theology, which incidentally is also big on service. It was my birthday, and the whole congregation sang to me. It was a wonderful moment, and I was incredibly happy. The pieces of my life as a woman were starting to gel. I liked this person, Bobbie, and I took some comfort in her skin. Another grain of Bob fell to the ground so that Bobbie could live.

A day after my forty-ninth birthday Monique wrote a letter to Dr. Bowers, whom I was leaning toward as my gender reassignment surgeon. I needed a letter from my therapist, as well as a psychological evaluation to make sure that my motives were sincere and that I was psychologically fit. Monique wrote:

> Even though Bobbie has chosen the fasttrack in her transition, she is doing exceptionally well. As a psychotherapist who has worked with transgendered individuals for fifteen years, Bobbie is clearly one of my stellar "students!" We have followed the standards of care in as many aspects as possible, making adjustments due to the fact that we live in Montana. I have every reason to believe that her commitment to future compliance is total and unwavering. I find Bobbie mentally, emotionally and psychologically healthy and an excellent candidate for sex reassignment surgery.

I had come a long way in one year.

Chapter Sixteen

More than a Metaphor

I will garden again in that far away place
I will dig fingers deep into loose soil
Feel its coolness, breathe its dusty perfume

Mother of Earth see my soul and give solace
Mother of Earth call me from winter

I will stretch in the sunshine of that time
I will hold my face to its light
Drink in its seductive warmth

Mother of Earth see my soul and give solace
Mother of Earth call me from winter

I will shake my hair in the breeze of a dream
I will be warm and whole and happy
In that place, in that time, in that dream

Mother of Earth see my soul and give solace
Mother of Earth call me from winter[55]

It was the winter alone I dreaded, the short dreary days and dark nights. I may have been naive in many ways, but I knew about Montana's long, cold nights and silent gray days of winter. I knew too that this winter I would be alone. By late October, I had already given up hope of making new friends. Even though in September, when I moved here, I had resolved to get involved, it was not always enough to shelter me from my own thoughts. I had done a few things at church and met a few folks, but they had children and jobs and other commitments. I had made a few friends in recovery, but those connections, I came to find can be loose and fleeting.

Then there were the people who knew me before, some of whom I thought even understood. It never ceases to amaze me the different re-actions I get when I come out to people. Some people that you thought would run off screaming were fine with it. Others that I thought would get it politely evaporated. Whatever it is that happens in communication, whether it creates understanding or merely passes information, my coming out during the summer did not produce friendship and support in the fall.

I wrote a letter to my daughter, one of those that Shane used to sing about from the Moody Blues, *never to send*,[56] although I was far from a knight in white satin. Meghan had been plain in her demand that I not only drop dead, but also that I refrain from contacting her. I guess that makes sense. I did meet her mortality demands in many ways, but, lest I be accused of criminal stalking, I also honored her wishes to have no contact. However, I needed to preserve the truth as I understood it then, in hopes that she may one day look for it. I wrote,

"If we do not communicate, how can we ever understand one another?"

And I was not referring only to my stuff, as I could see that she was still resentful over my divorcing her mother and what I think she felt was abandoning her and her brother. I wanted her to know that from the first day I held her in the palm of one hand on the day of her birth, such a small, fragile and beautiful miracle, I had loved her. I always will, no matter what. As surely as God brings good from every bad, I began to glimpse the love of God for me. *'Cause I love you, yes I love you*[57]. . . as only a parent can.

I wonder if when I was in the depths of my box if God kept a picture of me in God's office the way that I do of Shane and Meghan, a poignant reminder of that love and the hurt that I suffer as surely God suffered from the rifts between us. I keep thinking of them, as I trust that God did of me. I will keep the pictures up despite, as Wm. Paul Young so aptly described in *The Shack*, "the Great Sadness."[58] I remain hopeful that just as I walked through the spiritual door into the arms of God that Meghan and Shane will walk through my door and see that I have never stopped thinking about them, that I have not abandoned them, that they are not alone and that I love them without fail.

People might toss off flippantly in light of my pain,

"Well, you asked for it."

And that's just the thing I did not ask for this, for any of it. I did not seek gender confusion nor even know of the prescribed treatment until I started. I just knew that my sense of self was very wrong and covering or hiding would no longer work. I did not choose to lose my family, my home, my job. Who would?

I could not make the girl in me go away. I could not change her nor escape her, though I tried. Asking me to deny who I am would leave me like a stripeless tiger. I am *transexuelle*. I was born that way, and I will die that way, no matter what I do in between. I cannot change who I am. The only choice I have is to live with it as best as I can.

"So why should I not be happy?" I reasoned.

That's a deal I can make. But what baffled me is why other people, who have so little to lose or gain by rejecting me, do so.

As I have examined in recovery my own judgments of other people, I have realized that judgment of others is just another form of my own fear. In my own insecurity, I constantly compared my-self to others. To escape my self-loathing I disdained others instead. Conversely, as I have embraced love and tolerance of others I have let go of both judgment and fear.

Trans people are both male and female, both before and after transition, in my opinion. Oh, the boy in me sleeps now for the most part, and I feel whole without him, unlike I did with him. However, I suspect that he is still there somewhere. I am living now as a woman. In truth, genitals have little to do with it. It is so much more psychological, emotional, spiritual and intellectual. It is about reconciling body, mind and spirit.

Gender is not only physical, but it is much more social. Transition is about joining how I think and feel and how I present to the world with how the world perceives and relates to me.

I lived for many years as a man, yet never felt comfortable or complete in that role. And it almost killed me, perhaps would have had I not begun transition when I did. Now, I am a woman. I wake and work as such - dress, walk and talk as such, socialize as a woman, sleep as such and even dream as a woman. It is peculiar that I used to dream as though from the outside looking in, like watching a movie about me in which I did not play a part. It is not like that anymore.

I dream as a woman inside looking out upon her world in which she is actively doing her part and loving it. I had often used a somewhat popular phrase to describe difficulties and disappointments.

"I hate my life," I would blithely state, though I meant it.

I stopped saying that for it was no longer true. Instead, even though it was still very hard, I started to love my life.

The world of women in which I am included without reservation is different than that of men - duhhhh! It is more intimate, interconnected, seemingly acknowledging, as if by intuition the common experience and attendant need for emotional safety, comfort and warmth. As an expression of this, women often smile at one another as they pass, even if complete strangers. At least they do in Montana. Even though unfamiliar, women seem to intuit their commonality and shared solidarity. Again, sue Monk Kidd said it best:

> Solidarity is identifying with one another without feeling like you have to agree on every issue. It's unity, not uniformity. It's listening without rushing in to fix the problem. It's going deeper than typical ways of talking and sharing going down to the place where souls meet and love comes, where separateness drops away and you know these women because you are these women.[59]

I am these women. Not only did I come to know this, I came to feel it. Often, when with a group of women friends, I would sit back and look at them. I love them for who they are and for just being there. It does not matter that we do not share all our beliefs in common. What matters is that we are together, depending upon each other as we share the daily grind that we call life. My sisters are my family.

This solidarity is sometimes manifested only in a glance or knowing smile, and these same women who will offer and return such simple gestures to other women will not do so with men. I have had such nonverbal exchanges as a woman with women I had known for years but who did not recognize me. That never occurred when I was living as a man. Maybe it's just Montana, but these days I can scarcely walk down the street without exchanging eye contact and a smile with another woman. I do not know why or what such exchanges mean or how they came about as social phenomena. However, I think it has to do with who and what we are as women.

For my part, I simply do not in most circumstances feel as secure with men as I do with women. I never did. I am concerned about how such gestures might be taken by men, particularly those whom I do not know. That is to say that many women do not feel entirely safe, even with men they do know. It is often not the same with other women. I immediately and intuitively feel safe and understood by other women, often without any words. Sometimes, I want to reach out and connect with that innate relation, sometimes for her sake and sometimes for mine. Thus, women do not so much compete, need to dominate, or feel a sense of vulnerability around other women.

Men are not the same. Can you imagine two men passing each other on the street exchanging warm, sweet smiles? I do not think so. They would be called gay, again a stereotype. Men may say hello, nod their head or mumble some exchange like,

"How 'ya doing?" or "What's up?"

However, the posture of men towards each other is often of a baser, competitive nature. By their very nature, most men seem to need to compete, to show strength and independence and to establish dominance over one another. As I reflect back on my relationships with men, as a man, one or the other of us became dominant, the alpha male as it were. It is small wonder that I was usually conflicted in my friendships with men.

However, even as I scribble out these stereotypes, my experience with gay men, who are not any less masculine in my view, has not been like this. Gay men in my experience seem to be far more genuine, sincere, congruent and less competitive, without sacrificing even an ounce of their masculinity.

The women that I call friend care about me, as I care about them. We love each other as sisters, even though I am not as present to them as I once was. While we may be angry, hurt or saddened by each other, we will always be concerned about each other and have each other's happiness, health and well-being at heart. We do not care about who is the stronger or better at anything. Perhaps I am merely fortunate to know a great group of women, but we often rely on one another, or even the group as a whole, for strength and comfort. We may only be chatting with each other, but that is seldom the extent of the exchange that our presence brings to one another.

Just being amongst such women brings comfort and confidence. Not only does the company of women inform me that I am alright, but it also serves to define me and shape me into yet a more secure, caring, loving, giving, happy and peaceful woman. That feels so much better and more authentic than the interactions I would have with men that often left me reeling, hurt and disappointed.

People often ask when I knew, as if a date certain lends credibility. How do I answer? There are moments that stand out with clarity, but in truth I always knew. From the time I was old enough to realize a gender distinction, I knew that a little girl lived in me. I remember that I was four years old, because that was the time that I became afraid. I was wrong and did not want to do the wrong things. I did not want to feel like a girl when everything around me suggested something different. The world around me defined me as a boy, and I did not want to disappoint. I was afraid to be the wrong person. I was afraid to be.

From the tender age of four, I learned not to be, but to adopt. I watched my older siblings and tried to do what they did to escape my father's wrath. Be aware. Watch the circumstances. Watch others and do what they do. That was the right thing to do, the right way to be. The best that I could do was watch the other boys and try to be the best boy I could be. For more than forty years that drive remained as constant within me as the blood that coursed my veins.

As I began to morph, I learned that even the most liberal, open-minded people would prefer that I stayed in my box. People just have a tough time with those who try to escape those social confines. They saw me more as a snake shedding my skin or like a wishful leper rather than a butterfly learning to fly. I felt like more than a metaphor.

I was alive and struggling just to be. I despaired under the weight of struggling alone. I feared that it was just too much to do alone, and I wanted to give up. Then, like a desert sunrise, understanding brought hope and strength. The light showed the way, and the way was alone. How else could such a journey be taken, when even the person closest to me on the planet could not come with me?

Many had gone before me and left a path, but the steps along that path were mine alone to take. I could lie down and die or keep putting one foot in front of the other. Instead of looking around to see who was coming, I looked ahead to the goal. It was still far off, but I had come so far. Six months earlier, living a new life in a new gender seemed an impossible mountain to climb. Yet, as I began living full time as a woman I looked for the next peak. I was a male-to-female transsexual transitioning to the gender of identification and away from that of birth and upbringing. That was not so bad.

So, into the mainstream I joyfully jumped that fall to live full time as a woman. I legally changed my first name from Robert to Roberta, signed a lease in her name, got bank accounts and revised my social security card, school records and credit cards. I got a driver's license with Roberta's name, picture and proper gender marker. It did not require actual movement of the heavens and earth to accomplish, but it did take a lot of phone calls and almost two months.

When I traded vehicles for the Subaru, my landlord had set me up with his golfing partner who was a car salesman. I presented as Roberta of course, as I had already been living as such for the previous two months, and my landlord knew me as none other. He was an older man who lived upstairs. His balding hair was gray, and he was shorter than I, with a bit of a gut. Oh, but he was charming and always treated me like a lady. He was indeed a ladies' man, and often had women over for the evening.

"Do you hear anything upstairs, I mean at night?" He asked me once.

Not wanting to appear judgmental, I quickly deduced that humor was called for.

"I can hear you pee," I said, as his bathroom was right above my bedroom.

The car salesman was a few years younger than I, but his mother was chief legal counsel for the Department of Corrections, and I had contact with her on a few cases as a prosecutor. I knew her to be both professional and reasonable. Her son showed signs of that sort of upbringing. He made me a good deal, as my landlord said he would.

Of course, he treated me like a lady, which was very interesting indeed in the context of buying a car. I was waiting for him to show me the vanity mirror on the passenger side, but to his credit he did not. I signed all the transaction documents as Roberta, and we were progressing swimmingly until he had to call the bank in Butte for the pay-off on my other vehicle. Plus, I had to sign off on the title in Robert's name. I was growing anxious as I knew the gig was up.

"Um, my name used to be Robert, and now it's Roberta," I simply and earnestly explained. "I understand," he said and downplayed it.

"Would you keep my confidence?" I asked, and have no reason to suspect that he ever revealed a thing to anyone.

I will remember that occasion as one of the rare moments when humanity prevailed. Where the world might hold little regard for a used car salesman and perhaps less for people like me, this transaction of a type typically characterized by motives of materialism and profit became transcendent. Here was a successful business person who needn't be moved by the vagaries of a troubled soul in recovery and gender transition. He could have laughed as others had, or jeered or looked askance. He could have responded with bewilderment, judgment or disdain. He did none of those things. He said he understood, without missing a beat, as he completed my credit check, which dovetailed seamlessly with my new name and social security number. Roberta had credit, so she must have been a real person. She is now the happy owner of a car registered and titled in her name.

The import of such transition milestones often did not occur to me until several days later. I felt as if I could then take a rest on my mountain trail as I continued my ascent. I could sit and survey my progress on the journey and the miles ahead. The mountain no longer seemed impassable, nor its height unscalable. I knew that if I kept putting one hiking boot along the trail just one step ahead of the last that I would reach the peak. I would know who and what I was. I would search no longer. I would be.

Continually, over time a slow metamorphosis took place. The changes seemed to emerge from within, and my confidence grew right along with my self-image as I presented to the world as a woman in speech, movements and actions. I did what women did. I walked as such and I talked as such, and the world began to perceive and treat me as such.

When I saw through the eyes of convention alone, I should not be surprised that convention was all I could see. But, when I began to see through the eyes of possibility, shit happened. I was perceived as a woman by all I encountered at work, in stores, in public restrooms, gas stations and grocery stores everywhere, even Safeway. It was more than outward perception. It was realization on the inside, too. I am a woman, no matter how I look. It is good, like the sun shining on my face with clarity, warmth and peace. I am happy and comfortable. Mostly, I know the inside of my skin.

As I continued to emerge, my marriage did not. It was winding down, to coin a phrase used in conjunction with the affairs of a dissolving business.

Divorce is like that. Peggy and I had sometimes held hands as we slept, and I knew I would miss that. As I continued with my transition, I knew in my heart that Peggy and I would not be together again. And I missed her, even though we spoke on the phone sometimes two or three times daily, and I saw her at least every other week.

It amazed me how little Peggy and I fought after February. Was it because I was no longer living in secrecy and dishonesty, or was it because I was sober? It was probably both, as transition and recovery seemed to dovetail, each producing hope and clarity of heart and mind. Still, we did have some hard discussions. Peggy rightfully felt betrayed when she asked,

"Did you know about this before we were married?"

She went to a few counseling sessions to help her deal with her emotions. She had to grieve the loss of her husband and lover with whom she thought she would grow old. I had promised her as much, so I could not deny the validity of her feelings.

"I have to give myself permission to be angry with you," she said.

But I could hardly be angry in return and tried to just listen and validate her feelings.

"No married trans person thinks their secrets will ever become their reality," I managed.

"I believed you would rescue me from them."

We exchanged some hard words, with no clear resolution. I went to a meeting in Butte. When it was over, Peggy was waiting outside after leaving a note on my car windshield.

"I apologize." she said. "I was harsh and mean."

I was astounded.

"No, Peggy, I deserved it. I betrayed you."

I knew it, but I also knew that it could not be helped.

I had truly fallen in love with Peggy. I married her believing that she would save me from myself, even as unfair and unrealistic as that was. I believed that this curse I had carried throughout my life would one day go away and that I would indeed grow old with Peggy. I could not have known that the belief that I could escape who I am was even more unrealistic. As Shakespeare had foretold centuries ago, if I had been true to myself, I would not have been false to Peggy or anyone else for that matter - my children, my brother and my friends.

I felt fortunate to have had at least one such love in my lifetime and equally unfortunate to lose it. We both lost as much. When I longed for love, I prayed that Peggy would find it too. She was too young and loving not to have someone to take care of, to share herself with and to grow old with. I had intended to be that someone. I thought our relationship, our marriage and our love would be all that I needed to live without my "other self." When it was clear that was not to be, I harbored a hope that Peggy would be able to accept it - and me as a husband and lover, as unlikely as that sounds. Peggy tried, for her part.

"Thank you," she said, "for informing me of two things at least. I know that I am not an alcoholic or a lesbian."

Though I was grateful to have Peggy's acceptance, understanding, patience and unwavering support, without which I doubt I could have started, I missed her terribly and felt great sorrow and guilt each time I thought of her, which was often. I think God gave us that time from February to September as a kind and graceful end to our marriage so that we could go on in dignity and love. I thank God and Peggy for that, even though we would soon be divorced. And we knew it as we packed to move in August. We too argued about who would get what, but not in the selfish way that accompanies most divorces.

"Here, Honey, you like this, you keep it," we often said as we sorted through music, artwork and other valuables that we had collected, which described and defined the moments of our life.

It was the most amicable divorce I had ever encountered. Still, divorce is traumatic for anyone. It turns your world upside down, no matter what your views on family values, marriage, love, etc. are. When you are married, even if the love has faded and you do not get along, that other person is always there. Though I had many problems, we had a good marriage. We could talk, shared common interests and values and could laugh, love and fight. It was not always easy, but we could live together, and when the day was done, sleep together, with a kiss goodnight and good morning. Loving a person is one thing, but living with them day in and day out is what makes a marriage work. And ours did. On December 22, 2006, the First Judicial District Court in Lewis and Clark County entered our dissolution of marriage. It had been hard that morning especially. We were both anxious and almost argued about something trivial. We "got 'er done" though and had lunch together.

Chapter Seventeen

What are You Afraid of

I know I ain't nobody's bargain, but
hell a little touch up and a little paint . . .

- Bruce Springsteen[60]

In the first year of sobriety, many of us mark different occasions, especially the passing holidays. We mark with wonder and amazement the first sober St. Patrick's Day (which meant I did not go to Butte), Memorial Day, Fourth of July, etc. New Year's Day 2007 was the first sober New Year I had in so many years that I really could not say how long. I rang it in at a friend's house in the hills. She had a potluck party with an array of treats. The main course was chili. For dessert, my friend made these triple chocolate brownies which, since my new addiction was sugar, I had the same "one or two" as when I was drinking. I can now admit that while there may be one and there may be two, there is no such thing as "one or two."

There was absolutely not a drop of booze. We ate well and sat around a campfire to watch fireworks in her yard at the stroke of midnight. The fire burned hot enough to keep us marginally warm in the depth of a Montana winter, what I have always thought of as the wee, small hours of the year. It melted all the snow around its perimeter, and though the ground was frozen, it was dry. Just after the stroke of midnight, I got a New Year's kiss from a couple of guys, just as I had at a Halloween party after my first dance with a boy, a slow one to be certain. I had liked it all just as I imagine a teenage girl would with her first forays into romance. However, it was not yet time for such frivolity. I still had all the wrong equipment, and some trans women, like Gwen Arroyo, had been murdered in sexual encounters that may have begun as innocently. Even though I had longed for closeness and romance, God had thus far relieved me of its burdens.

We hold hands and say the Lord's Prayer at the end of meetings to signify, as some say, that together we can accomplish what we cannot do alone. At one meeting, I had been sitting next to a guy that I had a huge crush on. We held hands and prayed, but I was in no way prepared for what he whispered in my ear. He said, as I later discovered that he was married,

"You can lead me into temptation."

"Anytime," I mumbled in my naiveté.

All the way home, Springsteen's lyrics rang in my dizzy, hopeful brain: *If you're tough enough for love, Honey I'm tougher than the rest.*[61] God spared us both from that fiasco.

I had actually imagined when I set out that I would have suitors who would want to know me for who I am inside, and once blinded by that light, would accept, understand and love me. The realization of how unreasonable my expectations were was hard to swallow, and I had taken such a huge bite all at once. It was insane, but a psychologist I saw in January concluded otherwise. To be approved for gender reassignment surgery, gender correction surgery, sex reassignment Surgery, all politically correct alternatives to "sex change operation," I had to obtain two letters, one from my therapist and one from a psychologist with an evaluation included.

I had seen numerous psychological evaluations in my professional lives, both in the group home programs and as a prosecutor in child abuse and neglect cases. I knew that they involved clinical impressions as well as conclusions drawn from test results. For instance, I knew that much about me would be gleaned from a MMPI, and I knew what that acronym stood for - Minnesota Multiphasic Personality Inventory. I do not know for sure how long the MMPI has been around, but it seems I recall it from the 1980s in the residential child care setting. Just to demonstrate how small of a world Montana can be, at St. Labre we had relied upon a psychologist from Billings for our child psychological evaluations, and yet he turned up in my kid cases in Virginia City as an expert psychologist for the State a decade or more later. His daughter married the friend and colleague who did my name change.

My "psych eval" revealed only a few surprises. I knew that I was depressed, alcoholic, borderline anorexic and had trouble with math. However, I would not have described myself as narcissistic (who would?) or having a learning disability. I knew the MMPI's reputation for reliability, and since I got my recommendation for surgery, I was not going to quibble. In fact, much to my surprise, I was able to accept things about myself revealed to me by others that before would have caused great resentments with fierce arguments in the darkness inside my head, where the committee would soon be picking out curtains and furniture as if they would be staying a while. They did not even get inside the door this time.

I emailed my friends that it had been a defining moment, where you know that life will not ever be the same, and that is a very good thing. On January 16, 2007, a mere eleven months since the "crash," it was no longer a question of if, but a question of when. Mom told me that she prayed daily for my "intentions" and that her thoughts were with me. I was still considering both Montreal and Trinidad, Colorado for my surgery, although I had already applied to Trinidad.

Mom wrote me in an email the story of a shrine to St. Joseph in Montreal, and the story of a "Brother Andre of Mount Royal . . . a lowly brother who fostered and promoted throughout his lifetime devotion to St. Joseph."

"I hope to be with you when the time comes," I read in her email as I cried happy tears.

Could I ask for more? I was never so assured of my mother's love than I was in that moment.

Mom also attached religious significance to Trinidad, wondering whether it devolved from "the Trinity." I did not know, but I learned that due to its Hispanic influence, there was a great devotion to Mary. And there she was again; *Standing right in front of me, speaking words of wisdom, let it be.*[62]

On February 8, 2007, Dr. Marci Bowers called me from the LA airport, having been in Los Angeles to tape a segment of the Tyra Banks show, as her notoriety continued to grow. She gave me a surgery date of October 4, 2007, but felt certain she could move it up. October 4 is the feast day of St. Francis, which had been important to me since the born-again days of my youth. Fr. Paul had arranged a field trip for my class at the end of my junior year in high school. We walked from Watterson High School the length of the baseball and football fields along Cooke Avenue to a theater close by to watch *Brother Sun and Sister Moon*, Zeffirelli's rendition of the story of St. Francis. Perhaps it was my developmental stage, or the music by Donavan, but I definitely heard something:

> *Brother Sun and Sister Moon*
> *I can hear you calling*
> *I can hear your tune*[63]

I heard that calling and the first notes of a tune that has resounded in my soul ever since, sometimes quietly and sometimes with a joyous crescendo, not unlike Beethoven's *Ninth Symphony*. The October 4 date struck me as somehow significant, although I asked for a summer date in hopes that my sisters could be there too.

As I struggled through another Montana winter, I was doing well. My job was going well. I had won an appeal after the State read my brief and simply capitulated. It was not my doing, really, as I just pointed out all the many missteps at the trial court level. I admired the Attorney General's staff for just throwing in the towel instead of forcing the issue on a losing argument. I kept the pleading by which they conceded the case and felt as if I should frame it and hang it on the wall in place of my *Juris Doctorate* diploma. I did not have my fancy, framed diploma on the wall as many lawyers do, because it bore the masculine name, and that just would not do. Instead, I hung up photographs of flowers that I had started from seed. Thus, I liked to say that I grew photographs.

Macy's did not keep me on after the holidays, and I was looking for another part time job because the OAD just did not pay enough to cover my bills, medical expenses, old debt, etc. Transition was going well. The physical changes included fewer whiskers, smaller facial pores, softer skin tone and sprouting breasts - about the size of plums, which is about the size they would grow to. I had estrogen and no testosterone coursing through my veins, for which I was exceedingly grateful. However, the hormonal changes in my body no doubt enhanced the emotional roller coaster I was on.

On a bright, chilly day as I walked along 11th Avenue toward St. Paul's, I noticed the driver of a white Chevy van staring at me as he drove past.

"Is he reading me?" I wondered as that same old fear gripped me.

But it was not disdain that registered on his face. It was more like interest, as I noticed his head move up and down with his eyes in wandering approval. Suddenly, I recalled how safe I had felt to gawk at women while I was driving. Peculiar how we feel so comfortable behaving inside a vehicle in ways we would not countenance while on the street, flipping off another driver for instance. I began to fear for the driver of the van as he stared back at me over his shoulder while driving past. I smiled and wondered if young girls like that kind of attention too, and if that was not why they often giggle between each other.

Everything was in place, and I was just waiting for Dr. Bowers to give me an exact date. I had paid her $500 deposit with my earnings from Macy's and had saved some money from the proceeds of the house sale to pay for some of the surgery. The rest of it, along with traveling and living expenses, would be from a credit card advance of $17,000. It was hard to believe that it was really happening, all in the space of about a year, but everything was coming together. I had a wonderful faith community in the United Methodist Church as I found myself changing all my paradigms. My understanding of God no longer blocked my understanding of God, as God continued to reveal God to me in so many ways. St. Paul's was active spiritually and socially, and I could not have been in a better place.

Recovery and transition continued to walk hand in hand. I had developed many friendships in that community, and the women were a great source of comfort and strength. Nothing like a few good women, I thought. I had a sponsor, and that was central. I had struggled along for sometime without a sponsor, as I was still afraid of revealing myself. I knew intuitively that it would be necessary and just could not yet bring myself to it. I thought I was so different.

I felt like I did not fit in any of the meeting groups I went to. I said to a friend,

"Helena recovery just does not have a place for me."

"I'm thinking about quitting meetings," I said, dejectedly.

Two people kept me from it. I called my friend who first brought me to a meeting and explained my problem to him. He listened with great concern and attention. He was the one who had said,

"Don't drink, and go to meetings. Don't drink even if your ass falls off. Just pick it up and go to a meeting."

"I think you need to go to more meetings," he told me.

Another friend listened to my complaints and asked,

"What are you afraid of?"

I tried to explain that I was not afraid. I just did not fit in. She asked again,

"What are you afraid of?"

I mumbled a lame excuse, like,

"They don't know what it's like to be me." Again, she repeated herself as if there was nothing else to discuss,

"What are you afraid of?"

She was so wise that it pissed me off as she knew it would. Nevertheless, she was unrelenting and I knew that she was right. My problem was fear. I was afraid of the part of recovery that required me to look at myself and admit my part in all the misery in my life.

I had Christmas dinner with a friend and her family. I met her dogs, birds, fish, turtle and all the other accoutrement of her country life. I had agreed to housesit for her and her family when they went on their January vacation. They had a gorgeous home that they had built in the hills east of Helena. It was quiet, with the gurgling sound of fish tanks constantly calming in concert with the breeze blowing through Ponderosa pines that grew so tall outside the windows. The house was furnished with overstuffed antique furniture, and the sun lit on the hardwood floors with abundance through many large windows. It was the perfect retreat setting in which I would attempt that fearless soul searching.

I had not realized the full extent of the "stinking thinking" I had built up behind my alcoholic dam over nearly thirty-five years of practice. As I started to pull the finger of my fear and defenses out of that dam, I literally broke down behind a flood of tears, as I could see only my pain. I had started with my Dad, and of course, I could not even begin to see my part all by myself. My journal entry that day read:

Forty-five minutes of self searching and I am devastated. I suck. I have no idea who I am, and even if I did it is likely nothing more than the deception I have created. I have done well and I do not like myself. It is too painful to empty myself out on this table to see.

The exercise was valuable nonetheless, as it became painfully clear to me that I could not do it alone. Also, for perhaps the first time I could plainly see that I had not been completely honest with another person in my life. My dishonesty in relationships was selfish and entirely self- centered. Was I like that in all my relationships? Clearly I was, as my every effort was geared at projecting an image of someone that I was not. It is selfish to never give yourself away.

I went to a meeting because the first thing I saw when I arrived at my friend's house was a fifth of whiskey in the kitchen and a few bottles of wine in the cupboard. In such a state, for me to drink would be for me to die.

I continued to pray over that week for God to lead me to a woman to ask for help. I contemplated several whom I admired for what they said at meetings. Two seemed like the most likely candidates. I was still too nervous to ask directly, so prayed one morning that God would lead me that day to the woman I should ask to be my sponsor. It is odd that God should answer such a demanding prayer at all, let alone as quickly as God answered this one. As I drove up for the noon meeting, one of the women I had thought about asking for help pulled up in her car right next to me and parked.

"That was fast," I said silently to God as if surprised that when I pray to God my prayer might be answered.

"Okay, you asked for it," was the answer to this prayer.

We walked into the meeting and sat down together. She spoke to me like I was alright, even though I was still scared as hell. It did not dawn on me that she had been a sponsorless new comer once too. She was comforting me as if I had asked God for that blessing also. It is amazing when God answers your prayer with blessings gratis, but, God is like that.

As my understanding of God began to change, mostly by letting go of the dogmatic and book-based God in favor of a dynamic, present power, I was not certain that I knew God at all. I came again to that place where I could not trust God, or lacked faith that God did want me to be happy and whole.

As luck would have it, somebody announced that day at the meeting that they had brought forms into the meeting that would help with a self inventory. They left them on the table directly behind me. I turned around and grabbed one. As I was reading it, my new best friend looked over at it.

"I can help you with that," she said matter-of-factly.

I could have cried. How she knew that was precisely what I needed right then and exactly what I had asked God for, I do not know. I wanted to write that it remains a mystery to me, but that would not be true. God is like that.

My sponsor has saved my butt countless times. She seemed hard-hearted at times, but only because she loved me enough to tell me not what I wanted to hear, but what I needed to see.

"Your eyes glazed over," she said later.

I heard what she said but could not accept it. But, she had what I wanted. She had years of sobriety and was as calm and even as a snow-covered peak on a cold winter morning. In Montana, on such a peak, the only movement is evanescent snow rising like a spirit on the breeze. Her happiness was self-contained, and she did not wear it on her sleeve. She was never really too far up or down. She was stable, neither too big nor too small.

"She was right-sized," a very wise woman, Nancy would have said.

She helped me understand my character flaws and how they had influenced my choices and relationships over the years, as well as my actions. She heard all the secrets of my soul and did not go running away in fear or disgust. She did not judge or reject any part of me, at least not outwardly. And, to her credit, she has likely forgotten much of that which was wrong with me, embracing instead the person that I was becoming. She was my wise woman, my inspiration and my friend. I had thought that I could never repay her, but with the realization that she likely feels much the same way about her sponsor, I have sponsored several other women because that reciprocal, almost symbiotic relationship is just how the deal works.

On March 2, I went with the office attorneys to a workshop in Butte. I stayed overnight at Peggy's house and enjoyed her cooking as always. It was a Friday, so we watched her Friday shows on TV, "Monk," "House," and that other one about the detective and pseudo-psychic friend who always seemed to luck into the right answer. This guy from Helena started calling my cell phone number. I had naively given it out wanting to be helpful. He wanted help of another sort. He was drunk. He had found out that I was transgender.

"Why are you in Montana?" he slurred over the phone.

"You should be in San Francisco," he said, probably not intending to sound as cruel and judgmental as he did.

"Why don't you come over?" he asked, not realizing that I was sixty miles away.

I was not interested but thought that I should try to help him anyway.

"Let's go for coffee and talk about it," I suggested instead.

But he was unrelenting in his crude comments, barely veiling his sexual agenda. I hung up but he kept calling back. I thought about turning my phone off but did not.

I went back to the conference, and at a break one of my coworkers approached me and told me she had just heard about my transition. We had been working together for months and she did not know. That was very affirming. She was supportive, and as I was telling her all about it, the phone rang again. I suspected it was that same drunken, horny and rude guy from before. I thought about not answering. I had just spoken with him though, and it would be of no service to be rude. I checked my caller ID, and since it was a different number, I answered.

It was the clinic in Trinidad.

"Can you be here May 1st?" the assistant asked.

I knew it was less than two months away but said,

"I've been waiting forty-eight-plus years to be. Yes, I can be there."

When I got home the next day, I sent Monique an email.

"The only way to describe how I am feeling right now is incredible excitement and deep peace both at the same time. It's amazing. Thanks for hanging with me."

PART THREE: NEW LIFE

Chapter Eighteen

Would you Like to Dance

There's a place in the world for a gambler
There's a burden that only {she} can bear

- Dan Fogelberg.[64]

Monique had assured me that the universe would call when it was time. As 2007 began, a trans friend called, suspecting that her job was at risk.

"I got your name from Christine Kaufman," she said.

Christine was a local state legislator whom I had met at Pride the previous year.

"I'm not sure what I want to do or even if I can do anything," she queried.

"There's not much you can do. Transpeople are not in a protected class," I informed her.

"But, sometimes it's enough just to call people and talk to them about it. It's the J.D. behind the name," I assured her.

"I'm not in a spot to represent you. I have no employment law experience. But, I will try to help you keep your job."

Like many trans women, she was afraid ultimately of losing her job on some pretense, so did not want to rock the boat. By the same token, if she did nothing she might be unemployed anyway. They had scheduled a meeting, and she wanted me to go with her. I was reluctant but agreed.

After advising her to contact the ACLU, the Human Rights Bureau and a private lawyer, we agreed that I would go with her to the meeting so long as we went prepared with a copy of the employee handbook and her HR file. We got together and reviewed them, and I called her employer, a student loan organization with whom, incidentally, I had an account. So much for stealth, I thought. I called them and they decided to cancel the meeting, and take corrective action with her, which included a letter for her file involving some pretense.

In another situation about a year later, a trans woman named Kyndra called me and asked me to speak to a trans woman in Livingston that was having some early transition employment troubles. I was very reluctant as I wished to remain in whatever stealth I had at that time. However, as I continued to talk with Kyndra, I was impressed by her intellect as well as her desire to help someone else, and she seemed to have her head on straight. I decided I would talk to her friend.

Male to female trans women just are not that pretty as they begin transition. They have beards, and hormones have not yet softened their faces. Kyndra's friend worked in a grocery store, and I suppose stood out like rotten fruit. She had to interact with the public in her job, and evidently the good grocers of Livingston thought that might be a problem. They were making sounds about terminating her employment because she wanted to dress as a woman at work.

People in gender transition must do this in order to complete the real life test pre-surgery phase of transition. To a certain extent I am not without sympathy for employers in such circumstances, but on the other hand I had been victimized by discrimination, and it seemed very wrong to me. I called the store's corporate headquarters in Boise and spoke with a woman in their HR department. She assured me that she would address the problem. I do not know what she said, but Kyndra's friend had her job back if she wanted it.

As it turned out, she did not. I cannot say that I blamed her. I also cannot say that I really had any special talent, skill or knowledge in employment law. I think the changes in attitude by the employers were due in part to the J.D. behind my name and my willingness to call the people in charge and point out what was going on in a veiled suggestion that they had more to lose than to gain by taking adverse action against an employee based upon their gender identification, which in many corporations was becoming a protected class. Even though I did not see myself going into private practice in employment and discrimination law, the universe had called.

As uneventful as February was, March was just the opposite. I got the call from Trinidad giving me just under two months to get ready for surgery. I was psyched, yet vacillated between great joy and high anxiety. Frankly, I was scared. There were so many things going through my mind, not the least of which were all the arrangements for travel and my stay in Colorado.

I had transgender issues to consider as well. The Steve Stanton story in Largo, Florida, about the transgender city manager about to be fired due to her transition plan, was at its peak. I recalled the Reverend's report to the Montana legislature a couple years earlier about transsexual pedophiles and peaking at women under the restroom stalls. It did not matter that these reports were inherently inconsistent. Pedophiles do not take sexual gratification from grown women. What mattered is that they represented a prevailing attitude that showed no welcome to me. That climate scared me, and I was not certain that I wanted to remain in Montana after surgery.

My journaling became most prayerful. My sponsor had suggested that I just talk to God, so I did as I wrote. I wrote to God that I was afraid. I speculated that it might be self doubt or second thoughts about the surgery, or perhaps the loss of control, since it was moving so fast. I knew that I would do well to wait and examine those maybes. But I did not want to, and I would lose my $500 deposit if I cancelled. That was a loss I could ill afford.

It was not the physical change I feared. I borrowed from Rod Stewart when it came to that particular appendage, often thinking that the attachment was "purely physical." I could not say that I hated it as many trans women do. I just had no use for it and no desire to keep it. It was merely functional at best, and then only for urinating, as I had not had any sexual activity in almost a year. So, what was I afraid of? Was it life as a woman? I had been very comfortable and never once regretted my transition. My only regrets were that I did not start sooner and for those I had lost along the way. I felt very good in my female skin.

"I am afraid of you," I said to God.

I always was because, just as with my father, I was afraid that God would not approve and thus would not allow me to live peacefully as the woman I felt I was. Some religious views held that I was violating God's law. Yet, since the journey began, I had asked for God's will. I prayed,

"Here is my transition, Lord. I give it to you in accord with your will."

I was afraid that God would not approve, and I worried that I could not survive. I tried, but just could not trust God enough to let go completely. I had to trust, face my fears and surrender completely.

I thought of the "trust falls" we used to do at encounter workshops where you get all warm and fuzzy with your coworkers. I would do that free fall into God's arms. I asked God to "catch me please, and set me down where you want. Bless me in accord with your will, Amen."

It reminded of the Thomas Merton Prayer:

My Lord God, I have no idea where I am going.
I do not see the road ahead of me.
I cannot know for certain where it will end.
Nor do I really know my self, and the fact
That I think that I am following your will does
Not mean that I am actually doing so. But I
Believe that the desire to please you does in
Fact please you. And I hope that I have that desire in all
That I am doing. I hope that I will never do anything
Apart from that desire. And I know that if I do this
You will lead me by the right road though I may
Know nothing about it. Therefore I will trust you
Always though I may seem to be lost and in the
Shadow of death. I will not fear, for you are ever
With me, and you will not leave me to face my perils
Alone. [65]

I had loved that prayer since I first discovered it in college. I prayed it earnestly now. How could I be sure that sex reassignment surgery was God's will for me? I prayed and sought the counsel of the women I respected. I talked to my sponsor, my friend Barb and my pastor, as well as Peggy and some others whose faith I respected. Of course, no one could tell me for certain. I knew as well as they counseled that God's will for me was between God and me.

I had been making arrangements with a trans woman friend of mine in Missoula to stay with while I had electrolysis, not on my face, but in a rather sensitive spot in preparation for surgery. We did not want ingrown vaginal hairs after all, did we? She invited me to a LGBT gala event in Missoula known as the Black and White Ball. I was very excited, as I had not yet been to a formal dance as a woman. I bought a little black dress that I wore so sexily well, and off I went with expectations par usual exceeding the possibilities actually presented. It was fun, though sobering and discouraging.

My colleague who had been so encouraging and comforting early in my transition was there and invited me to dance. I couldn't quite get the hang of that Montana favorite, the jitterbug, but I tried and he did not mind. It was disconcerting to have someone else lead in such a fast paced dance. My life was much the same.

Someone took a picture, and when Peggy saw it said,

"That is really sweet."

I agreed, but it meant so much more. In the space of a dance with no words passed, I understood that I was accepted, even valued, for who I was and not the façade of a person I had been. Here was a man who had faced his fears and dared to live authentically. In doing so, he showed me the courage to do the same. I did lose the anxiety and doubt over my rapidly approaching date with the surgeon, but another friend reminded me of just how different we transsexuals really are. It seemed especially so in Montana.

Even in the gay and lesbian community to which I ostensibly belonged, I was the proverbial redheaded stepchild, accepted for the solidarity of our societal struggles, yet apart. The mainstream flowed about us with interrelationships like the microcosm of a LGBT dance in Missoula, Montana, close enough to dive in, yet elusive. We stood just outside looking in, hoping and waiting for another dance.

It was Lent for the Christian world. St. Paul's had a weekly Wednesday evening community dinner that I had been attending and a short Lenten service afterwards. I enjoyed the services and Marianne's usual superb messages. On Wednesday, March 15, 2007, I was much at peace as I sat in the pew at St. Paul's. It was a small group so Marianne cajoled me away from my usual seat by the pillar. Thus, I would not even have the chore of holding up the church that evening. It is a joy to be present in church without worrying about the kids, the car or the budget, the whatever. Often when I really get that God is present, I mean God is here and God is now, I can rest in God's presence. It is such a happy, peaceful place. The 15th was such a night, and I closed my eyes as a pianist and flautist began to play.

I should not be surprised when God answers my prayers. It is the how of it which sometimes astounds me. I had asked for God's blessing on my surgery, for that is what I truly wanted. It was my final step into womanhood, the crescendo of the symphony of my life to that point and assuredly, God was the maestro. I did not expect a voice, a thunder clap or a bush afire. God could have answered me in any of a thousand ways. Yet, when I said "yes," believing that it was God I affirmed, God honored me, honored my decision and my femininity.

I never really thought much about visions, but that is the only way I can describe God's response to my prayers. The musicians began a plaintive rendition of "Ave Maria." I closed my eyes, devoid of thought or emotion. I was as much at peace as I ever have been. As the flautist continued with the melody with the piano accompanying, I saw myself dancing. I was wearing a long flowing cotton dress and sheer white cape and scarf. I have tried to recreate that sense of billowing white flowing spirit in photographs of white flowers. It is elusive. As I danced round and round in wispy whiteness, I saw a man approaching me. He was young and stylish. His hair was dark and cropped short. His eyes were dark and his skin olive. I knew at once that it was Jesus who approached. He held out his hand to me and said,

"Would you like to dance?"

He smiled as I turned and swirled. I was as fully feminine as I could be, and Jesus was happy. I had my blessing.

Ave Maria! maiden mild!
Listen to a maiden's prayer!
Thou canst hear though from the wild,
Thou canst save amid despair.
Safe may we sleep beneath thy care,
Though banish'd, outcast and reviled
Maiden! hear a maiden's prayer;

Mother, hear a suppliant child!

Ave Maria!
Ave Maria! undefiled!
The flinty couch we now must share
Shall seem this down of eider piled,
If thy protection hover there.
The murky cavern's heavy air
Shall breathe of balm if thou hast smiled;
Then, Maiden! hear a maiden's prayer;
Mother, list a suppliant child!

Ave Maria!
Ave Maria! stainless styled!
Foul demons of the earth and air,
From this their wonted haunt exiled,
Shall flee before thy presence fair.
We bow us to our lot of care,
Beneath thy guidance reconciled;
Hear for a maid a maiden's prayer,
And for a father hear a child!
Ave Maria!
- Sir Walter Scott[66]

As March marched on, Mom and I completed our travel arrangements and plans to stay at the Tarabino Inn in Trinidad, a Victorian bed and breakfast. Of course, much of my stay would be in far less comfy accommodations. Mom wrote in an email,

"I know you are feeling some trepidation now. That is why I have had you in my prayers for lo, these many months, and I shall not cease."

I don't doubt that she is praying still, as am I. I told my friends and sisters about my "vision," and none were too surprised. My friend Syl wrote,

"How beautiful. I feel by you relating the story . . . like I share in the blessing."

She could not know how true her statement was, as she had been through so much with me online that allowed me to survive and this moment to arrive. Another friend said,

"Jesus accepts you for all that you are and will be. It is only society that tells you differently."

Knowing what a Christian man he is, I believe he was right.

I needed another couple visits with the electrolysist and would need to take a day off of work to drive to Billings for an appointment. I wrote this email on March 23 to my boss, as much for the shock value that I knew it would arouse as for anything else:

Jim in preparation for my surgery I must undergo a little proce-dure that may make you wince. Genital hair removal. Are you wincing? I do not know if I told you the medical science involved, but in the vernacular my "outtie" becomes an "innie." The surgeon does not want me to have hair growing inside, so recommends that it be removed ahead of time. I checked with my laser hair removal doctor and she says too little, too light (pigment wise). So, I have to remove it through a series of electrolysis treatments one at a time. It's a painful ordeal but very necessary. Add to that the op-erator is in Billings. I have an appointment with her next Friday. Would this have been easier if I had said: "'Hey Jim, I need next Friday off, ok?"

Jim said yes.

The operator, Rose Ellen Paris, was wonderful. At seventy-one, she looked more like fifty-five, and drove a pink Cadillac.

"Trans women are special to me," she said when I met her.

She did not say why, but she had a very steady hand, thank God. She had told me to get a prescription numbing agent called EMLA and slather it on and then cover it with plastic wrap. Genital electrolysis was painful for the three hours or so that Rose Ellen worked. I think she would have kept going if my body could have taken any more. It would not hold out, so I had to go to Missoula the next weekend for more.

At the end of March, I got a call that threw me. In my county attor-ney days, there had been two newspapers serving the county. The *Bozeman Chronicle* catered to the east half of the county and the *Montana Standard* serviced the west half out of Butte. We called them the "Comical" and the "Substandard," respectively. Madison County geography features two wide valleys, the Madison to the east and the Ruby to the west. Virginia City, the county seat, sat in between in a low spot between the Tobacco Root Mountains to the north and the Gravelly Range to the south.

Alder Creek, where Bill Fairweather had discovered gold in 1864, flowed north out of the Gravelly's right past Virginia City.

"What Bill had discovered would prove to be one of the richest gold deposits in North America, and would be the seminal event in the history of Montana."[67]

I had hunted both ranges extensively and knew them fairly well. I took my first bull elk and a bull moose in the Gravellys. Much of the time and activities surrounding the kids and Peggy was spent in those mountains or their shadows. We went camping up Mill Creek out of Sheridan a few times. We would sit around the campfire and tell stories by one of us starting out and then stopping almost mid-sentence where the next person would pick up. The stories always began with,

"It was a dark and stormy night."

I am fond of those mountains.

On the twenty-seventh of March, Nick Gevok, a reporter who wrote for the Butte paper, called me. He lived in Ennis and covered all my cases just as his predecessor, Perry Backus, had done for years. While I trusted Perry and considered him my friend, I did not enjoy that sense of comfort with Nick. I did not completely trust him. He had referred to me more recently in print as Roberta R. Zenker, f/k/a Robert. He had obtained my office number and addressed me as Roberta. I wanted to say, "f/k/a Robert at your service," but restrained myself.

My past was chasing me. Nick wanted to interview me for a story about my transition, and I wondered to myself when he would catch up with me. Following the Stanton story in Florida, I feared that same kind of sensational coverage on a local scale. After almost seven months living in semi-stealth as a woman, I was jettisoned back into fear. I reasoned that someone from Madison County tipped him off as to my whereabouts, although it had been no secret. He had publicized my new position with the Public Defender's Office when I left Madison County, so why now? I wanted to think about it, so stalled Nick.

The simple fact was that I had become accustomed to my life as a woman, even grown to like it very much. I was comfortable in my own skin for the first time in my life, and I was worried about screwing it up.

I thought of my trans girlfriend in Missoula and the whole notion of activism, which cannot be done in hiding. I had hidden my light under a bushel basket. I thought about doing the interview for, as my mother the cliché queen might say, "the good of the order." Monique had more than subtly suggested as much due to my position in society as a trans lawyer. There are other trans lawyers, just not in Montana. I did not feel that I was up to it, which left me feeling guilty and selfish. I cried half the way home from my electrolysis session in Butte that night. I wrote my friend an email:

> You know, all I ever wanted was to live as the woman I am inside in the mainstream. Perhaps it was naïve of me to think it would last forever, but I have that life now even without further surgeries. The only people who know anything else about me are those I let in. I have a church community where they know me as this sweet, articulate middle-aged woman. I have friends at Macy's where I can go shopping as that same woman. Same for Goodwill, hehe. I have a lot of love and respect in the recovery community. I do not want to forsake that if I do not have to.

"You cannot change your past nor make it go away," she replied.

I could not get mine to leave me alone. I had been asked recently by a public defender who had taken a sentence review case to assist him. It just happened to be a meth lab case I had successfully tried to a jury in Virginia City almost two years earlier. In Montana, the legislature enacted into law a process called "sentence review" by which a convicted felon could challenge the even-handedness of his or her sentence. It is not an appeal to a higher court. Rather, a sentence review committee consisting of three district court judges appointed by the Supreme Court reviewed an applicant's sentence for consistency with the sentences of other similarly situated defendants and affirmed it, lowered it or even increased it.

It was a system that I had great reservations about, inasmuch as criminal defendants had an adequate remedy of appeal to review the legality and correctness of their sentence that in no way justified this extra procedure that appeared to be little more than second guessing district court judges. It was odd, too, that their peers sat in review. I guess it was a way to keep them honest, a sort of self regulating peer review. However, I doubted its necessity and efficacy.

One case I had is a good example. It was an incest case in which the defendant, an over-the-road truck driver, determined that his stepdaughter required home schooling and that he would be the best teacher. So, from the time she was thirteen until she was eighteen and made her break, he taught her in the sleeping compartment of his truck. He had made a video tape, complete with lights and other "props," cue cards and music, oddly enough, Karen Carpenter's *"Top of the World."* He is not there any longer, as Judge Boyd, a wizened and beloved jurist from Anaconda sitting in for Judge Davis, sentenced him to about seventy-five years.

It had been a difficult and emotionally raw case for all involved. Perhaps the most difficult for me, though, was watching that video tape, knowing that I would have to give it to Judge Boyd, a Catholic family man, to review before sentencing. He returned it to me just before the sentencing.

"I didn't need to see this," he said angrily as he handed it back to me.

"Well, I wasn't sure, Judge. I'm sorry you had to see that," I managed meekly.

It was the last sentence Judge Boyd imposed, as he passed away a short while later. The defense attorney wisely counseled his client to withdraw his sentence review application, as it did not seem likely that Judge Boyd's peers would reduce his last sentence. In fact, given the egregious facts of the case and respect that Judge Boyd had amongst the bench and bar, the sentence likely would have been increased.

In the meth case which the public defender asked me to assist him with, *State v. Rolleau, et al.*, Judge Tucker had imposed a particularly tough sentence. At the time, I did not really care about the sentence, as my job had been to obtain the conviction and leave the judgment to the court. Inasmuch as there were three defendants, each with their own public defender selected from a pool of my most respected colleagues, I was still beaming with self-righteous pride at sentencing.

It had been a particularly contentious case, as the victims were vociferous in their insistence upon retribution, and the defendants refused any and all plea-bargain offers. Some cases just have to go to trial. I squared off in front of a Madison County jury against a formidable three-lawyer defense team, including my friend, Stephanie. Even though she put me through my paces, the jury quickly convicted, which of course is how it should have been. Remember, I had the law, the facts, including eye witness testimony and lab reports (real CSI stuff), and the power of choice on my side.

Something happened to me, however, at the sentencing hearing. Rolleau's girlfriend, a codefendant who had been pregnant throughout the proceedings, showed up with a beautiful baby in tow. I asked him to let me see the baby, which he did while beaming with goodness. I had always had a certain sense of compassion and tried to treat criminal defendants with dignity and respect. In that moment with Rolleau before sentencing, I crossed some sort of bridge of humanity where I realized that he was not all bad. As Randi Hood, the state's chief public defender said,

"There is something good in everyone."

I wrote an affidavit for Rolleau's sentencing review attorney that was used to get his sentence reduced. The victims soon after called me to register their objection. They too called my new office in Helena and referred to me as Roberta. I basically sent them away inasmuch as I was no longer a public official. I fear that in their anger and frustration, they contacted Mr. Gevock.

I was afraid of all that was before me and most of what lay behind. I was afraid of telling people the truth about me. My fear of rejection, now that I knew I had no choice, was as strong as it had ever been. I felt like a leper, even though no one could see my bloody, oozing sores. They were there, and if anyone could see them, they would surely turn away. Who could embrace a leper? People would not understand me. They would not accept me, and I would gain nothing from disclosure. I was polarized with fear, but I had a solution. Pray, and leave the result to God.

I consulted with trusted friends and colleagues. I called Perry Backus, who was very surprised and even a bit dismayed to hear from me.

"They can do a story with or without my participation, right?" I asked.

I thought I might be able to shade it sympathetically, instead of sensationally, as the Stanton story had become a media circus in the national media.

"They can, but it won't be much of a story," Perry told me.

I called my Missoula trans friend.

"Some follow the activism path while others live in stealth. It's up to you," she said.

My ability to live in stealth was not lost on me, and I was not sure at all that I wanted to give it away. It is a dilemma that all trans people must go through as they transition and beyond. "Only you can make the decision about how you want to live. The path that you choose will be the right one for you," she said with an air of wizened truth.

I talked with a few other newspaper people I knew just to make sure.

"No, it won't be a story worth printing without your participation," said one editor at the *Independent Record*.

I declined the interview and explained my decision in an email to Monique:

After talking with several people I have decided to decline the interview. They may print a story anyway, but I am told that it will not be much of a story without the interview with me. Part of me really wants to be the activist and do the interview for the good of the cause, so to speak. But I am just not up to it right now.

I have worked so hard and gained so much that I do not think it wise to jeopardize. Right now, even without the surgeries, I am living the life I have always wanted as the woman I have always been. It brings great peace and joy daily. I fear I would lose that in coming out to the world. Perhaps it is a risk that I eventually must take, just not today.

It is not easy to turn the page on your past. Mine gave permission to let it go only grudgingly. I fear that many people thus grow discouraged and abandon the attempt to grow and change. It is just too painful. Yet, if we are ever to break free of the roles in which our life and our world have cast us, if we are ever to recognize and become our true selves, we must change. I had to cross the desert that my soul, heart and mind had become. I had to give up family, friends, home and a whole way of life to begin that journey. I had traveled far with no regrets but the loss of family members. My soul breathed life again. My mind was open and my heart was free. I had not yet arrived, and my journey would go on. But, I did not crawl. I soared.

The classic Three Dog Night tune, *"Pieces of April,"* kept playing over and over in my mind as April ushered in, and all I could think about was May. I know it's backwards, but the one line that fit for me went,

"It's a morning, it's a morning, a morning in May."[68] It was April, but all I could think about was a morning in May. The first few weeks of April

brought a flurry of activity, but then the countdown began in earnest. April 17 was "T-minus-14 and counting." I had learned that phrase growing up in the sixties as we watched the live broadcast of NASA space rocket launches.

I had often used it in play to signify some magnanimous, if not imaginary, moment from which my life would surely be launched. I could not turn back, nor remain the same. Once on board and locked in, I could only hang on as I was hurtled forth by some inner inertia. Like Thomas Merton, I could not say where I was going. I had no question, however, but that I must go. Then, it was real. It was indeed momentous, unequivocal and would soon be upon me. Surgery would not be a launch catapulting me into a new life, for that journey had begun long ago, the seeds of which were always there inside, steadily germinating, whether I consciously recognized it or not.

I wondered if genetic women get to experience such a metamorphosis. Surely they do not arise one day different than the day before, filled with grace, beauty and wisdom. These traits all must grow from a source outside us that plants and nurtures virtue. I am like the sunflower for the time it has taken me to grow, and it is only spring. I am on the verge of blossom. My barren stalk will now yield its flower, opening to the "sun as my soul to God."[69]

I missed several meetings because of electrolysis in different towns two nights a week (one for my face and the other for, well, you know). It is amazing how self-pity creeps in to fill the void. I actually thought about taking pain meds to escape. It was crazy. So, I went to more meetings and improved greatly. If I ever doubted the status of my disease, the evidence was never far away. All I need do is stop treating it for a day or two.

Life got better it seems, almost daily. Peggy was coming to do our taxes from the previous year, as we had still been married and would file a joint return. Taxes were the bad news. The good news was that she was bringing dinner. I was truly blessed to have her in my life, along with several women from the recovery community, all of whom, I realized with deep gratitude loved and cared about me. My sponsor emailed me a scripture about the truth setting me free as I began my first feeble attempts at a personal inventory. I understood why she had wanted me to complete the inventory prior to my surgery, though it would not come to pass.

"I feel like I'm digging up the dirty bones of a dead man," I told her.

"I cannot truly have a new life without putting the old one to rest I guess - will you let me know when the funeral arrangements are complete?" I asked her, tongue in cheek as ever, trying to mask my fear.

Oddly enough, my sister, Kathy, had suggested as much a year earlier. "We should have a memorial service for Bob," she said.

I almost regretted not taking her up on the idea. The scripture was from the John gospel where Jesus is quoted as saying, "The truth shall make you free." My sponsor told me:

Freedom is on the other side of this dark walk. Sometimes it is hard to work toward a goal you cannot relate to but just as you have experienced a variety of firsts in your recovery so far, you will be able to experience a new level of freedom . . . you'll just have to trust that I am telling you the truth on this . . . well me and approximately 3 million other alkys.

I trusted her to tell me the truth, and she did. She told me the truth directly, even when she knew it hurt. It is an uncommon love that forsakes self-interest in favor of another's well being and growth. She taught me honesty. Oh, and Jesus was right too.

At 3:30 a.m. on April 18, 2007, I awoke and thought that sometimes my life gets the stuffing knocked out of it. The previous day was like that. I had to stop all NSAIDs that I took for chronic back pain, vestiges of two spine surgeries. As much as I had been stuck by doctors I was a veritable surgeon's pin cushion by the time I would get to Marci Bowers, M.D. She likely preferred that my blood was not thinned as to run out all over the place when she sliced me up. I am sure that even the prospect seems barbaric to most, but for me the physical aspect of gender reassignment surgery seemed the natural fix for what had always ailed me. Others are just born right, and everything follows in place and time.

Finding my way to my true self has always been a struggle, and I wondered then if it would still be so afterward, or would I rest peacefully in wholeness? It seemed likely, as surgery was a destination of sorts along a road filled with joyous discovery and comfort. I liked me. I no longer searched. I knew I could live, which for so long had been in serious doubt. There was no longer a need to anticipate living as if it would begin at some uncertain day ahead. I no longer had to reach the mountain peaks just to see what was on the other side. I knew, and I enjoyed the view.

In the third week of April, I had several email exchanges very much of moment, which inspire me even now, more than five years later. One was with Peggy's Mom. On April 20th, she wrote:

Although you have made your decision and are comfortable with your choice as well as being happy with it, I am still struggling with my sense of personal loss where you are concerned. Even though I know the kind, loving, helpful person is still there and finding satisfaction well in this new role I still feel the loss.

I understand the time is coming near to take that final step. I do wish you well and pray your surgery will be complete without any glitches and that your recovery will be quick so you can get on with your life.

Making peach pies will never bring me the same joy it once did, but life goes on, and I shall try to make every moment that the Lord allots me worthwhile and may everything I do be done to the Glory of God my Savior.

Though she struck a nerve, Dorleen succinctly and poignantly touched upon the core emotional dilemma of gender transition. Although the inside person, their heart and soul, the essence of who they are, does not go away, all outward manifestations are seen as different so that those who are closest feel a deep sense of loss. It was true. I wrote in response:

Dorleen thanks so much for thinking of me. I know my gender transition is hard for you to understand and accept, as it has been for so many people in my life. I too have lost much. I deeply regret that. I especially regret losing my relationship with you, for I have always greatly admired you. You are such a special gift from God to all whose life you have touched, and there are so many. However, as Peggy would most assuredly tell you, turning back was never an option for me.

For me the choice was simple. It was truly one of death and life. I could not continue living as I had. I chose to live. In so choosing I have daily, sometimes hourly sought God's will. It has been hard, but also wondrous and miraculous. I realize that invoking God in my transition is difficult for some to grasp, but, in the end that is entirely between God and me. However, I have never been so convinced of the power and peace of God's presence and loving will. And, I know that you share in that knowledge. I know that God yet has a purpose for me, and I pray that I may come to know it and receive the strength to carry it out.

I am so grateful that you are as you are. Thank you for praying for me even though you do not understand or agree with my choices. Thanks again. Hugs, Bobbie

It was again like explaining the darkness to children of the light with no hope that they could understand because they had not lived in the dark. I did not see a great light, but I sure as hell found the switch. I could not return to darkness. Dorleen wrote back:

Bobbie I was truly glad to hear from you. Peggy has told me how you have felt and you have reiterated it. I do appreciate your kind words and I shall turn my thoughts and prayers to God and will know that He answers all prayers maybe not in our way, but as he deems best for each of us. As for thinking of you, I do that often; i.e., when I see a pretty bouquet of flowers, when I see the plot for the wild garden, when I look at your beautiful cabinetry and observe your wonderful talents. I also realize that you have lost some valuable relationships, but I pray those most important to you will be restored.

I also realize that your chosen path has not been easy and that there will be unhappy times, but with faith in our Lord and Savior Jesus Christ, that path should be more bearable. I send my sincere love and friendship – Dorleen

There is nothing like the pure connection born of love between two people. It is something like grace. The path was difficult, but because I had chosen a spiritual path as well, it was possible and at times, even joyous.

April 19, 2007 reminded me as the old-timer said in the movie, *Jeremiah Johnson*, "Spring is slow in coming to the mountains."[70] Montana spring, so painfully slow in arriving, seemed like the perfect metaphor for my burgeoning new life, where newness and change had been reluctant and uncertain. I did not fear surgery, for much of the change had already occurred, and the operation was more of a catching-up procedure as far as I was concerned. My new life had begun the day I decided that I wanted to live and had the grace and strength to step out of fear.

April 20, 2007 dawned a good day I thought as I awoke. I had been given another day for which I was grateful. Another day in my new life was God's gift to me, and living it with gratitude was my gift to God, then as it is today. I had so many days that began just that way. I was grateful for that awakening, and glad it had come before my physical changes. I was greatly blessed to have such full preparation for life-changing events.

Another week and I would be sitting on the plane to Trinidad. I was as happily nervous as a person could be. Naturally, questions remained.

"What will it be like? How will I manage the pain? How certain could I be that surgery was God's will?"

It all tumbled round and round inside my head.

I think I knew, but what God has to do to convince me. It is small wonder that God does not talk to people flat out. I would probably argue. And, just why would God do that? I am only a single human, one of billions over the course of time. Have you ever spoken to a single grain of sand? It is better that I pray, trust and believe the answer I feel in my heart. That, I think, is the trick of faith. I can never know with absolute certainty the rightness of an answer to my prayers, but I can believe. I believed that this was right. It was what God wanted me to do. Gender reassignment surgery was God's will for me. If that notion leaves another incredulous, perhaps they will want to ask God about the why of God's will. "Why" is not a question that I ask anymore or can answer as far as God's will is concerned. It is God's purpose after all that I seek, not mine or another's.

April 21, 2007 marked one year since I had begun hormone replacement therapy. It was a good day to take stock. I had been euphoric, barely waiting to get back to my car to take my first dose of Premarin and Spironolactone. I was in male mode, and the pharmacist looked quizzical and dubious. I felt like a drug addict seeking relief as I tore open the prescription bags. I was happy and relieved to have taken only a single step up that mountain trail that was gender transition. It seemed an impossible height to which to ascend.

Yet, a year later, I was nearly at the summit, and the view was tremendous and exciting. I must concede, however, that at the summit I felt a little like Lewis and Clark at the summit of Lolo pass. They were indeed daunted by the many mountains that lie ahead of them. Life is like that I suppose. We feel so overwhelmed at times by the journey ahead that we fail to celebrate the summit under our feet announcing how far we have come. I had recognized only hopelessness and demoralization in the past. Now, I recognize the summits for what they are - one peak between two valleys upon which to stop, rest and enjoy the view before plunging with hope, trust and faith into the next valley. While the peaks are now not quite as high, the valleys are not quite as low.

I made a promise to myself that after surgery when I was physically recovered I would climb a mountain to celebrate my spiritual climb as well. And, I did. A year later I moved into a beautiful apartment at the base of Mount Helena, a lower mountain recreation area to the southwest of the Helena Valley on the eastern slope of the Continental Divide. I could literally walk out my door, cross the street and begin my hike. From the peak, you can see the whole Helena Valley and beyond, for as far as the mountains will allow.

To the west lies the Great Divide, and to the north lies Sleeping Giant. The first white settlers, mountain men and explorers, who likely gave the Rocky Mountains their first "white" names, could be quite literal, if not crass and demeaning. Thus, the forest service has, rightly in my view, gone about renaming some of the more offensive ones, like "Squaw Tit Peak" west of Missoula.

It is with a deep sense of gratitude, peace and joy that I make those climbs for so many reasons. I am not drunk and not dead. I am whole and loved. I am relieved at the arrival of wholeness, oneness in mind, body and spirit, to lose the duality and bonds of gender dysphoria. I have no confusion, guilt, fear, ambiguity, doubt or confusion about who I am. I am a woman. From this summit I can look ahead at my life and see as I have never done so before.

April 22, 2007 left only one week of work before I would board the plane to wholeness.

Monique would take me to the airport, as any one of a group of women would have been glad to do. I chose Monique, though. It was a way of honoring her and telling her that her job was done. She already knew and had been slowly withdrawing life support for months. Though always ready to assist, she had set the butterfly free and knew that she would fly with her own wings.

"I am the midwife," she had often told me.

Her skill had made ready the birthing.

"I would be delighted and honored to 'deliver' you to your flight home," Monique told me as she assured me the date was marked on her calendar.

I did not make any journal entries the last week before leaving - too busy I suppose with lingering details at work and trip preparations. The last entry before leaving was on the 24th. I wrote:

5:25 a.m. Seven days. Everything is ready. It is so good. I am happy and at peace, for I will be one, whole person. I can't wait.

On April 27th, the day before I left for Trinidad, my sponsor turned prophet with her blessing:

God is going to take very good care of you. Remember, if you can, to think and go to him first during the insecure times ahead. You are creating a great foundation for yourself in sobriety. I'm very proud of you and admire your dedication and stamina in following your path.

"The first thing I would do is pray about it," she had often told me in response to some sudden and deep crisis of mine.

How could I forget to turn to God first? I tried to make it my practice, and God did indeed take very good care of me, despite my failings.

Chapter Nineteen

There She Is

Be not afraid. I go before you always.
Come follow me, and I will give you rest.

- St. Louis Jesuits.[71]

April 28, 2007 dawned bright and clear, as if I had ordered it so. A young tree out front just began to bud. I grabbed my camera and took a few shots of the pink buds against the blue, blue Montana morning sky. I was blessed and said good morning to God as I thanked God for the day, this day, my day.

I had asked my landlord to pick up my mail for about ten days and set it inside in a basket by the front door. I had picked his mail up on many occasions. In fact, I think he rented to women exclusively for this purpose and to do minor office tasks for him when he was on extended sales trips. I did not mind, and he even threw in a few dollars to help me out.

"I have to get my plumbing fixed," I told him.

I knew that would discourage more questions, as it would for any man. I would not have used such an archaic, patriarchal phrase with another woman, but I did not want to have a discussion about my surgery with him.

He came outside the morning of the 28th as I waited for Monique and took my picture. The sun was bright, though the late April air was still cool. Crocuses, tulips and daffodils were in full swing. I wore a blue flowered skirt, light blue shirt and vest I had purchased on sale at Coldwater Creek in Missoula. I love anything Coldwater Creek, and blue is my best color. I would wear my best blue outfit to Trinidad, with blue and white Silver Forest earrings and the blue butterfly on a silver chain that Kathy bought me the previous summer to welcome me to the world of women.

My landlord took several pictures of me as I waited outside with my face to the morning sun, greeting the new day as well as my new life. Only the day before the Chief Justice of the Montana Supreme Court called to wish me well as did one of the associate justices. I was humbled, but inasmuch as I knew them both and greatly admired their respective characters, I should not have been surprised. Nevertheless, I was deeply moved to have that kind of acceptance and support from the highest levels of Montana's government. And so I was off, never again to be the same.

The trip to Colorado was uneventful and did not take long. I saw Mom and my niece, Jessica, waiting by the baggage claim just as they saw me. Mother does not hear well. I fear that some older people who cannot hear the volume of their own voice sometimes speak without this realization. They say what they think or feel without realizing that they are not whispering. From several feet away I heard Mom say to Jessica,

"He looks the same."

That could have been a blow if I let it, but that's Mom - you gott'a love her. The plane went only as far as Boulder, so I had to rent a car after meeting Mom and Jessica. Terry could not come but sent her daughter as her emissary and to take care of Granny. Since I lived so far away, I had not been much a part of Jessica's life. She was Meghan's age, and I marveled at how she "got it," got me, but Meghan could not grasp or want to have any part of it. I was grateful that she would be there as a sort of surrogate daughter and sister. We now have that as a special niece-aunt bond, as Jessica said the moment I arrived,

"Hi, Aunt Bobbie."

We ate Chinese that night at a local restaurant. I don't recall the name, but they had placed a small bouquet of fresh cut flowers in a small vase on each table. Jessica, Mom and I took turns taking pictures of each other with the flowers in the foreground. We enjoyed light conversation and I marveled at how much I now enjoyed such simple pleasures. We settled in at the Tarabino Inn, the recommended B&B in Trinidad. Our suite was well appointed in Victorian fashion. It had two bedrooms and a bathroom with a large claw foot tub. The food and service was great.

Mom made friends with all the other guests as we explained that we there for a little get together. Hm yes, well, it worked. We discovered Trinidad the next day like tourists. I even found a meeting to go to. One of the great comforts of recovery is that I can go anywhere on the planet almost and find a meeting and be treated just like another drunk no matter what else is true about me. If it's not about alcoholism, it's an outside issue.

I'm sure the group in Trinidad had seen its share of trans women, as Trinidad had become the de facto "sex change" capital of America due to the notoriety of its most famous surgeon, Dr. Marci Bowers. Marci had tutored under the instruction of Dr. Stanley Biber who introduced the procedure she employed and perfected; however, not until after she had gone through it herself.

Marci is tall and very good looking with long wavy hair. In many ways she exemplifies the male to female trans ideal. She is passing without doubt. She is pretty, but more importantly, she is professional, articulate and intelligent. She is a surgeon, for Pete's sake.

I met with Marci the next morning for my presurgery consultation.

"You have plenty to work with," she said.

I knew that her thoughts were purely perfunctory as she must consider such things, although it hardly felt complimentary. I was planning on having breast augmentation during the same operation, so Marci had to examine my breasts as well.

In scheduling my surgery date with Marci's assistant, Robin, we had discussed what implants to order.

"There are two varieties, the regular and the modified," she informed me.

"The regular implant is for people who have some natural development," she said as she described the difference.

I imagined they were not unlike the silicone falsies I had been wearing for the last year. I cleaned them daily with some special cleaner made for the purpose that turned the homemade pine jewelry box I used to lean them against a rustic shade of green. No, it was not mold, but I often wondered what was in the cleaner.

"The modified implants are specially shaped for women who basically have no boobs to speak of," Robin said.

"I think the regular version will work," I told her.

"I have little plums and hope for a little more growth."

Besides, the modified ones cost more, and I was plumb out of money. Every cent more would just expand my revolving credit which, realistically, was already beyond my means to ever repay, although it would take another couple of years before I would be able to admit that. Robin ordered the regular implants.

However, I had to discontinue my hormones two weeks before surgery, and in that time, even my plums disappeared. The promise of hormones was that they would produce in me breasts a cup size smaller than my mother and sisters. I should have realized that I would have little growth, but again I allowed my expectations to exceed the ability of real circumstances to deliver.

My sister, Terry, required a mastectomy as the result of her breast cancer. When she went for her implant, the physician did not have one small enough to match her remaining breast. Mine were a cup size smaller. To coin the vernacular, I was flat and ruminated on the justice visited upon me for teasing the girls in middle school who were similarly situated. It was terribly discouraging after a year of hopefulness, and I wondered if pubescent girls did not go through the same emotions. At least I did not miss out on everything that growing up female allowed.

"You may want to get the modified implants," Marci flatly suggested.

"I think you are right," I readily agreed.

That brought us to the question of size.

"What size would you like?" Marci inquired as the visit began to take on a surreal quality.

I had always dreamed of having natural breasts. I often wished for breasts, if even for just one day.

"I wear a 36B bra with the falsies, and my entire wardrobe revolves around that size," I responded, and "I do not want to draw any more attention to myself than I have to."

I was still afraid of being read, as it had only been eight months since I started living full time as a woman. Marci did not respond. I suspect that she is used to such expressions of timidity and the reasons for them. Like so many fears, mine were not based upon reality. Fear is often about events that have not yet occurred and are based on what we think *might* occur. That fear of social rejection is so compelling that we often allow fear to control our decisions and choices. Thus, many of us live our lives based not on present realities, but on events which have not, and may never actually occur.

"You decide when we get in there," I said. "I'll leave it up to physician discretion."

When I awoke after surgery I had 38C breasts. I suspect they had run out of the smaller implants, but have never regretted the larger size or all the shopping I have had to do to accommodate them. Marci drew half moons on the bottom half of my areolas to know where to cut and a midline for reference, and that was that.

Trinidad has a large Hispanic population, and though I do not wish to invoke stereotypes, it seemed that many were Catholic too, as evidenced by a significant presence of Mary statues. One front yard featured a claw foot tub turned on one end as a make shift grotto. The flat end was buried a foot or so, and the curved end gave cover to Our Lady. That afternoon I went to a grotto high on the hill overlooking Trinidad and the valley beyond.

Two years later on the day before her surgery, Kyndra, Kynni for short, and I visited a Buddhist temple high on the hill overlooking Chonburi and the sea. They were both vantage points from which to take in the scope of things outside, all around and internally too. The grotto was a place to ponder and pray. I thought of Jesus as a person who, when troubled (which must have been often, given his great capacity for compassion and the tendency of humanity towards suffering), went alone to a high place to pray. I thought too of the psalmist who wrote often about finding God in silence, and about patience and waiting upon the Lord. I thought too of Mary.

I knew that it was not too late to back out. I prayed, for I wanted to do the right thing. I had the desire to seek God's will. I knew that God would not appear physically before me nor speak in human words. Still, I wished for it. In my heart I knew that the decision was mine to make. The moment of true faith was one of solitude. All the arguments had been made and mere words would no longer do. Did I delude myself into believing that I was following God's will, or was I merely seeking my own as I had done for so long?

No one could answer these questions, and God seems so silent at times. I suspect that God's apparent silence, God's quiet way of guidance, is so by design. God wants me to have faith, to trust. So I prayed and left the results to God. Having had my vision, my blessing through the dancing and smiling Jesus, and having not heard nor felt anything to the contrary, I was confident that I was following God's will. I was joyful and at peace. Hail Mary, Ave Maria, Let it Be.

That night I felt serene as I wrote about a curious mix of some fear, but mostly peace and calm. I felt what I had come to recognize in recovery as joy. Arriving early at Tarabino's was worth the extra money for two days of relaxation, visiting and mental and spiritual preparation. We had been tourists with a cause, and I felt great. I enjoyed a bath every morning, wonderful meals, and full, restful nights' sleep. I had emptied my mind of worry and stilled my soul.

I prayed. I asked God to remove anxiety and fear, and they were gone. I asked God to take away sorrow for all that I had lost. I asked God that I may be willing to accept God's will, as I had every day over the last several months. I was still obsessed with the thought of being alone, as I had had no one in my life romantically for over a year. I knew, however, that I would have all that I needed. I would be whole and at peace. If I would be alone, I would give myself to loneliness. I would discover and embrace the fullness of myself alone. I would work and serve and pray and play. I would take the richness and rewards of whatever life I was given as I surrendered to God.

"Count from one hundred down to one," the anesthesiologist said.

"One hundred, one," I said, determined to out-smart the fentanol and versed about to knock me out.

I thought about Dr. "D."

I awoke from surgery feeling just a bit euphoric. It was the morphine, however, as emotionally and spiritually I felt no different than I had the day before. I almost allowed myself to be disappointed, as I had heard many stories of women who were completely overwhelmed with joy after GRS. I was not, but I felt pretty darn good before surgery.

I was awake in my room for some while. It is hard to tell how long in that state. The first person I saw, though dimly, as I did not have my glasses on was my Mom. I could think of no one more appropriate or wonderful to attend my rebirth than my mother.

"Well, there she is," she said.

Terry sent a beautiful bouquet of flowers. The card said,

"Here's to dancing for the rest of your days. Welcome, sister! Love, Terry."

I smiled and thought of Jesus and dancing.

My roommate in Trinidad was Chrisy, all of seventeen or eighteen years old, and in need of repair of a previous GRS that had not worked. The wall inside was too thin and basically broke. Marci would somehow have to sculpt a new vaginal wall using skin grafts and synthetic skin, as I was told, of the sort used for burn victims. Chrisy was young and pretty and sweet, if not still a bit naïve. I liked her tremendously and she seemed selfless as she encouraged me those first few days instead of worrying about her own upcoming delicate surgery.

Mom became the self-appointed combined candy striper, grandma and den mother for five brand spanking new Brownies. It is not easy to be down when Mom is around or to remain so for long. Everyone seemed to get on well.

Peggy arrived a few days later. I am not sure she was thrilled to be there, but I had asked her to come. It meant a great deal to me that she again was there for me. She had lunch one day with one of the other "wives" who had yet to reconcile all the changes in her life and marriage. Peggy could share her experience, but really, what do you say in such a circumstance when all that you have known and hoped for has gone?

"Life goes on. Start over. You'll be okay."

It sounds well and good and is certainly true, but as I saw the grief on that woman's face, I had to wonder how hard it had been for Peggy and how much she stored away for my sake. In her card to me she wrote,

"Only through love's constant changes does love remain constant." And so it was with Peggy. She had been there for me throughout, in spite of her own pain and loss - guiding, talking, consoling, cooking, protecting and in countless other little ways. Peggy is a remarkable woman, one whom I am proud and grateful to know and have been influenced by. She was once a lover, now a friend, forever a soul mate. She gave me a white rose that I set in a glass in a western window, and as the sun went down, I was filled with the bittersweet realization that I was losing much even as I gained.

The pain was not nearly as bad as I had feared. I was happy and much at peace. But my boobs hurt like hell. They had given me a jacket sort of bra that I had to wear for weeks afterward. I thought of the 1998 movie, *The Man in the Iron Mask*, in which Leonardo Dicaprio plays both, King Louis, XIV and his twin brother, Philippe. Philippe, it seems, was somewhat vexed with his brother's position, so locked him away in a tower with an iron mask on his face. The bra was as constricting as that iron mask.

I understood that Marci had to shave a sort of pocket in the tissue in which to seat the implant, and that, much like a cracked rib - it would take a while to heal. On the other end, so to speak, much of the nerve endings in my newly formed vagina had been deadened in the surgery, so it did not hurt at all. The soreness in my chest and too-tight jacket bra more than made up for it. My breasts were certainly bigger than I had anticipated, and since they were underneath the muscle, they were really firm. I had these huge granite boulders crushing my chest. I loved them. They came with a sense of me-ness, of belonging and being part of me, such that I said to myself,

"Where have you been all my life?"

Women who go through GRS often experience depression not unlike the post partum blues that genetic women experience after childbirth, both supposedly stemming from vast hormonal swings and imbalances. I did too, but I knew what to do with it. I worked my program as soon as I was conscious enough after surgery to read my literature and pray. I said, as I had every morning for months, and every morning since,

"Good morning, God. My name is Bobbie. I am an alcoholic. Thank you for this life and way of living."

I would not dream of starting a day without turning to God in gratitude for another morning. In those mornings in May, 2007, I was happy to be alive, to be a woman and able to greet the day in exactly that way. I could not remember a time when joy awoke me.

When I was young and waging the war of a troubled soul against all visible signs of authority, at the time manifested in the Pope's black and white minions, they told me that I would have a calling in which God would tell me what he wanted me to do with my life. I had searched for the answer to that elusive mystery. For instance, I went to Ashland as a Jesuit volunteer as I believed I was answering that call. I stayed for the same reason and likewise went to law school. I made a career as a prosecutor like a soldier for God, not holy enough for sainthood, yet still possessed of the bitter sanctity of fighting the good fight. I had a purpose. *Here I am, Lord.*

If I had learned anything during the previous winter of recovery - sort of my winter of discontent - it was that it is purpose enough to just be present to those around me. At the hospital I smiled or gestured to passersby.

I even dared to look at strangers in the eye as they passed. To some I spoke, as they seemed to want to have someone to talk to about the weather and the beauty of the day and their husband dying of cancer. I had little to offer, but I knew that kindness always returns, often as soon as it is given. And so it went for my seven days as a patient at Mount San Rafael Hospital.

Chapter Twenty

Tat on Her Ass

A little girl, who had more courage than she knew,
who found her dream is that not happiness?

- *Memoirs of a Geisha*[72]

T he sinking feeling I had in the pit of my stomach was more than the plane's descent into the Helena airport. It was more than the let-down a person feels after accomplishing an important goal or project. It was something deeper, more fundamental and vital. I did not want to return and fought more and more the closer we came to the ground. I thought I should have a new place to start this new life and ached again for the sea coast. Peggy bought me a few bags of groceries and dropped me at my 11th Avenue nest. It was bittersweet, as I had everything I wanted, yet possessed so little.

I did not want Peggy to go but knew that she must. I did not want to be back in Helena, yet here I was. I especially did not want to go back to the same job.

"My job on a good day was keeping the courts and prosecutors honest, and on a bad day, it was helping convicted felons to escape responsibility," I used to say with resignation.

Some people said in a conciliatory tone that they deserved representation. I never felt that way. It seemed to me that they were entitled to a competent defense under our laws but seldom got what they deserved. I had seen some heinous crimes, including rape, child physical abuse and molestation and one particularly grizzly homicide on Billings' south side where the defendant, on the day after he was released from prison, slit his brother-in-law's throat.

He relied on a self-defense theory at trial, so there was no question but that he had done it. His problem, however, was that ten eye-witnesses did not see it as a matter of self defense, particularly in light of the evidence that the defendant said to his brother-in-law that he was "gonna' cut your jug." Evidently he missed, because he cut through the victim's carotid artery, which has a more direct route to the heart, resulting in quick, massive blood loss and death.

I had the entire file at the appellate defender's office, and I dutifully looked through every paper and scrap of evidence searching for an issue for appeal, including photographs of the victim. Criminal lawyers, like medical professionals, are sometimes forced to confront gruesome realities that most people do not even think of, and would just as soon remain blissfully ignorant of. In this case, the medical records stated that the first responders "massaged the heart."

Most of us think of a massage as something done on the top side of the skin; however, here it was quite literal. The first responders had actually cut into the victim's chest cavity to squeeze the heart. The crime scene photos displayed a horizontal cut across the neck, and a vertical cut in the middle of the ribs and torso. The photos were chilling and extremely difficult to look at.

While the elements of homicide are straight forward, homicide trials are always complicated affairs. Thus, it is difficult for even the most learned of jurists to get through the entire matter without making some error, even if they do not often rise to the level of reversible error. The thing that many criminal defendants do not understand is that an appeal is not another trial. Appeals are based entirely on what happened at the trial level as demonstrated by the record - the pleadings, motions and briefs, as well as the hearings and trial transcripts. That's it. There is nothing more, and if trial counsel did not raise an objection, the issue is waived for purposes of appeal except in rare circumstances.

Fortunately for the defendant in this case, trial counsel did a masterful job, reserving several issues for appeal. The most notable was a jury contamination claim involving a telephone call to a juror from a friend at night while the jury took a break from deliberations. The caller inquired whether the juror was aware that the defendant had been released from prison only the day before the murder as reported in news accounts during the trial. The juror reported the call to his fellow jurors, thus contaminating the entire pool, or so the argument went. When the trial judge caught wind of the taint, he inquired of the foreman and the guilty juror and determined that the pool had not been contaminated and could still serve its function of reaching a decision based solely on the testimony and evidence. The Supreme Court agreed, and I was not too disappointed, even though I worked very hard on that case when I returned from Trinidad.

The simple truth was that while I loved appellate research and writing, my heart was just not in criminal defense. As long as I approached it as an academic exercise, I could do it. However, given my notions about purpose and doing God's will, I had a real disconnect that, no matter how hard I tried to embrace criminal defense philosophy, I could not wrap my head around the notion that guys like this deserved quality legal representation. They did not, as they deserved what they gave.

However, I do understand in our society ordered by law that justice is not such a cruel keeper. Justice in our culture does not demand that criminal defendants get what they deserve. It does, however, require that trials are conducted according to the rules we have devised to be fair and humane even in the face of grave inhumanity. Former Montana Governor Marc Racicot prosecuted a case in the Madison County Courthouse in the early 80s. As an Assistant Attorney General he tried the Mountain Men, Dan and Don Nichols for the homicide of a would-be rescuer of Kari Swenson, the decathlon skier they abducted for the younger Nichols' bride. He said, "We must keep that balance true."

I tried hard to do that, and found that my clients were better served through my intellect rather than through my emotion.

However, given that I was still taking pain killers for five weeks after surgery, I must question whether they got even my entire intellect as I resumed work at home at the end of June. My work showed it, resulting in a motion for an extension that I submitted to Sarah that was grossly incompetent. Jim wrote me the one and only letter of reprimand that I have ever received. I was devastated, exacerbated by the fact that when I appeared at the office that first week home to pick up files, no one said a word of sympathy or offered a single get well wish. It was another elephant-in-the-room moment that everyone but the secretary chose to ignore. Jory was not bound much by social convention and did ask how I was doing and wished me well.

It was very hard at the time, but looking back, I understand how uncomfortable most people are talking about gender reassignment surgery. I mean, what do you say?

"Everything come off alright?"

Diabetes and cancer we know about, and social norms allow us to talk about these, even if we are uncomfortable. However, when it comes to GRS, there are no social conventions and almost no experience for most people to draw upon. I get that and harbor no resentments.

On the other hand, some of the cards I got were hilarious. My sister, Dede, sent me a Zena, Warrior Princess, card that let out the warrior cry when you opened it. It also said,

"Don't try to fight it. Celebrate it."

She got it. Another card, from Wise Woman, Nancy T., had a drawing of a man with plucked and shaped eyebrows leaning on a hoe amongst a row of eyebrows with the caption,

"I see you've raised some eyebrows."

Nancy got it too. My sponsor got me a card that showed some thought. It featured a rather distraught woman on the cover with the caption,

"I exhaust myself trying to be me."

Those first weeks after surgery were perhaps the most difficult of my entire transition, but through the support, wisdom and selflessness of the women around me, I knew I would make it, in fact already had. Though I still had a great many difficulties that I hoped by the grace of God and my program I would overcome, I had redemption. I no longer felt confusion, fear, guilt, shame, doubt, ambiguity and uncertainty about something as fundamental as self. I was one whole person, a woman, and I was happy. I still had a long way to go in my program and my life, but I had made my peace with myself and the world.

At some point in transition and recovery, both cease being critical. It was no longer about progressing through objectives and instead was more about just living. I had done all the things that were necessary for my transition. I had made the climb that only a year before seemed impossible. I was now on the other side. Though I did not realize it at the time, I still had to build a life from all that I had lost or given away and whatever scraps remained. I had to take it all and makes things right and put them into a way to live that made sense.

Even though I felt good, I still had much to change. I could at times live in the moment and embrace the good things each held. However, there was much about me yet to be revealed, and my sponsor had the instructions to help me see. I wanted what she had - the peace and even temper in all things. She treated problems like they were just part of everyday living, like Peggy's father had done with things mechanical. I wanted to live like that too and for over forty-nine years, the way had eluded me. My sponsor held the key and was willing to share it with me. I kept going back.

I struggled as she explained to me the themes my personal inventory revealed. I was self-centered and dishonest, in that I was deluded in what I believed was the truth about myself, and held unreasonable expectations of others. I couldn't see what she was saying and felt a great disconnect. She said later,

"Your eyes glazed over, and that's how I knew that even though you said yes and nodded your head like you understood, you did not agree."

It was similar to when she taught me the vitality of gratitude. I would call, overwhelmed by some problem, and she would carefully listen.

"You know, sounds like you need to make a gratitude list," she said.

I was incredulous. Didn't she hear me?

"I feel like shit and you're telling me to be grateful?" I thought to myself once and said out loud as I got off the phone.

I thought I could not do it but devised a way to try anyway. I would start at the tips of my toes and thank God that I could stand. I thanked God for legs so that I could walk and kept working my way up my body, thanking God for all the parts that worked and the functions they allowed me to perform. When I got to my hands I started to really feel it. I thanked God for opposable thumbs because they allowed me to ride a mountain bike. Having fingers alone would allow me to eat and perform many tasks.

"But, can you picture riding a bicycle down a mountain trail and clipping along pretty fast holding the bars with only your fingers?" I said as I described the exercise later.

"Try slowing down or holding on to the handle bars without opposable thumbs. It's possible, but so much more difficult and probably dangerous."

When I rode, I flew, at least my spirit did. I soared above the world, above my life. I could look down and know that my purpose would become perfectly clear. I was not bound to a place or profession and did not have to push or worry. I just had to fling my arms wide and be open to the universe. I had the happy, comfortable and peaceful knowledge that no matter what else, I would live and die as a woman. Everything else was thus temporal.

I had to let go of the cocoon and freefall into life, humanity and the universe. Over the coming year I began to see that the terms of my life involved four main categories.

"Finances, romances, employment and children," I would repeat like I was Eleanor Rigby, living in my dreams.

I added new prayers to my morning routine. I asked God to remove my difficulties as a witness to God's active influence in my life, as well as a vital truth that my sponsor kept reminding me of.

"God wants you to be happy," she said.

My eyes must have glazed over because I had never allowed myself to believe that. I had always thought that I did not deserve to be happy. I had done so many things wrong, made so many bad choices and hurt so many people. Besides, there were so many other broken and hurt people in the world, how could God possibly have time for me? I had some work to do.

First, I had some house cleaning to do, and with my sponsor's tremendous help, patience and encouragement I set about doing so. I sent letters to family members, called my Mom and met with Peggy and her Mom to make my peace and apologies for my self-centeredness, dishonesty, betrayal of trust and my fear to let them know who I really was. Mom, saint that she is, forgave me instantly. However, it is no small thing to me. Since that day I have had a clean slate with my mother and an honest, open and loving relationship as the result.

Peggy's mom was harder. When I first came out, she had told me honestly what she thought about my drinking and my choice to transition.

"You threw up a wall and put us all on hold," she pointed out.

"You have chosen a hard path that will never be understood nor accepted by a lot of people."

"I am grieving Bob," she wrote, "to put it mildly."

Her only solace was that Robert did not have to experience the same pain. She was angry and saddened, not only because her daughter lost her husband, but she felt as if she lost a son-in-law. It hurt a great deal, especially because every word was true. Pain, when not wallowing in self-pity, becomes a teacher and great motivator. Because Dorleen had been honest enough to share her pain, the door was open for me to understand my part and make amends. She accepted them and let me do her estate planning and will as her kind gesture of acceptance. She is still part of my life, and although the bond is diminished, we still love one another. Peggy's siblings were equally magnanimous.

However, Dorleen was right that I could not expect everyone to understand or accept me. One person, in order to convey his disappointment in me, wrote,

"God does not make such mistakes."

I had heard the "God don't make mistakes" theory before, but his reliance on God to discredit me, however, did give me pause. I did not resent him for it but instead gave great thought to my transition and spirituality, for they fit together as surely as my recovery did with them both. There is a saying which asserts that there are no mistakes in God's world. It's quite a claim really. Just imagine - wars, disease, hate, violence, birth defects, etc. are not mistakes.

It may be so. However, it does not follow that these are all God's doing. I heard an old timer say,

"I was born with free will and bad judgment."

I think that is the case with evil in God's world. People make war. Germs make disease. People drive drunk and kill other people. People die every day, sometimes naturally and sometimes not. Many people blame God for not intervening in what they see as terrible, painful circumstances. While I believe that God is active in the lives of people and does influence circumstances, I do not believe in the great Gepetto in the sky. I do not believe we twist and turn on strings dangling from the divine plan. What about birth defects? They are not so easy to explain. Why does God not intervene and take them away?

I think that God created the world and all that exists. God put it all into motion - the earth, the sun and all the planets, all life. God made the building blocks, DNA and the genetic code, but I do not believe that God begins or ends every single life. As Rabbi Harold Kushner writes, God has chosen, ostensibly in accord with God's overall scheme of things not to interrupt natural laws and the exercise of free will. Hence, it is a theologically correct statement to say, shit happens. I believe that God creates each and every soul and spirit, nontangible, ethereal and mystical, as is God.

It is our soul that is created in the image and likeness of God. The rest is open to interpretation, critical study and theological discussion which do not begin to countenance gender identification.

I am no mistake. I am as perfect as any of God's children, born both male and female, perhaps the result of over-exposure to particular hormones at a particular point of development in the womb. Again, as Dorleen said, many will not understand or accept. Even so, none, not even science can dispute my transgender nature with any greater credibility, as there is no empirical study or evidence to the contrary. It is possible to be born both male and female. Some babies are born intersexed, having genitalia of both genders.

I realize that I was born physically male, but I was also born female in heart, mind and spirit. It is a truth that only those who are so blessed, or can suspend judgment with an open mind, can grasp with certainty. And, I am certain - as certain as I have ever been. I did not make it up, or choose it or fall prey to a cult or scurrilous influence. Who is to say that God did not intend it this way? What part of science or theology proclaims that it is impossible, wrong or morally reprehensible to be both male and female? I am not an abomination, for God does not make mistakes.

This enigma that is my life is exemplified in comparisons to various celebrities over time. For instance, when I was in college, a young woman said to me,

"You look like Robert Redford."

Yet in late May, 2007, the clerk at the post office said,

"You look like Marlo Thomas."

I have no delusions about ever looking like either one. However, it still begs the question if you stood them side by side, what comparison might be drawn? There are likely not many. Yet, when I was twenty, I looked like a young man with blonde hair and ruddy features. And, when I was near fifty, I looked like a fortyish woman with bangs and light hair. Both were me.

When I was little I loved the show, *That Girl*. My "Oh Donald" imitation is still pretty good. I wonder now if I identified with the protagonist as everyone else did, or was she more of a role model. I watched a *That Girl* marathon recently on TV and was enthralled, so I concluded the latter and take the clerk's comment on my hair style as high praise indeed.

Since I had changed so much in my life, I wondered if Marci should not have stamped some sort of seal on my backside after the surgery, like US Grade A, No. 1 Premium Transgender, for instance. She did not, so I thought a lot about getting a tattoo. It seemed the ideal way to mark my transition and celebrate its conclusion. The butterfly had been my metaphor throughout and would be the perfect symbol. Its stages so resembled my own changes and growth. Monique and I often discussed it in therapy. I even gave her a photograph of a butterfly perched on top of a pink coneflower that I had planted in the front yard in Silver Star. When I packed up to move the previous year, I had to go through all the things my children left behind. Among the keepsakes that Meghan left was a plaster decorative mask with the right eye painted as if for a ball and the left eye adorned with a powder blue butterfly profile dominating that side as if it had emerged from the cocoon within. I looked at many butterfly designs for a tattoo, but the one from the mask is the one I settled upon.

I could not trace the design with tracing paper as I had many wildlife scenes for transfer to wood projects. The curves of the mask would not allow tracing. So, I drew the butterfly freehand and was satisfied enough with the results to sign it. As I began to inquire about getting the body art applied, I found out just how expensive the proposition was, and had all but given up when I sat next to a guy at a Sunday noon meeting. He was tough and hard, as was his girlfriend, and I loved them both because of the way they had overcome their struggles, found each other and carved out a life where none was before. He showed his wear.

He often wore sleeveless tanks and tees that exposed the muscular arms of a body builder. He referred to the ink markings that covered those barrels as a singular tattoo. They belied the fact that the gym in which he spent many hours was likely owned by the state. I was amazed to learn that he had done most of the skin artistry himself. The location of his former studio notwithstanding, the beauty and artistry of the work was readily apparent. I had listened to this guy and his girlfriend for nearly a year at meetings. I grew to see them with admiration and respect, unlike the many persons, places and things I had formerly and precipitously judged and reviled.

I took my butterfly design to this guy a couple weeks later, and we discussed a price. It was more than I wanted to spend, or even had, but seemed more than reasonable compared to what the studio artisans were charging. We set a date for early October, 2007. I arrived at the appointed hour in gym clothes that could be easily removed.

They lived in a small house at the end of the road. It was humble, almost cottage-like, tidy in appointment and Spartan in appearance. The studio consisted of a massage table, chair and tools, and was entirely makeshift amongst computer desks. However, I was most impressed with the talent of this artist when I saw his drawings inside, including highly detailed pen and ink drawings of an eagle and a hawk. They truly were the best I had ever seen, and I told him as much.

His girlfriend sat working at the computer during my entire session. I was glad of that, for the *corpus locus* I had chosen. The irony of this circumstance, whether arranged by fate or God, began to emerge as we talked. Here was the ex-con, having been screwed, glued and tattooed, as it were, by the system and the former prosecutor lying bareassed on the table before him, seeking anointment for having overcome her own demons. If either one of us had realized beforehand that I had actually prosecuted him in his youth in Ennis, this circumstance surely would never have arisen. He had spent his formative years in Virginia City, the very town where I had worked in my previous life. He spoke of his brushes with the law, including a DUI. He even remembered the officers and the judge.

"Who was the prosecutor?" I asked, knowing full well from the time frame that it could only be me.

"Some guy," he responded.

I enjoyed those quirky circumstances and the apparent contradictions. Only in Montana, where individual journeys so resemble concentric circles closely orchestrated one with another, could these magic moments occur. It saddened me to realize, as the only one appreciating the moment, that I had been so closed-minded in that former life. I was so intent on the trappings of a life not my own, locked in fear of facing the truth of who I was that I nearly missed my life altogether. As piteous as is the life not lived, so too are those not found or shared. I have missed so many other lives through judgment and condemnation. I thank God for this physical reminder of how happy, rich and full a life lived openly and honestly can be. I did know a new freedom and a new happiness. But for this gift, I might not have known that from the cocoon of an ex-con could emerge an artist with talent, integrity and grace, and from an ex-man, a demure woman with a beautiful tat on her ass.

Chapter Twenty One

Finances and Romances

Look at the birds in the sky
They do not sow or reap
They gather nothing into barns
Yet your heavenly father feeds them
Are you not more important than they?

- Jesus.[73]

If I could only follow Jesus's next words of advice and give up worry. Yet, I was the one that could let go and let God only as soon as I had it ready for God. I struggled with the notion of a loving God that only wanted me to be happy. I understood the concept but could not for the life of me believe it. Yet, trust in God was the precise answer to all the questions that bothered me, like the winds of April in Montana unendingly whipping around my ears leaving my head ringing and feeling hollow.

Money had been a problem almost from the day I left Madison County. The decision to go when I did was brash and short sighted. In typical fashion, my expectations of my ability to cope far exceeded the reality. I had been poor before, which meant that though I had no garbage bags because I could not afford to go to the grocery store, it did not matter, as I had no table scraps or packaging to throw away. It was not quite that bad, although, it got pretty thin the last few days before payday. Paying my bills, though, was becoming increasingly more difficult.

Way back at the beginning of therapy Monique asked me where I saw myself in five years as if, I thought to myself, I could divine such matters. I was worried about the money aspect of transition which so many just cannot overcome. I was fortunate in that I was not flipping burgers, but had a professional degree and corresponding job and salary. Well, the salary was definitely on the low end of the spectrum but I could expect no more under the circumstances. Public service lawyers are grossly underpaid in any event. I also had a pile of debt.

"Do you think you will have food and a place to live?" Monique asked.

"Yes, I do," I said, thinking she was making light of my circumstances.

Yet, after my surgery, as the months that I could not find a better paying job stretched well beyond a year, I was having trouble paying bills.

I have never been good with money. I had managed my own since I was ten years old and had an income such as a paper route affords. Up until that time my siblings and I had learned to do without the things we wanted in favor of those we needed. As soon as I had my own money, though, I could spend it anyway I wanted. I saved up for things like cool clothes and a Schwinn ten speed bicycle. It was green and I raced around the town for five or six years on it until I was old enough to drive. If I was not saving for anything though, I spent money freely just as soon as I had any in my pockets.

As a lawyer, I was spoiled by a pretty good salary and money habits I had carried with me from my youth.

"Whenever you can, use someone else's money," my father had once said.

I got pretty good at it as I grew more and more self-centered and compulsive. Take a desire, add credit and shake. Presto, I got what I wanted when I wanted it. I did not wait, for I had no patience. I did not suffer for want of food, clothing or shelter. Neither did my children. I kept piling up things like cars, tools and other boy toys. When I did not have the cash I did have the credit. I purposely used my American Express card just to earn Sky Miles. I could keep up with the monthly payments then, and I allowed small balances on several credit cards to accumulate.

Peggy and I had ideas about building a house on the adjacent acre lot we had purchased next to the manufactured home we lived in. It was a good idea, even if the neighbors did not like it. Years earlier we had gone to a day-long workshop on straw bale building techniques, and spoke often about building our dream house in that style. We collected floor plans that we liked and put them in a basket of dreams underneath the coffee table. We thought and thought and talked and talked. We dreamed and I prayed for it on the strength of Peggy's goodness, for mine was surely not enough to merit consideration by God. I could conjure up feelings of selflessness in that fashion. If someone else would be benefited from my requests, why should I not also benefit? It is good that God denied my self-centered requests long enough for me to learn some humility and see how selfish I was.

The house never amounted to anything but a straw dream in the wind. We could not afford what we wanted to do, as we both had become unwitting prisoners to revolving debt. Peggy often complained of not having enough money and would sometimes go into a funk because of it. I had had a few funks of my own years earlier, but with a certain sordid satisfaction,paid my bills every month with money to spare. Instead of reacting to Peggy with understanding and charity, as my alcoholism got worse, so did my selfishness. I reasoned that since Peggy could not contribute to our common dream then I would indulge a few of my own until she could. So, I bought stuff.

I had always preferred Craftsman tools and built up a balance on my Sears card that hovered around $5,000. We took a few trips to allow me to "de-stress," and the AMX balance got away from me to the tune of several thousand dollars. I had a few other cards with similar balances. Plus, I carried two car loans and the kids' college loans. But, it was all manageable.

When I started gender transition, everything changed. First, I took a $10,000 advance on a credit card to pay for follicular hair transplant surgery. Then I moved to Helena and took a nearly forty percent pay cut. My plan was to complete transition, at least through surgery, and then find another, better paying job. I thought it might take me about three months to find another job at my former rate of pay. I was badly mistaken, another example of my expectations grossly, if not naively, exceeding reality.

Then I started to finagle, taking lower percentage credit card offers to pay off higher percentage balances. Stealing from Peter to pay Paul is an alcoholic's birthright. I had some of the cash I would need for surgery from the proceeds of the sale of the house. I tucked it away in a CD. I would still need to borrow to get it done. So, I struggled financially right along with all the other changes. I had prayed for patience and humility, and I was getting a crash course. Somehow, though, there was always an answer to my income shortages, like an old gift card here, and an insurance pay-off there. It was always timely and unexpected. I ate, paid the rent and somehow made it. I had borrowed $17,000 to make up the remaining financing for surgery, plus a little extra for living expenses afterward. Somehow, the financial road opened before me.

Yet, I continued to struggle for the next two years under the weight of revolving debt that ballooned to the neighborhood of $65,000 as I started using credit cards for living expenses. I had a whole pile of Sky Miles and just enough grocery bags to handle the garbage I generated. I perfected the art of using someone else's money. I determined to run out the string, still hoping I could find another, higher paying job.

I sent out my first job application on the 16th of May, 2007. I discovered usajobs.com on line and applied to countless federal jobs for lawyers all over the world. Some replied that I had not been selected, but most did not. I perfected my resume, had fifty printed professionally and developed several cover letters for the types of jobs I was applying for, in stealth or out, depending on the degree of openness to diversity I perceived from the ads. I could crank out five-to-ten applications a week, and often did.

I applied for every state attorney job that came up. I interviewed twice with the Department of Public Health and Human Services, knowing that my qualifications far surpassed the level sought and the rest of the candidate pool. Yet, I was not hired. One interviewer treated me with open contempt. I was disappointed and could not determine why I had not been hired. What did I do or say that they did not like? Instead of wallowing in self-pity, though, I worked my program. I prayed, talked to my sponsor and looked for someone to serve. I got out of myself and filled out more applications.

I went to a weekend recovery workshop, and if I was not in a funk when I arrived, I was by the time I left. The speakers gave such great emphasis to all that could be, all that seemed to be, missing from my life. The well-intentioned presentations undoubtedly meant to be uplifting, left me little more than disheartened. Okay, my initial expectation of a three-month job search had been unreasonable, but I was beginning to think there was a little more to it.

The federal jobs all required background checks and I knew that the first thing that would come up, even with only a Google search, was *Rosenthal v. Roberta R. Zenker, f/k/a, Robert R. Zenker*, and the gig would be up. I asked Jim about the state jobs because I had long ago been told that lateral movement once inside state government was the norm, and I had a great resume. We agreed that my secret was probably common knowledge and that the word was out on me. It made sense, after having met with the governor's office and the department of administration and being well-known at the AG's office. There are only about 3,000 members of the Montana Bar, and I had been well-known both as a county attorney and as a member of a few State Bar committees. If any would-be employers cared it is likely that they did not want to have the dubious distinction of having the first transsexual lawyer in Montana history working for them.

So, there I was, nearly on the eve of my fiftieth birthday, stuck in a job I did not want. It did not pay enough to rescue me from my dire financial affairs, nor anywhere near what my professional skills and experience should have been worth. I should have expected as much. So few trans people had professional employment at all. I had actually become quite fond of, and caring, about my co-workers. The work was challenging, albeit one-dimensional. I enjoyed research and writing just not all day every day. I wanted direct contact with people. I wanted to have a sense that I was helping and serving them.

I applied for countless jobs all over the country. I did the work. I had to wonder whether God was responsible for the result because I just did not seem to be getting one. Gone were the days of cursing God in a tantrum when I did not get what I wanted. Gone were the days when I believed that my prayers went unanswered. The answer on employment seemed to be no or maybe later. I came across several of the Psalms in my daily meditations that suggested that I needed to be patient and wait upon the Lord. That was a new experience, yet I prayed and practiced patience. I did not have to wonder why I got adversity.

It had been twice as long as I thought it should take to find a job, and I had nothing to show for it. Money, money, money. I was buried under a mountain of someone else's. My payments, together with living expenses, were greater than my income. I cut credit cards, but a higher paying job would surely help. I lived in a basement apartment. It was cozy, but small and did not allow enough winter sun. The allure of Montana had faded. Its sheen was lost, perhaps in the smoke and heat of its recent summers, which seemed to have become a new season called fire. I wanted a garden, like Bilbo Baggins of Underhill. I wanted the sea and thought that I needed it too.

My children still did not speak to me. I was almost fifty and living, as James Taylor sang: *Down in a hole.*[74] I was alone, with no partner to share life with, both its joys and its burdens. I could not pay my bills. I was not fulfilled in my work or my life. I lived in a town, a state, a region that held so little of what I wanted. And, I could control none of it. I had to rely on and trust God for answers. If God wanted me to have a different job with a higher salary, it would be so. If God wanted me to live somewhere else, it would be so. If God wanted me to reunite with my children, it would be so. If God wanted my debt reduced, it would be so. If God wanted me to have a home of my own, it would be so, and if God wanted me to share life with a partner, it would be so. I sang in my head, seeing my wings stretched wide as I soared higher, my soul still reaching for God.

At about the same time, the "Prayer of Saint Theresa" started making the rounds on the internet, and I believed it.

May today there be peace within.
May you trust God that you are exactly where you are meant to be.
May you not forget the infinite possibilities that are born of faith.
May you use those gifts that you have received, and pass on the love that has been given to you.
May you be content knowing you are a child of God.

Let this presence settle into your bones, and allow your soul the freedom to sing, dance, praise and love. It is there for each and every one of you.[75]

I had heard that line before, the one about trusting God that I was exactly where I was meant to be. I had been told twice and I believed it. I am who, what and precisely where I am supposed to be. I still did not think of God as the great puppeteer, the big man with a plan. I believed that God takes me as I am and builds with me as God will, according to the degree to which I give my will and my life over to God's care. This too I have added to my morning prayer,

"God, please accept my will and my life into your care. Grant me knowledge of your will and the power to carry it out."

In December, 2007, I learned that a young woman I was working with would have the basement of her house available to rent. I could save three or four hundred dollars a month if I moved in. Her live-in boyfriend was a senior at Carroll College in Helena. I lived there for six months and did save on expenses. I made it as comfy as possible, but it was still pretty dim. The only windows were two typically small basement windows with outside window wells below ground level. They allowed very little light.

When summer rolled around, I took over half of the patio space for a planter garden. It was doing quite well but evidently interfered with my housemates' designs.

"We'd like you to move out," the young man said.

I was there by their leave, so what could I say?

"Alright, give me a chance to find something," I meekly replied.

It dawned on me just how low I had fallen.

"I sub-leased a basement apartment from college kids, and just when I thought I could not get any lower, they kicked me out," I told friends.

I did not resent it, much to my own amazement. I just prayed and started looking for another place.

I had been having my hair done at a posh, chic boutique called Hair Hair since I moved to Helena. It is owned by two successful, entrepreneurial male stylists who also live together and rent out a few places in the buildings around town that they own. Joe and David had been very supportive of my transition. I had an appointment at Hair Hair with Robin, my stylist, that even though I really could not afford, I dared not cancel for the time it takes to get another one. Robin had worked wonders with my hair since I began transition. She performed no less than coloring miracles as I changed from wig to piece with my own hair blended in.

"Robin, you're the color queen," I told her once after she had worked her magic.

No one could ever tell. As the line from the old television commercial went, "Only your hairdresser knows."

"Hey, you don't know of any places for rent, do you?" I asked her as I sat where she directed me.

I hadn't yet washed my hair that day, so once I had my apron securely pinned around my neck, she directed me to a chair with its back against a large black sink with a hose and spray nozzle sticking out. I love having someone else wash my hair and I completely relaxed as soon as her firm hands began to work up a lather.

"Is this too hot?" Robin asked as she began to spray the shampoo out of my hair.

"No, it's just right," I said, hoping that she couldn't detect my disappointment that the shampoo was over almost as quickly as it had begun.

"I think the boys might have the place next door coming open," Robin confided.

As luck would have it, the modern upstairs apartment on South Park Avenue came open.

"Can I see the apartment?" I asked Joe the following week.

"Yea, I think Gina has the key. She's upstairs."

When I opened the door and saw all the sunlight from multiple windows shining on the hard-wood flooring, I nearly cried. I was home and realized at once I could be happy there for the rest of my days. By the end of July, 2008, I was in, lock, stock and planters. I put in rock gardens outside and even made a space for the cement St. Francis that I had been packing around the last three years. It had been my Grandmother's, and she had placed it on the eastside of her garden shed. I bought a portable shed and let Francis take up shop. I stored my deer decoy just above Francis on the hillside, and later that fall, the deer's head fell off, or something. Perhaps a young buck had challenged it and knocked its head off. I found it lying at Francis's feet and said with mock disdain,

"Francis!" I took a picture of the oddly ridiculous sight of St. Francis with a deer trophy at his feet. I loved that upstairs apartment, and it was perfect for just one. It was my sanctuary, as safe and warm as could be.

At the beginning of 2008, I started to check out the online dating sites. I met several guys, and one even asked me out. His name was John and he lived in Helena. He was some sort of independent real estate developer. We went to dinner at Benny's Bistro, a chic restaurant downtown that I really enjoyed. We talked a lot, and the mutual attraction was clear.

Somehow the conversation turned to alcoholism.

"I have fifteen years of sobriety," he said.

I knew he would be eligible.

We had written emails back and forth for a couple of weeks and learned that we both liked to dance. I did not tell him about my past.

"Do you want to go dancing?" he asked after dinner.

"I think the Eagle's Club is still open."

"Where's that?" I ventured, trying to sound interested but not eager.

"It's several miles north of Helena on the Lincoln road." We continued to talk as we drove.

"I'm in real estate," John said.

"I haven't been that involved lately because I'm taking care of my parents, but I've got a few irons in the fire."

"I am getting tired of criminal law," I replied, "and would like to do something else. I just don't know what."

The Eagle's was closed so we took the long way back to Helena to the west of the Scratch Gravel Hills. We had been talking so much that I did not realize it as he drove into a new subdivision project on Mt. Helena, immediately west of town. It was snowing, and Journey came on the radio: "*When the lights go down on my city by the bay.*"

"Would you like to dance?" John asked as he stopped the car.

He came around and opened the door to his Dodge Durango, and I noticed that he wasn't as tall as me. But, if I stood downhill as he held me it was just about right for a kiss. The snow fell softly as we swirled around in an embrace. I had often recalled the scene from The *Sound of Music* when girl meets boy. When they kissed, she picked up one leg. I did too.

I should have known better than to let it go further, but I paid no attention to any warning inside. I needed to know what my sexuality was, and I wanted this experience. He kept kissing me and touching me all over, and I loved it. I wanted it. We got back inside, got naked, and I got what I wanted. So did he.

"Alright, that's enough. I am not comfortable with this," he said as we finished.

As I rolled off I knew that I had been read in bed, a very dangerous situation for many trans women, like Angie Zapata, that even resulted in murder. Fortunately, John remained calm.

"When did you have your surgery?" he asked.

"In May, how could you tell?"

"I felt the whiskers when we were outside kissing," he said "but thought what the heck."

"But your boobs are really firm, and it feels different down there."

I did not try to hide or lie, but just told him my story. He took me back to my car.

"It's too bad, because I really liked you," I said as I got out.

He didn't reply, so I closed the door and walked away, turning my collar up against the January cold.

I drove home, hurt emotionally, but unharmed physically. I called my sponsor and my other wise women the next day.

"He only wanted to get laid," they said.

"It was predatory! They each declared.

"But you were foolish and very lucky that everything turned out as it did."

I vowed never again to put myself in that position. From then on I would tell all would-be suitors my story before the first date. I did not get many dates and recalled what my trans friend had told me a year earlier in Missoula.

"There is no man for you in Montana."

There were no dates after that, until I met another guy named John.

"Would you like to go to lunch?" he wrote in an email.

"I'd love too, but I must tell you something about myself first," I wrote back.

I wrote a coming-out email, a condensed version of the letter I had sent to friends and family a few years earlier.

"I've heard of that, but can we still have lunch?" John wrote back.

He brought me flowers. We dated all that spring, or what passed for dating I suppose. We tried sex a few times after the first several dates, but it just did not seem to interest John ultimately. And I had the nagging feeling that I was not heterosexual after all.

Plus, our dates usually consisted of me driving to Missoula because I had a vehicle that was much more economical than his pick-up when gas was nearly $4.00 a gallon. We mostly stayed at his house and watched TV. We did a few things out doors in the spring, but romance just did not blossom. We stopped dating but remained friends, even to the extent that he drove over and helped me retire the Bob mausoleum in East Helena by delivering my heavy, bulky table saw to a friend and setting up the rest in my garage below the new apartment. I still call John to see how he is doing.

"Hey," I say as my usual greeting.

"Straw," John says in response like I was a long lost friend.

I was a little sad that try as I may, I just could not seem to find romance with a man. I was grateful too, to have been treated as a woman with kindness and respect. I especially enjoyed riding in the front of John's pick-up, holding hands like his girlfriend.

I went back on-line, and got lots of bites, until I told them about me. A pattern developed where these guys would profess great love for me until I told them the rest of the story. Then they vanished. A friend advised to try to have fun with it, so I did, and did not take the rejection too seriously. I knew who and what I was. I was happy with the woman in my skin, even if men were not. Still, I enjoyed the fruit baskets and flowers, like Harry Chapin stashing the bill in his shirt in the song, Taxi.

In the spring of 2008, the Montana Attorney General's office advertised a position opening for a lawyer in the Prosecution Services Bureau (PSB). It was a job and bureau I knew well, although John had retired, and the colleague who had run from me that first weekend at St. Paul's was now in charge. I sent my application in before the deadline in March and waited. AG, Mike McGrath, was waging his campaign for Chief Justice of the Montana Supreme Court. I waited some more.

I called the woman in charge and inquired what was up with the position. She responded with an offhand comment.

"Even though we advertised the position, we are not yet sure we are going to fill it."

I thought that odd and waited some more.

I have an idea about how the AG's office works from my years of working with them. A colleague from a case years before was the civil attorney for the office. It would be his role, if asked, to research questions like whether or not antidiscrimination laws extended to transgendered people. He would determine and advise the attorney general about liability exposure in a discrimination lawsuit. They would likely know that the law afforded no protection against discrimination on the basis of gender identification. Still, I applied because I knew I was very qualified with sixteen years of prosecution experience and superb references. My record was sterling. I waited some more.

I finally got an interview on June 25th, three months after I applied. I was the first one to be interviewed, at 8:30 a.m. I was early and waited again. The bureau chief and another attorney corralled me into a conference room as we waited for the third interviewer who was supposed to be there. After waiting for ten minutes or so, she decided to begin anyway.

"This won't take long," she said as she sat down.

Twenty minutes later I walked out the door with the usual conclusory comment,

"Thank you for your time and interest in interviewing me."

The next day I wrote a followup thank you letter to express my continued interest. I did everything right, answering all their questions without fail, what few there were. I learned later that they hired a woman from in-house who had practiced in child abuse and neglect cases. She was a classmate. I knew that she had nothing close to the kind of experience I had trying all manner of criminal cases together with abuse and neglect cases, as well as youth court cases. I had been a career prosecutor, yet was passed over in favor of a candidate who did not have half my experience.

I was sure it was discrimination and contemplated a Human Rights complaint. I talked to my sponsor about it. She advised against it.

"It would be a long fight, the kind that some people drink over," she pointed out.

I decided she was right, and besides, suing the attorney general as he ran for Chief Justice might be perceived as a political stunt in any event. Also, it would mean coming out to everyone I knew in Helena, some of whom might feel betrayed. I did not want that and the harm it may cause. I swallowed my pride and sent out more applications.

Chapter Twenty Two

Winter Solstice Kiss

You've got a whole heart
Give me the hard part, I can love that too

- David Wilcox[76]

In July, 2008, I turned a corner. Like a soft breeze on a warm summer night, the promises of recovery were happening. It started with the move to my new apartment. It wasn't just that it was such a beautiful sanctuary for me. What was more significant was that I had not worried about it a single bit. I trusted God that all would be well, and it was, beyond what I could even have thought to ask for.

My peace of mind had been steadily growing since May from what seemed like bad news. My boss told me I could no longer take long lunches to accommodate meetings.

"You're taking too long for lunch and people are noticing," he flatly stated.

"Can't you go to a night meeting?"

"Sure, but I have a home group that I am accountable to," I asserted defensively, though I knew the importance of such things was lost on him.

So, I stopped going at lunch and opted for night meetings instead. Yet, in the sands of disappointment, I found a pearl. I had the time to meditate at lunch now. May is a beautiful month in Montana, if for no other reason than the warmth of sunshine on my face, having waited since October to feel it. There was a courtyard with a playground right outside the Park Avenue Building. A day-care center was right next to the playground, so there were often young children running, screaming, hitting, crying, playing and just being children. I would sit on the other side of the park, as all that childrenness made it difficult to be quiet, though I thanked God for their sweetness and innocence just the same. I suppose being around children can be a meditation in just that way. Every chance to see the presence or action of God and give gratitude is an experience of the divine. Meditation for me involves being quiet and experiencing God, both in big ways and in small ways.

I sat in the grass under the budding quaking aspens making that trickling sound like a running mountain stream, and focused on one of two mantras. One was "thank you." The other was "God." Both worked, for they brought me peace. I began to understand the presence of God, like wind, always present in time and in space. When I felt like God was not there, it was I who was not present. God's presence abounds, like the air around me. All I needed to do was breathe. God was not a static being in some far off heaven that I might make it to one day. God was in me and all around me, not visible or tangible, but real nonetheless. Nothing else seemed to matter. I began to understand serenity.

Like turning a switch inside, I was resigned to accept whatever fate my life would offer. I began to think about Mary, you know, Jesus' Mom. I pictured her as she is often portrayed, the supplicant. I looked up the word, "supplicate," and found that basically it means to humbly beseech. I thought about that as I contemplated Mary's words when Gabriel told her she was to be the mother of God. She said, "Let it be . . . ." (Luke 1:38). I could not conceive of a better model for my recovery program as we prayed daily, indeed many times throughout each day, for God's will. Had not Mary been speaking those words of wisdom throughout the ages? Yet again, she spoke them to me.

I had a job, food and a place to live that I loved. I would be okay, just as Monique had intimated. I still had difficulties with finances, romances, employment and children, but something I heard stuck like glue holding me in this good place.

"God's time and my time are not the same time," my sponsor had often said.

I was beginning to understand that change and growth take time and experience. Imagine yourself the triune God acting in the lives of a few billion people. Often the needs of all those people conflict and require compromise to accommodate them all. Someone has to give while another must take. Heredity, habits, disposition, behavior and a whole host of human inclinations often must congeal simultaneously to bring about a result. If humanity were not both blessed and cursed with free will, it should not take long for the proper pieces to all come together at once, but just let a person make up their own mind, and see what happens. God is the janitor of humanity, and our messes are so bad sometimes that it takes a while to clean them up. Finally, I understood patience. When I actually learned to wait and trust God, good things happened.

I had a new place. I had my friends and routines. I had my recovery group, my spiritual community at St. Paul's, and I was just voted on to the Emmaus Board of Directors. My life was rich and full, even if I did not have all that I wanted or felt that I needed. I no longer feared loss, nor feared failure to gain the solutions I sought. I learned how to let go and let God. I learned that there was nothing I could do to improve upon the readiness of circumstances for the action of God. Stand back and let it all be had taken on a whole new meaning.

I realized that gender transition, even under the best of circumstances is unequivocal and unforgiving. It required of me everything I had, and then some. I was still paying for it. Yet, there was no compromise, no half measure. I had to make my way in the world as a woman or not at all. I had been blessed and fortunate to have done so as quickly as I had and with relative ease. Still, I was resigned to accept the fact that some pieces would never be complete. I doubted that I would overcome gender identity discrimination in the workplace in Montana, and it did not seem likely that I would find a man who could accept me and love me as the whole person that I am. I had a whole heart, and I wanted the person who could take the hard part and love that too. I wanted the person with whom I could share every secret, so that secrets would be no more. That person was not to be found.

I began to accept that too, as I mused about just who would want a trans woman for a partner. In the ordinary course, a heterosexual male is looking for a heterosexual woman, not a heterosexual trans woman. Guys, with few exceptions, think it's just too freaky for them to accept. A lesbian woman likewise does not want a lesbian trans woman, as we are sometimes perceived by lesbians as something less than a real woman. And I get that. Even though I have this hunger to be known, I'm not like the girl next door. Thus, the field seemed pretty narrow. The only option for romance that began to appear to me was another trans woman, if for no other reason than that she would likely be in the same position and would understand me intuitively.

As those conclusions sifted through my consciousness that fall, I got the email announcement for the first ever Montana Transgender Day of Remembrance. It is a national event in which trans communities all over the country get together to remember those of our members who have been killed, or undertook the task themselves, each for lack of tolerance, understanding and acceptance. Montana's Day of Remembrance would be held in Billings. I thought it was time that I got hooked up with Montana's trans community, and this would be a perfect opportunity. The thought occurred to me that I might meet someone to date, but I had long since learned that my expectations were my biggest enemy.

I got a call in early November from the event organizer. It was Kynni, whom I had spoken with over the phone before. She had asked me to help a trans woman with workplace discrimination problems during her early transition. I was happy to help out, and I was impressed with how together Kynni seemed to be.

She too was a professional, an engineer by trade, and I looked forward to meeting her. We spoke a few times to make arrangements for me to stay with her friend in Billings. So, Saturday, November 22, 2008, found me on a Montana road trip, doing my nails as I drove. Montana was wearing her best Andrew Wyeth brown, and snow had gathered on some of her peaks as I drove east to Townsend to take the Deep Creek Canyon to White Sulfur Springs, on past Martinsdale and Two Dot, Harlowton and Lavina, then south toward Billings. I had made the trip many times. It was an unfettered three hours of Montana, vast and open, with a chance around every bend of spying wildlife of great variety. It was a chance to think, too, to take stock and be grateful. I love Montana road trips, always have, and by the grace of God and the redemption of this place, I always will.

A local church was hosting the event, so I went there first. As I walked down the isle to the front, there she was, busily finalizing everything for the service. Yet, she stopped and gave me a smile and her full attention when I softly spoke her name.

"Are you Kendra?" I said, learning later the spelling of her name was actually Kyndra, with an "i" sound, not an "e" sound.

"Yes," she said. "You must be Bobbie."

She held out her hand confidently, although I learned later that it belied a deep shyness, endearing on one hand because it showed humility and lack of pretense, but almost irritating on the other as it fell so far short of the beauty and grace I saw in the woman who clasped my hand.

We spoke only briefly before she was off to take care of other last-minute details, but I had fallen head over heels. I knew in the first instant I saw her that she was thoughtful and giving. She would go a great way, whether out of a sense of guilt or charity or both, to make things right for others. Having spoken with her over the phone, I knew she was intelligent and articulate. Plus, she was kind of cute.

I never believed in a love at first sight, but then again, it had never happened to me before, or at least not in many, many years. But when I saw Kyndra, selflessly creating this event for others to remember and take courage in who they are, I was already impressed. Then she stopped everything, gave her whole attention to me and smiled. I was smitten. I was in love. During the ceremony, Kynni got up to light candles as a memorial for each person who had died. I got up to help, as it seemed a simple way for me to be of service. Someone took a picture that I cherish as the first of many magic moments that have passed between us.

"Would you like to have lunch tomorrow?" I asked Kynni, as she had wanted to talk.

She was in early transition, having tried valiantly to live the male life for forty-three years, as a son, brother, father, husband and friend. Her story resounded well with me. We had a lot to talk about. We had lunch at Denny's after the service at the UCC church that had sponsored our Day of Remembrance service and welcomed us with wide open arms, hearts and doors.

Kynni was dressed in what she called "drab," a sort of androgynous look that Kynni employed to hide her emerging breasts and still fit in as a man. She wore a flannel shirt, jeans and sneakers with no jewelry or make-up. After lunch, we went shopping together at the Billings Mall on the west side. We continued to talk, and Kynni got her ears pierced. I bought her first pair of real earrings, silver tear drops with inlaid mother of pearl.

We talked about relationships and sexuality. Amazingly, I could be completely honest and candid for perhaps the first time in my life. I did not have to hide anything, and whether by mutual design or accident, we have communicated in that forthright manner ever since. It is the first completely honest relationship that I have ever had. There is great freedom in truth it seems.

Kynni wanted a friend for support, to hang out with and go out with as she continued to transition. It quickly dawned on me that while my emotions could easily run away with me, Kynni was not looking for a relationship.

We started emailing songs and pictures back and forth. Kynni came to Helena one night and slept on an air mattress on the floor. We went out for Mexican and talked late into the night, I with my love in check, she with her searching for herself. I told my sponsor about my feelings for her, and she gave me this prayer that has also been added to my daily routine,

"God, I ask for your will for Kyndra as well as for me. Please take this relationship and allow it to become what you want it to be, and show us the truth."

I prayed and we continued to email.

Every year the Imperial Sovereign Court of the State of Montana, a drag troupe that does shows to support numerous charities and service groups holds its annual holiday show in Butte. Kynni asked me to go with her, and I gladly accepted. We both wore red formal dresses and my Grandma's old fur coats that my Mom had given me years before. Hmmm. We looked great and enjoyed the evening. Peggy came for a while, as she had for many previous holiday shows with her girlfriends.

Kynni and I shared a motel room that night and talked late, about transition and after, about relationships and spirituality. I told her about my morning prayer routine, as I would be doing it the next morning. We talked about relationships, and I read to her the relationship prayer, sans names. Even though I was really trying to just be a supportive friend, I think the light began to dawn. We enjoyed shopping the next day, and when it was getting to be time for us both to drive home, neither of us wanted to part.

I came home for lunch the next day, as my office was across the street from my South Park apartment. As I was checking my emails, I got an instant message from Kynni. I was anxious and anticipatory as we exchanged the usual greetings, before Kynni wrote a line that has changed both of our lives and opened doors to love that neither of us would have thought possible.

"I have grown rather fond of you," she wrote.

"Do you want me to tell you the truth?" I typed out in response and hit "Enter" on my computer keyboard.

I wrote her this poem just before Christmas.

A WINTER SOLSTICE KISS

You took my hand as we walked away knowing
there was no one to see as we stopped in the snow.

It lightly fell as in dreamlike romance.
Could we, dare we? Yes we must, we cannot stop.

Is it the cold, or the entire world against which we
embrace, or nothing at all, as we surrender

unto each other, so long starved by our own truth,
sated at last, full to overflowing, sweet release.

Bodies pressed, you bending, me stretching, grabbing
like life may cease before it is lived.

No space, no air, no reserve between us or the world.
Lips, tongues, wetness, a caress, silent screams.

If snow could fall joyfully, it did on that winter's
Solstice eve in the snow with you.

Some would doubtlessly decry us as abominations. That is okay. I cannot judge or argue another person's beliefs. I believe that God has reserved judgment unto God and recommends unambiguously that we not spend our time in judgment of others. I have run the gamut of Christian belief and dogma, from Bible thumping fundamentalist *handing tickets out for God* to relativistic Catholic, from judgmental right wing nut to flaming humanist. I have drawn a few conclusions about God, faith and spirituality that inform every part of my life today.

I will say this about God. First, God is, and requires no further explanation than that. God is present in time and in space. God is here and now. God is dynamic. God knows me, loves me and accepts me in all my humanness. God delights in my happiness and is sad when we are apart. There is no grand plan of God for my life, for God meant for people to take the harder road afforded by free will. A life lived marching lockstep with dogma, and even scripture, is not possible for all the inherent contradictions. There are simply not enough stones, nor blameless ones to throw them.

I love the image in *The Shack* of God as a black woman chef, sleeves rolled up and knee deep in the sometimes laborious tasks of life and humanity, yet working everything out through patience, tolerance and love. God loves and tolerates me enough to allow me to make my free choices, but patiently reminds me that God's design for living would bring me joy, happiness and freedom. Ultimately God tells me that my purpose, however I choose to fulfill it, is to be happy and serve others, to suspend judgment and embrace all of humanity as even God does.

In the end I cannot know with certainty what God's will is. I have to trust that because I have given my will and my life over to the care of God and asked for knowledge of God's will and the power to carry it out, that it will be so, even as I do my part. I must believe, when I ask such things of God, that it will happen. Faith is not knowledge or certainty, but a leap off a high ledge in the dark, trusting that there will be light and safety before I land.

I had made arrangements months in advance to spend Christmas, 2008 with John in Missoula, and, though I would loved to have been with Kynni, John was a friend who placed a premium on honesty and forthrightly living up to promises. John had honored my femininity in the kindest of ways by not pursuing romance when it would have been easy to do so if for nothing else than to cure loneliness. He respected me and treated me well, and I wished to keep such a friendship.

Kynni captivated me my heart, my soul, my whole being. I could not believe that it was true, but, there she was. And she knew me from the inside out, from all my dark corners to my bright hopes, and still wanted to be with me. Kynni understood me intuitively. She got me. She accepted me. I could not ask for more. Then she said she loved me.

We knew it would be hard at times. I was afraid to face an unfriendly, unaccepting world, but I promised to take Kynni's hand and do it together if she would have me. There were no rules, no guidelines or social norms for us to follow. That is very freeing on one hand and frightening on the other. But when I was with Kynni I was not afraid. I had joy and peace in my life before we met. I was filled with gratitude just to be alive and whole. Of a sudden they knew no bounds. I wanted her soul, not just to be awake, but to soar. I knew that she had suffered, and I did not know the half of it. I also knew that she need suffer no longer. Kynni was on the cusp of a wonderful new life, as far as I could see, and I want to help her get there. I was grateful just to be part of it. I was sure that I was some sort of insane just then. I couldn't think. There was nothing I could do. I had truly chosen not to fight. I surrendered completely, and it was not just a feeling. As I said, she had captivated me.

Chapter Twenty Three

God Moments

*There's a song in the heart of a woman
that only the truest of loves can release.*

- Dan Fogelberg[77]

Kynni was just beginning to sing the song that I knew so well. She had tried to stay in her marriage and had been honest from the start about being a transsexual. She believed she could keep it in check as I once had. She told her wife as much but alas, she could not. Sometimes I think that the wisdom of the ages is nothing more than resignation to the certain knowledge that there are some forces that we cannot control, try as we may. Shakespeare was right about being congruent, and a life lived falsely to others is doomed to failure. We simply are unable to control or contrive who we are. Kynni and I both tried repression and denial for many years, and it simply did not work. The girl in her had to live as surely as she did in me. This truth was plain to see, and I soon adopted the role of gardener trying to help her blossom.

As she dismantled her marriage to a woman without the grace Peggy had displayed, I often held her as she sobbed bitterly. I could not fix it, I knew, but offered all the encouragement I could. Kynni had refinanced their home, so her soon to be ex could afford the payment, and moved out. She wanted her two children to have their family home and made every attempt to support her ex toward that end. She had a camper, which she moved inside a rental garage with a bathroom that she called home.

"I've heard of trailer trash, but camper trash is a new one on me," I quipped when I saw her place.

We were together nearly every single night for the next six months at her place or mine. We went out for Chinese or a McFlurry at McDonald's. We went to movies and LGBT events. The Montana Pride Network put us on their board, and just like that, we became LGBT advocates.

We took her kids out on weekends when Kynni had them. Kynni had told them much about who she was, but not about the culminating event of transition. She struggled greatly with that, as all trans parents do. She loved her children dearly and had been the nurturer all along. She wanted to keep them in her life, come what may. I liked them, and they liked me, although we did not think it time to tell them about me. They took me for the woman I am, and we did not discuss my past much, which oddly enough, I have not shied away from.

Kynni worked on the steps of transition all during the spring of 2009, and I helped her as much as I could with things like her legal name change. I represented her at her final hearing in front of Judge John Brown in Bozeman. He was a gem and treated us both with dignity and respect. So, Ken became Kynni legally, got a new driver's license reflecting as much, together with the proper gender marker, and worked on her divorce.

Kynni planned to have her surgery in Thailand with Dr. Suporn for several reasons, one of which was expense. It would be several thousand dollars less there, even after factoring in travel expenses. She had studied several clinics, as she is the studious type. I remind her of her native intelligence with a quotient of 150, which she denies in typical self-deprecating fashion. She had concluded that Dr. Suporn's approach yielded more satisfactory results, and given my somewhat unsatisfactory results, I could not disagree. Her surgery date was July 1, 2009, two years and two months to the day after mine.

She had not yet told her children of the reason for her trip to Thailand when we left for Kalispell in mid-June for Montana Pride Inc.'s principle event, the PRIDE celebration and parade. Not only was it necessary for Kynni and me to attend as Board members, but we also signed up to give a presentation about gender transition in Montana, which I dubbed, as one might guess, Transmontana. Kynni brought an element that I could not, as she had grown up in rural Montana in the very town in which we have now taken up residence.

Her parents ran a store there, in which they made and marketed a Montana made product all over the world. I had seen the work for years and came to recognize it as what I refer to as a slice of "Montanacana." I look for their pieces at garage sales and thrift stores, knowing that Kynni helped to produce them. She showed me the very spot where she dug the clay as a child. Of course, I collect every piece of pre-1989 Clays in Calico that I can find.

I met Kynni's parents at the Day of Remembrance, which gave a powerful message in itself. I have seen them many times since. Kynni's Mom is not that much older than I am. She is more like a friend than a mother-in-law. I took to her immediately, as her compassion, caring and support for Kynni was readily apparent. Kynni's Dad is the same way, even though they both have trouble with the pronouns.

They are both from old Montana stock, he from Big Timber and she from Columbus. They have that same pragmatic, live-and-let-live nature that would sooner accept a person than scorn them and suspend judgment on their character and make up until the work is done. Kynni's Dad and I have enjoyed many a clever remark at each other's expense. I cherish Kynni's parents as if they were family, for he has told me as much.

June is the best month for a Montana road trip. The flora and fauna are all dressed up in their best coats. Green up has usually reached its peak by the middle of the month, and the blossoms of many plants are at their most glorious full bloom. Bear grass is one such flowering perennial, despite the nomenclature. Most of the time it looks like grass, but once every five to seven years it flowers at sub-alpine levels. When it does blossom, the plant dies and propagates by dropping seeds and through rhizomes, a maze of root-like structures not unlike those in grass or cottonwood and aspen trees that seem to litter the landscape in which they appear for that very reason. June of 2009 was one of those magical times when the bear grass blossomed all over the Sealy-Swan Valley as we drove North to Big Fork and on to Kalispell for the PRIDE Celebration. It was a wonderful weekend, punctuated by the parade on Saturday.

I had been worried for months about our safety at such events, as we were in close proximity to neo-Nazi and white supremacist groups, hiding out in the Idaho panhandle and Northwestern Montana for generations. A sort of alarm went off in my head sounding strangely like the theme from *Deliverance*. However, to our very pleasant surprise, the Kalispell community came out in far greater numbers of supporters than detractors. I could not help but notice the vitriol exhibited by our opponents, and I wondered which teachings of Jesus they had been listening to. Didn't Jesus embody the new covenant between God and humanity? Did he not teach that we should, above all else, love one another as he loved us? I did not see love, peace or joy amongst that small group. They were bitter and antagonistic, yet, our supporters, indeed we ourselves were happy, smiling and waving with something like what my mother called "brotherly love."

I wondered who that God was who held its followers in fear of a certain degree of heat in which they would burn eternally. I wondered who that God was who could call any of God's children an "abomination." It was not the God I knew, nor the one I wanted. It was not the Jesus with whom I danced, who smiled at me and honored my femininity. As Mpho and Desmond Tutu write in their new book, *Made for Goodness*:

> Perhaps we too are shaken by the thought that our enemies will not burn in Hades throughout eternity. But, ultimately, the reality of heaven cannot tolerate the existence of hell. Even our worst enemies are God's beloved children. What kind of God could endure the sight of God's own children screaming in eternal pain?[78]

God is not going to fry me for eternity, even if a street side poster states something to the contrary. Is it the words of scripture that are wrong or out of context, or the ones who wield them as a weapon to castigate the marginalized whom they seek to cast out, against whom they spread hatred, judgment and condemnation? They say, "love the sinner, but not the sin," as if God granted them the power to divine what sin is and what it is not. Rabbi Kushner says this:

> The false prophets who invoke God's name to endorse what they are inclined to do anyway, the religious and moral ventriloquists who pretend that God is saying the words that originate with them, are talking to themselves[79].

Several months earlier, shortly after I met Kynni, three new job announcements appeared in the newspaper and on line. I prepared my resume, cover letter and other application materials for the City of Bozeman, the Montana Department of Labor and Industry and Disability Rights Montana, all seeking an attorney. To my surprise, as the New Year arrived, each contacted me to set up an interview. I was particularly surprised that the City of Bozeman contacted me, as I had left blank a question on the application that I deemed objectionable on several grounds.

The question asked applicants to list all internet social networking groups they had been members of and other associated personal information, like usernames and passwords. I knew intuitively that the question sought to ferret out people who might use the internet for criminal purposes. However, it was not the typical question that sought only criminal history information, like felony convictions. I thought it a gross invasion of privacy that our Supreme Court would no doubt abhor. It also looked like a vehicle which, though innocuous enough on the surface could result in discriminatory practices depending on whether or not an applicant was a member of a protected class and whether they were members of corresponding internet support groups for instance. I also knew that even though the interim city attorney was an old colleague that my visits to trans support sites would out me. My response to the question was that I did not have a felony criminal record.

As an aside, I do have a federal criminal record, which always throws people, as it sounds so serious. About a month before moving from Silver Star, Peggy and I had gone up Fish Creek Road to cut some firewood against the possibility that we may be there another winter. I had intended to pick up a permit during the week, but was busy enough at work that I could not get to Sheridan by 4:00 p.m. when the United State Forest Service offices closed. That Sunday was the only day that looked like it would work for both of us. A former friend had told me that he never got a permit, and he had cut a lot of USFS dead trees to haul home.

We went without a permit and got a pick-up load of firewood cut, bucked and stacked on the truck. Sure enough, as we came to the highway, a pale green USFS pick-up was on the way in. He stopped by me.

"How you doing?" he asked, sounding rather friendly when his intent was suspect at the very least.

"Fine," I said in unthinking response as I too was more focused on his intent.

"Do you have a firewood cutting permit?" he asked as his intent became crystal clear.

I could see no point in trying to mask the obvious.

"No," I responded and explained the whole sordid tale, to which he listened kindly, perhaps with bemused curiosity.He appreciated my being forthright and honest so much that he let me keep the firewood. The permit cost about $6.00. The fine was $96.00. Counting gas, time and the federal record, it was the most costly load of wood I had ever retrieved. I sold it to the next door neighbors for $50.00 when we moved. I listed that crime on the application but doubted seriously that any self-respecting Montanan would hold it against me, except for the fact that I got caught.

The City of Bozeman has a modern city government leading a growing cosmopolitan city, at least by Montana standards, into this century. Their interview process was demanding, separated into three sections, each lasting an hour to an hour and a half. The first section involved different staff members, about ten people in all, sitting around a table. One of them was the city judge, who was also a former colleague.

"Hello," he said, not as much with a formal tone, but more the friendly tone we had always spoken in.

The next section was with the Legal Department, two of whom were also former colleagues. They showed no judgment or condemnation either. The last session was with the Mayor and department heads assembled in the council chambers. The table at which they sat was a bench really, in a horse-shoe shape, elevated so that they all looked down on me seated at a table in the middle.

I was not intimidated, but rather confident and poised. I knew that I was more than qualified for the position, having done the same kind of work for fourteen years in Madison County. I knew I could walk right in and hit the ground running and told them as much. Perhaps I appeared over confident, for they did not hire me, opting for a deputy county attorney with far less experience. I was disappointed, as this job was one familiar to me and would allow Kynni and me to move in together in Bozeman or its environs. But I did not let it get to me, as I was resolved to accept those things over which I had no control. I just did my best and left the result to God.

My next interview was with the Montana Department of Labor, and it so happened that the chief legal counsel was a lesbian. I should not have assumed, as I did, that she held no prejudice against me, because she may have, as she did not hire me either. It is entirely possible that, although she bore me no personal negative bias or angst, she did not want to be the one to open the transgender barrier any more than any of the other state agencies I had been turned down by over the previous two years.

I could deal with that disappointment too, but for the manner in which I found out. I overheard the hiring results by one of the interviewers as I walked behind him at lunch. He was talking out of shop. The director was good enough to phone me personally to tell me that she did not hire me because I was over qualified and would be bored and to apologize for the manner in which it was disclosed to me. I appreciated that, although thought to myself that I would gladly be bored for $65 grand.

The last interview was at Disability Rights Montana, and seemed the least likely, as I had little equivalent experience. I had a friend who was an attorney there, and he had been encouraging me to apply for over a year. I had already applied once before and heard nothing. They did not seem all that excited about me. However, I was resigned at that point, when my pride had been sufficiently pummeled to accept whatever position I was offered.

Once I walked into their office in late March, any negative vibe I had vanished. The affirmation and goodwill between the twenty or so employees was palpable. I was excited of a sudden and did my best in the interview. At one spot the Executive Director asked,

"How would you resolve a conflict between employees you supervise?"

I immediately thought of what my sponsor said to me about my conflicts.

"The first thing I would do is pray about it." I said to Bernie, who just happened to be the woman whom I had basically betrayed at the legislature in 2005,

"You are not supposed to say this sort of thing in interviews, but I am going to throw caution to the wind. The first thing I would do is pray about it."

Bernie later told me she knew then that she would hire me because she had said almost the exact same thing when she interviewed for her job. People often talk about such serendipitous moments that manifest the fruits of our prayers and trust in God. We call them God moments.

Bernie called a few days later and offered me the job. I gave my two weeks' notice the same day and left on as even a keel as could be expected. I carried no resentments with me in any event, and what other people thought of me was none of my business. I could let it all go and earnestly wish each of them well, and I did.

A week, or so, before I was to begin at DRM, Bernie called.

"Would you be able to get together for coffee? I have something I'd like to talk to you about."

I knew what was coming but did not fear it. Even though one of the interviewers knew me from my former life, I do not think that she had yet shared that knowledge. I met her at Starbucks at about 8:30, Thursday of the following week.

"I checked your references as I always do," she said. "The professor at the law school was very complimentary about you."

"I ran a Google search, and one result confused me," she said.

My old nemesis, Reid Rosenthal told on me yet again. The first hit was the lawsuit featuring the caption that listed my new female name and my old male f/k/a. Bernie knew that I was trans.

"I was waiting for the other shoe to drop," I said evenly.

"I am transgender," I said, not wanting to be coy or hide anything. Taking pride in who I am was more important to me than any job anyway.

"No, no, no," she said, "I just wanted to talk to you about it. It doesn't make any difference to me. You have a really strong resume."

"Oh, well thank you," I said, hiding my surprise.

"I don't know how to talk about this, so bear with me," she said. "So I will just speak frankly, okay?"

"Sure. I actually prefer it that way."

"Do you need any accommodation as you begin work at DRM, like addressing the entire staff about trans issues?"

I was relieved as a sense of gratitude washed over me. She just wanted to help ease my transition to a new workplace.

"No," I said, "that's alright."

I had long ago become accustomed to just being myself and letting the discussions and comments go where they would. It was not my business what other people thought, as I knew who I was and felt perfectly normal in every respect.

"I would be more than happy to talk about it if anyone has questions."

The big revelation, however, was that Bernie knew and did not care, did not even consider my being trans in looking at my resume or during the interview and decision making process. Finally, after twenty-two months of futile job searching, someone was willing to take a chance on me, like Henri J. Haskell did for Ella Knowles, because of my abilities. I was finally able to get a job as a woman, signifying the completion of my transition into mainstream American womanhood. I do not know if I have made it, but a young woman referred to me the other day as a "career woman." I was elated and more grateful than I could say. Plus, my new office had south facing windows that would allow my geraniums and Shane's tree to flourish.

My difficulties were being removed, it seems, as time and continued sobriety rolled along. Romance was resolved, as was the employment problem, and I had a plan that would resolve my financial woes too, ironic though it be. I had met with a bankruptcy attorney in September, 2008, just after moving into my new place. The rent was quite a bit higher, so I knew I had to do something to change my fortunes, or the lack thereof. I learned that I probably would not qualify for a chapter seven and would likely have to file under chapter thirteen.

"It's a Bush era addition to the bankruptcy code that will leave you in servitude," the lawyer said.

It was not as if I did not want to pay my bills, but try as I may over the previous two years to get even, I could not. The money simply was not there. I also learned that anything I had purchased using credit in the ninety days immediately preceding my petition filing date would not be discharge-able. Thus, I had to limp along for a few months before we could get serious about filing.

I filed for bankruptcy on February 17, 2009, three years, almost to the day after beginning this odyssey. I had my debtor's conference in April and my plan approval hearing in May. I would have to pay a certain amount of money to the trustee every month for five years which would be automatically deducted from my paycheck. That way, as long as I remained employed, I would not really miss it, particularly since I was going to be starting at a higher pay level at DRM, even after deducting the trustee payment. I had steadfastly paid my bills since I was ten years old, and it was difficult after forty years to admit defeat.

The thing that made it all just a bit surreal was that our government was in the midst of bailing out irresponsible banks and corporations to the tune of billions of dollars which, of course, begged the question,

"Who will bail me out?"

Indeed, who would bail out the millions just like me – the ninety-nine percenters?

Here we had these high expectations of the man who promised change, and his first official acts smacked of cronyism and Reaganomics. To save our economy we must save the big banks, the theory went, and in turn, they would make funds available to the masses. However, it did not quite work out that way, as corporate climates filled with greed and deceit did not change. The corporations believed their own rhetoric and took their junkets, bought their jets and gave out their ridiculous bonuses.

I had espoused a trickle-up theory that I still believe might have worked. Why not bail out consumers buried under a mountain of revolving debt? A tax rebate that could be used only for the purpose of paying down debt would have helped everyone. Banks would get needed cash, and consumers, relieved of onerous monthly payments, would have more disposable income to keep the wheels of capitalism rolling. Even though it will be years before I discharge my debts, I will come out of bankruptcy solvent, and, having five years to practice living without spending someone else's money, I hope to live without using credit cards. At any rate, I do not fear financial insecurity any longer. From my failures, financial redemption has arisen.

Finance, romances, employment and children - all my difficulties had been taken away, except that last one. That's a tough one. Hardly a day goes by where I do not think about Meghan and Shane. I cannot dwell on our rift and what we have missed. It would be too much. I have to let them go. I pray instead that God will bless them and that God's will be done. I have sent letters and cards with checks inside. They do not post to my account, so I know that the correspondence has not been opened. More likely, my cards and letters have been tossed on arrival. It is a sinking, hollow feeling, and I wonder about parents whose children have died.

I have no pictures of holding you
Singing to you about sunshine
And small white flowers
May you bloom and grow always

You are far away now
Still, I hold you in my heart
I do not let go as I am afraid
That you have taken my sunshine away.[80]
I cannot be angry at Meghan and Shane. I cannot curse God. I humbly beseech . . . Let it be.

Chapter Twenty Four

We are Changing the World

And now I live {by} a mountain top
And I'm almost {fifty}five
And I've found my peace I found my release
I'm happy just to be alive.

- Andy Pratt[81]

I used to say when I was younger that life at best is a struggle. I thought it profound. However, it was true at the time. It is not true now. I have a pink hat from the clothing line which proclaims "Life is good." I love that line, and it is good.

I am active in LGBT events and causes. I have been very active trying to persuade Montana's legislative contingent to pass the Federal Employment Non-discrimination Act, called ENDA. I try to influence other trans people to speak out as well. We need that law, and I sure could have used it a couple of summers ago. In the words of Martin Luther King, "injustice anywhere is a threat to justice everywhere."[82] I believe that injustice to anyone is injustice to everyone. I can no longer stand back and just let it all be. Even though, as Billy Joel sings, my survival has been "a noble fight,"[83] it is not enough.

We are changing the world. Leslie Feinberg wrote, "Together we are shaping a society that does not yet exist. . . . We are inextricably bound by our deep desire and commitment to win genuine justice and equality."[84] Just as I am trying to shape myself into the best woman that I can be, I pray that collectively we will shape the world into its best self. That is the challenge of our lives, the calling perhaps.

A fledgling trans woman who works for state government recently contacted me to inquire whether an executive order from the governor dealing with discrimination extended to gender identification. (Executive Order 412008). It was not express, so I sent my former colleague, Ann, an email at the governor's office.

> I have a few questions about the applicability of the above referenced executive order to gender identification as a specific class. As you know, it is not express in the order as it is in the personnel policies of a number of Fortune 500 companies, and on the verge of becoming federal law under the express provisions of the Employment Non-discrimination Act. Can protection from gender identification discrimination be implied from the order and the intent of its recitals? Noting that the Governor's express intent with this order is his 'firm and unwavering commitment to take a leadership role in promoting nondiscrimination,' does he want to get out ahead of the curve, or at least join in the groundswell in recognizing gender identification as a protected class in nondiscrimination laws?

> Obviously, knowing my history as you do, and by the nature of my questions I am promoting express classification of gender identity in such laws and hope that Governor Schweitzer would join Senators Baucus and Tester in doing so as well.

> We are changing the world.

Ann responded favorably, as I might have guessed, however, noncommittally, as I might have guessed as well. She did not answer my questions, but that does not matter. She got the message and did not reject it out of hand.

Advocacy has become an important role for me. A friend poignantly and succinctly wrote:

I know you were there in Thailand. I saw you in the photos. I also know that you were there in times before. That you were there for others, too, doing all that you could do to help. My comments about others helping us were about all of you there. . . . some by sharing their journeys, some by showing that there is power in coming together, that love really does exist, and that even being transgender cannot stop it from reaching you.

I'm still crying about it all . . . . Some of you were willing to go to the ends of the earth to help fix something that should have been all along . . . . I'm still crying because you all had the chance to feel that joy, to know that unity, to watch the miracle while it was happening. For me, to know that the totally impossible isn't; that love beat the odds and science found a way, and hope is not a wasted emotion if it can be put into action. All of you have proven that the impossible is possible. Thanks for letting us in on the miracle, too.

I cried too, as her words seem to put many things into perspective for me. They resounded like a clarion call. I have been blessed and very fortunate and must pass on what I have been given to others. It is miraculous and full of hope and love. Is that not our purpose, or at least some purpose, worthy of serving? It is a privilege for me to be present to others in my life, whether in daily affairs or larger challenges.

I have been active with the Montana Pride Network, as Kynni and I are serving on its Board. I have begun to work with the Montana Human Rights Network, The Pride Foundation, and others who understand that we are in fact changing the world as our society and our culture continue to evolve.

Advocacy groups often feature a "call to action" on their websites. I have responded often to support causes I believe in, which usually have something to do with advancing equality, justice or other improvements to the world condition. We have in Montana a loose affiliation with these and with others of similar ilk.

I received an email one day advising that the Bozeman City Council would that evening entertain on its weekly agenda expansion of the city's anti-discrimination policy to include sexual orientation and gender identification and to extend health insurance benefits to include spouses and partners within the same classifications. Kynni and I decided we needed to be present.

It was not lost on me as I sat in the growing audience before the meeting that I was now on the other side of the table from my days as a county attorney. I had appeared and presented at many public meetings in the past, advising on the finer legal points of one important issue or another, yet I had never testified as a citizen. It would be a first.

It was getting late before the mayor finally moved to the sexual orientation/gender identification policy issue. The council discussed it and seemed to favor such a policy as presented by the city manager, city attorney and HR director. Ironically, it was the same city manager and HR person I had interviewed with in the very same room only a year before, and the city attorney was the person they hired instead of me. His legal analysis as presented in a legal memo discussing the issue was posted on the city's website. It was thorough and astute. I liked him and realized yet again that I was right where I was supposed to be. I bore him no resentment, nor even jealousy.

Usually, when these issues arise at public meetings, there are a good number of religious right conservatives who testify about Biblical abominations and pedophiles and restrooms and such. There are also the liberal leaning lefties who propose such threatening notions as equality, justice and other constitutional precepts. Both sides showed up in Bozeman. Only the latter outnumbered the former about two-to-one.

I had been noticing similar dynamics recently and wondered about the status of love and hate in our world. In my view the distinction is clear. Hate is judgmental and exclusive, while love is patient, tolerant and inclusive. Where have I read a similar sentiment?

I testified too. I remembered my last appearance in front of a legislative assembly, and my fear then to speak my truth. I thought of Bernie and her son. I thought of purpose and calling. I prayed that God's will, not mine, be done. I prayed as I had on many occasions throughout my public career.

"God, please give me words to speak, not my own but your words." (A picture on the front page of the *Comical* the next day memorialized my moment of prayer).

I introduced myself.

"I am Montana's first and only out transgender lawyer, the only one in Montana history insofar as I know."

I have said this many times since in hopes that someone else will come forth, stand up and say it ain't so. It is a lonely distinction.

I announced to those assembled that both of Montana's Senators supported similar federal legislation, that the federal, state and many local governments throughout the country had adopted such legislation and that a majority of Fortune 500 companies had also.

"We are changing the world and can either stand idly by as change passes before us or get out in front of the curve and insure equality and justice for all," I declared, feeling like I was on a roll.

"After all, this country stands upon these principles, and our constitution demands no less." I commended the city manager, city attorney and HR director for their work and astute analysis, as well as the city for its progressive stance, and thought again about Montana's "western spirit of liberality." The city council adopted the policy by a unanimous vote and directed the attorney, manager and HR director to draft it for approval.

It was an important event for me, another in a string of such events of moment in my life. It was in some ways defining and redemptive. It was a living amends for my previous betrayal during the 2005 legislature. It was a fine hour for openness and honesty. I was a public LGBT advocate for the very first time, and Kynni later commented that another first occurred.

"Bozeman, the town where I was born, just passed the first inclusive anti-discrimination law in Montana history," she said excitedly.

While Missoula had adopted a policy of nondiscrimination that was inclusive of sexual orientation, it did not address gender identification. Bozeman was the first city in Montana to adopt a nondiscrimination policy that was inclusive of gender identification, and we were part of it.

"We are changing the world," I said.

I did not know that at the same time, the City of Missoula was working on a more sweeping LGBT anti-discrimination ordinance. The ACLU of Montana and the Montana Human Rights Network had drafted a proposed ordinance that would make such discrimination illegal in employment, housing and public accommodation. Council members Dave Strohmaier and Stacy Rye introduced the ordinance. The Council read the second draft at a public meeting on February 16, 2010 and set it for another public hearing for adoption on April 12, 2010.

On February 18, now four years almost to the day of my moment of truth in Silver Star, I got an email from Jamee Greer at the Montana Human Rights Network.

"I heard about your testimony in Bozeman," he said, "and I'd like to chat about the Missoula ordinance."

I had not planned to be so public and open about my being trans, but the universe had called and kept calling. The die had been cast. Jamee and I met for coffee at the Firetower on Last Chance Gulch in Helena.

For forty years or so, Helenans have been trying to fashion a shopping/tourist district in the Gulch, with varying degrees of success. There is even a walking mall closed off to vehicular traffic. The shops include high end galleries, trendy clothing stores and funky little shops and restaurants. My personal favorite is Toi's Thai because it is the only place in town that flavors its fare with Thai basil. The Firetower is across the street.

Jamee and I recognized each other right away for some reason, sort of a gay-trans-dar type of thing. Perhaps it was an activist, kindred spirit thing. I don't know, but we both have it. Jamee is tall, good looking and young. He smiles a good deal, endearing him instantly to me.

We spoke of the Bozeman policy and the Missoula ordinance. Jamee was the lead person for the Human Rights Network and was driving back and forth to Missoula from Helena almost daily. Before it was over, he moved to Missoula. He was both passionate and dedicated to justice and equality. It was infectious, and I very much wanted to help.

"Can you come to Missoula and tell your story?" Jamee asked.

I had learned in my program that when people ask for my help there really is only one answer. I say yes, so long as it is in my power to do.

"There may be opportunity for community meetings and radio broadcasts to advocate for the ordinance also," Jamee said.

The call was clear, like that of a Western Meadowlark, Montana's State Bird, so bright and strong that you can hear it even while driving down the highway at high speeds with the windows closed. I would speak out for justice and equality.

With so much time to think about it, though, I began to grow steadily more anxious. In the old days I would have quelled my anxiety with alcohol. My anxiety had grown so strong by March that I began seeing a therapist. At one point, Kynni and I went to soak at the Norris Hot Springs at the mouth of the Bear Trap Canyon just outside the tiny town of Norris,

Montana. Norris is one of the typical western outposts, featuring a gas station, the post office and a bar, and perhaps one or two entrepreneurial ventures.

The hot springs were just about as funky as they could be. The pool was lined with old fashioned 2 X 10 dimension lumber. My friend from law school told me they used to have a naked night on Sundays, heavily populated by virile, young bodies from Montana State University in Bozeman, an hour's drive to the east. The water was perfect, right around 103 - 04 degrees. The beer and wine flowed freely, and their odors filled my nostrils and left me with a strong and familiar sensation.

I won't say that I did not like it though, as I knew that their powers would take away my anxiety. I did not give into that sensation, that euphoric recall, because the rest of the story would be anything but euphoric. I knew that resumption of alcohol would come with a vengeance and take me right back to demoralization. I breathed deeply as my therapist had taught me, and prayed. I shared my feelings and sensations with Kynni, and she talked me through it all. The Cherry's Garcia after we finished soaking helped as well.

At about the same time, I discovered mindfulness meditation as taught by the Vietnamese holy man, Tich Nhat Hanh. Mindfulness is a way of becoming fully aware of my thoughts as they change from moment to moment without my interventions of control and judgment. It was similar to the teaching in recovery to "stay in the moment." It was a way to remain right here and right now, without my age olds fears of rejection, judgment and disdain, or my characteristic, yet unrealistic, expectations of future events.

Much to my surprise, my old friend Thomas Merton had taught the same form of contemplative prayer to the monks at Gethsemane. Since I drove two hours daily back and forth to work in Helena, I decided to get some audio CDs about mindfulness. My therapist had resisted my inquiries about anti-anxiety medications, and I was glad he did. The combination of mindfulness (such as I could muster) and controlled deep breathing were the only tonic I would need. I practiced them daily for the remaining weeks before the hearing in Missoula.

The week before the hearing I was invited to participate in a few public functions that again put me out there in the public arena. As I drove to

Missoula from Helena, I played an old John Michael Talbot CD from my first days in Montana, the words and music of which inspire me still.

"Can you be the light of the world, can you be the light? Can you give your love to the world; can you give your love?"[85]

The first event, on Thursday, April 8, was a panel discussion sponsored by the YWCA and NCBI of Missoula, two groups working towards a more just and accepting society. They billed the event as "Everyone Matters: Dignity and Safety for Trans People." They showed a film, which depicted some of the hurdles faced by trans people. I told them my story, as did the other panelists, in an environment that during the discussion I described.

"I feel safe here in this bosom of warmth."

It was a palpable feeling throughout the room of seventy people or so. The Missoula Police Department had hired a young lesbian officer as a liaison between the police and the LGBT community, who spoke as well. I was deeply moved by the humanity I witnessed.

"Yes, I *can* give my love to the world!" I said silently.

It was a glimpse of how an accepting community works, intent on love and support rather than judgment and condemnation. A person whose thinking and actions are devoted to the latter cannot possibly be filled with the former. I know which my God asks of me, and I pray that someday all persons of faith and good intent will come to the same place in their journeys.

Friday morning featured a radio appearance with a young gay activist and a sexologist, John Blake and Dr. Lindsay Doe, respectively, on a conservative call-in talk show. I was again taken by the passion, vitality and sincerity of my compatriots. As I have become more enmeshed in the LGBT community, I am struck by the inner fires I sense in those around me. Many have overcome great personal struggle to become their own true selves, to become whole as human beings at peace with their own identities within a world all too often hostile to them just because of who they are. Yet, these are happy people. They have loosed their fears and abandoned their pretenses. They are authentic, without judgment of others or demands for approval. They are passionate and dedicated. What exactly is wrong with that?

I had been warned that the some of the callers might be vitriolic. One in particular was the same evangelical preacher I had seen testifying before the State legislature in 2005, to whom I unwittingly gave my support. I was again introduced as the first and only transgender lawyer in Montana history. The preacher, my new nemesis, was introduced as a lawyer too. Thus, I should not have been surprised at his attempts to cross-examine me on the air.

"Where have you practiced?" he demanded as if expecting a dissatisfactory response from a person like me.

"I was in the Missoula City Attorney's office for two years, I've been in private practice, I was an elected county attorney for ten years, I've been an appellate defender and submitted numerous briefs to the Montana Supreme Court, and now I am a civil rights attorney," I said without having to think too much about what I have accomplished professionally.

He moved on to other matters, as I thought briefly about the O. J. trial and the Bischoff bail hearing. *Never ask a question on cross you do not know the answer to.*

Much to my surprise the strongest argument made by the opponents to the ordinance involved bathrooms. I was surprised because I thought it a weak and non-sensical argument, as I had been using the woman's restroom without as much as a sideways glance for the past four years. Still, even their protest signs outside the council building on the 12th belied some type of paranoia about men gaining access to women and children in restrooms by dressing up as a woman in a transgender disguise to assault them. It was disingenuous.

While I did not get the chance to share all of my thoughts about the bathroom non-issue at the hearing, it caused me to think back over my thirty years of public service. I had worked for nine years in residential child treatment programs that included victims of child sexual abuse. I had even studied for three years towards my master's degree in Residential Child Care Administration. I had been a prosecutor for sixteen years and had handled hundreds of child abuse and sexual assault cases. I had reviewed as many psycho-sexual evaluations, so knew something about the dynamics of child victimization and sexual assault.

The suggestion made by the opponents was that providing for the human rights of LGBT people would somehow encourage sexual abuse of women and children in restrooms. It simply had no basis in science, law or fact. Thus, it belied hysterical fear.

In the first instance, as my mentor from so many years earlier, Missoula City Attorney, Jim Nugent publicly pointed out, there was currently no legal restriction which kept any man from walking into any women's restroom. It is merely a social barrier not yet broken that provided any protection from such counter cultural behavior. In the second place, as many commented, people use the opposite sex facilities all the time to avoid lines or a pending disaster. Finally, the dynamics of control and power prevalent in sexual abuse and exploitation suggest that a perpetrator would be loathe to don a disguise to gain access to his victims, as subterfuge is antithetical to power and control. Similarly, sexual predation is seldom conducted as a random act. Victims are most often known to perpetrators.

Yet, if I followed the opponents' reasoning to its logical conclusion, we should not only ban trans people from public restrooms, but all men and priests as well. For, science, psychology, the law and the facts all indicate that offenders are most often men. As the clergy sex abuse scandals demonstrate, the clergy seem to bear this proclivity in significant measure as well. However, such a ban would not only be extreme, it would also be highly prejudicial. If it is not acceptable to pre-judge all men and all priests based on the actions of a few, then why is it acceptable to pre-judge a class of people merely due to membership in a class? It reeks of segregation and apartheid in civil rights struggles in other places and times.

The hearing on April 12 took seven hours with over three hundred people testifying.

One council member remarked,

"It is the most I can recall ever attending a Missoula public hearing."

Missoula residents were given the microphone for three minutes each, and non-Missoula witnesses had to wait till the end. I tried to sneak in after waiting three hours. An opponent from Florence up the Bitterroot, where many of the opponents hailed from, testified on behalf of a group she was in that was headquartered in Missoula. I thought I could do likewise.

I was rebuked by the mayor, and in my angst, went to that alcoholic place in my head of self-pity where others might have been angry or righteously indignant. I even thought about leaving and told Kynni as much.

"Don't let them win." she said. "Stay."

I finally got to testify at midnight.

"I am the first and only transgender lawyer in Montana history," I said again, with the challenging caveat,

"Unless or until someone else stands up to be counted, that's my story."

One council member chuckled and seemingly appreciated the humor amongst the emotionally charged atmosphere. I talked about the struggle for equality by Montana's first woman lawyer, Ella Knowles, and how it was resolved by the motion of a Missoula Legislative Councilman, intimating that Missoula had a legacy of egalitarian justice and equality. I talked about how my story resonated with Ella's and the employment discrimination I had faced in one of Montana's largest corporations, the university system and its highest levels of government.

I also mentioned that because discrimination is easy to allege but hard to prove, and that as courts had recognized there is seldom direct evidence of discrimination, that the law was needed to shape behavior by relying on the intentions of people of good will to follow it because *it is the law.* Finally, I told the Council, the audience and all the Missoulians watching on closed circuit TV that this ordinance was the right thing to do:

> In a pluralistic democracy we must embrace our diversity. In the cultural blender that is America, it is our birthright and our obligation. Culture is dynamic and will continue to shift and change whether we accept change or not. Missoula again has the opportunity to lead and to bring about positive change for the sake of justice and equality for all. We are changing the world.

The council passed the historic ordinance by a 10-2 vote, and I was proud to have been there.

Over the next few weeks, the Facebook internet waves were buzzing with posts and pictures, more than a few of them my own, of the momentous victory and where we might go next.

Just as all indicators pointed toward Helena, the *Independent Record* posed in its newspaper and on line, in its Question of the Week, whether Helena should adopt a similar ordinance. Sixty percent of the 800 or so respondents answered favorably. At the end of the week, Friday, April 23, Jamee had arranged with Montana Public Radio for me to appear for the evening editorial comment segment.

"God, please take my will and my life into your care," I prayed and gave a five-minute speech reflecting on Missoula's ordinance and Helena's sixty percent approval of it.

This is some of what I said:

Both this poll and the historic legislation are reflections of Montanan's sense of justice and equality - it is our heritage. A 1982 article in *Montana Magazine* recognizes that for more than 120 years, Montana has been known for its 'progressiveness and Western spirit of liberality.' The 1972 Constitutional Convention recognized this as well by producing one of the more progressive state constitutions in the country.

I mentioned the words of Coretta Scott King on her husband's legacy of advocating for freedom, justice and equality for all persons. She says,

"I have always felt that homophobic attitudes and policies were unjust and unworthy of a free society and must be opposed by all Americans who believe in democracy.'

"Montana has the opportunity to lead and bring positive change for the sake of equality and justice for all - to take a step forward, not backward - by supporting LGBT anti-discrimination laws," I said, and closed with,

"We are changing the world."

I had a terrible cold not long afterward and stayed home for four days. I went to the doctor on day four. I lived an hour away from Helena, so Dr. K was out of the question. In fact, we lived about twenty miles from Silver Star as the crow flies. So, I decided to go to my former doctor in Whitehall, in between Cardwell and Silver Star.

When I called I had a bit of trouble getting the receptionist to understand that while I had been a patient a few years ago and my old records are under Robert, that my name was now Roberta.

"I changed my name and my gender," I said, trying to explain my circumstances succinctly.

"Oh, we have an opening at 9:30," she said.

I caught a few of them looking me over to see what a transsexual looks like, but that was it. I was well and professionally received, unlike my experience a few years earlier with the neurosurgeon that fused my neck. His whole office had to stop and gawk. The physical therapist downstairs came running out as I was leaving and shot past me as I said hello. She looked like she had seen a ghost, and I suppose she had, as the person she had worked on before had been a man.

I cannot blame anyone for that kind of reaction. I do not like it, but I understand it. It is not something people see every day, because gender transition is not something a person does every day. Thank God. It reminds me of a magazine renewal jacket that came in the mail as a final notice for a subscription I had. It was typed in all caps with big bold print against a bright yellow background and said: THIS IS YOUR LAST ISSUE. I put it on my refrigerator as I said out loud,

"I hope so."

I recently made the front page of the *Montana Standard* for my Supreme Court appeal case involving the young man who stabbed the gang banger looking for a fight outside the bar in Butte. While I lost the case in a 5-2 ruling, the paper finally dropped the "f/k/a." *Mi yama est Roberta.*

I get up every morning and say:

Good morning, God. My name is Bobbie. I am an alcoholic. Thank you for this life and way of living. Please accept my will and my life into your care. Grant me knowledge of your will and the power to carry it out.

This prayer and way of approaching my day, indeed everything, is central to my recovery and my life. It's not that I think God needs reminding of my name. I am blessed and fortunate that God did not forget it as I feared God might want to. I remind myself that I have an ongoing addiction which, in the words of Emmy Lou Harris, "stays on tight like a glove."[86] It must be treated today.

I start my day in gratitude that I am not drunk or dead, that I have another day to see the sunshine. My mother starts her day this same way when she opens the curtains over her sliding glass door at the back of her condominium, which she calls, "My little Hobbit hole."

She lifts her arms to the sun and says a prayer of thanks. At eighty-five-years old, she is truly grateful for every day that she has. She inspires me to be the same. Even though I am sad or frustrated at times, I am still grateful to be alive, unlike the days a few short years ago when I asked God to take my life.

I used to think that giving my life to Jesus was a one shot deal, as if he would sort of carry me from there. I did not consider the continuing nature of my free will. At times that I thought too painful I had asked God to leave me alone for a while. God answered that prayer.

Oh, God tapped on my shoulder to turn me back and was never very far away, but God never imposed on me what I did not freely offer myself to. I offer my will and my life every day as I did in those first few months of sobriety whenever I saw all the numbers on the digital clock line up. It means waiving my free will.

Of all the mistakes I have made in my life, turning away from God's grace and love was the worst, with all the attendant shortcomings and hardships of living my life according to my own schemes and plans - my own will. It did not work, and made life so march harder than it ever had to be. Like the monk from Gethsemane, I hope I have the desire to seek God's will in all that I do. Even though I may know nothing of it at the time, I trust that I will be able to do what God asks of me today.

I am not an abomination or a mistake. One of the leaders of the Walk to Emmaus I attended placed her hands on my shoulders and looked at me directly and said, "Bobbie, you are a beautiful daughter of God."

It was a joyful blessing, one which I extend to every woman I sponsor. Though it is true, some may rightfully ask whether I might have been a beautiful son of God with enough time and continued sobriety. Perhaps, I may have. I cannot know for certain, for I followed another path.

I believe, as do others that I would not have survived but for transition and recovery. Of this much I am certain. It makes no sense and not a thing is gained by second guessing myself. I cannot go back even if I wanted to, and I do not want to. I love the woman I have become, and I know that God does too.

Like most women, I see her physical faults each time I get near a mirror. I have wrinkles from lots of smiles. That's not so regrettable. I have large pores and plenty of sun damage. That is regrettable. I have thinning hair and a too high hair line. When I had my hair transplant, the surgeon, a woman, said,

"I have a high forehead. In fact, it's a five or six head."

Mine is a seven. I have a Cro-Magnon forehead too, with emphasized brow bossing like many men do. It can be surgically shaved in a process called facial feminization. I would love to have that done. I would likely have my hair line lowered and a face lift in the process. Oh, and I might as well get a cute little turned up nose too. Of course, now I am really talking about money, and for what? I am already beautiful.

Though I pine wistfully for what I missed of girlhood, I like the idea of aging gracefully as a woman. I have a sense of place now, here in Montana. I know that I am home. I often think of that scene in the movie, *Legends of the Fall* where One Stab says about Tristan,

"The bear in him was asleep."[87]

I feel that way. I used to fight everyone and everything like an angry grizzly. Now, there is little fight in me and less need for it. The only Grizzlies I am concerned about now are the ones that annually chew on Bobcat butt. It's a Montana thing. I am content and at peace.

As Ann Lamott writes, quoting her pastor,

"Peace is joy at rest, and joy is peace on its feet."[88]

I understand this, and think it an apt description of serenity. I thank God daily for the chance to think so.

I am fond of saying that we *are* changing the world. I believe that it is true, whether we do so actively or passively. Our world is dynamic in space and in time as its very plates shift. Tides and winds move dust and sand. Rain wears down even the highest of peaks. The earth splits and new mountains rise. It has been said that the only thing which remains constant is change itself.

People and culture are like that too. Some, worn down by wear and age, fade, as yet others are born strong and vital with hope and ideas. People can and do change. If we do nothing, we change, even as our world changes around us. I could fight change, to no avail. I could ride it, at someone else's expense, or I could get out in front and help shape it. I can serve change by joining with others to give it a voice, or better yet, a song.

I used to fret over all the stuff of my life – what about this bill, what about this case, what about this person, what about this coworker, what about this job, what about the rent, what about . . . *ad nauseum*. Today, when I begin to think of those things, or about what I have missed or lost, what I want or fear that I will lose, I stop and fall. Unlike when we were in grade school and practiced for Russian attack with the "stop and drop" method, I picture myself falling into life, falling into the universe without fear. A little girl in the world can do something.

It's like those warm and fuzzy trust falls, only now I know that God has my back. I see myself with my arms wide, face to the sun, soaring. I let go and let God. I try to pray, do the work and without expectation, leave the result to God. It used to be that I would churn expectation, like the fire would go out if I did not constantly feed it with fuel. When my expectations were not met, I would be dashed upon the rocks (make that a double, please). Now, I just stack the wood and let God tend the fire. The flame does not dim.

It used to be, when I felt a greater sense of spirituality, it would not last. After a month or two or even a year, it would be gone, fleeting, like springtime in Montana. The fire went out. Yet, today it still burns, sometimes dimmer and sometimes brighter. Today I do not worry that it will go out, for every time I check on it, it has been tended, as surely the night follows the day.

Church and religion are good I think. However, I once said,

"Church is for the spiritually weak."

I regretted it almost as soon as the words passed my lips. But, I think it is true. I said it with a holier-than-thou attitude that I did not intend at all, for I am as spiritually weak or weaker than the next person. What I meant is this. God is always present in space and in time. Therefore, God must be in places other than books and buildings. Books and buildings help, but alone will not keep me spiritually fit. I must do more. I must consciously look for God in those other places. I must try to connect with God wherever I find God. Again, the words of my literary spiritual guru, Sue Monk Kidd, ring true:

> The ultimate authority of my life is not the Bible; it is not confined between the covers of a book. It is not something written by men and frozen in time. It is not from a source outside myself. My ultimate authority is the divine voice in my own soul. Period.[89]

When I hear that voice I am spiritually fit.

Since God is in all places at all times, God has no sense of place or time, or at least that they matter. Thus, I do not find God at all. When I was young, some people wore these little yellow buttons that said, "I found it," as if God were the one that was lost. I simply try to make myself aware of God and try to connect. The more I try, from those first feeble attempts at gratitude and morning meditation to soaring instead of fretting, the more it seems to be so.

In *Siddhartha*, Herman Hesse writes about the river and how it is present all along its course, both at the beginning and the end.

"That the river is everywhere at the same time, at the source and at the mouth . . . everywhere, and that the present only exists for it, not the shadow of the past, Nor the shadow of the future."[90]

Hesse wrote that the river always flowed "and yet it was always there; it was always the same and yet every moment it was new."[91]   God is like that, the alpha and the omega.

When I pray with the group at meetings and we hold hands, I think of God as electricity, sort of a charge firing amongst all of us. Scripture speaks of the Spirit as wind or a flame. I sometimes sit outside in the warmth of spring, close my eyes with my face to the sun and say, "God." Inevitably, the wind will rise.

My mother prays,

"May the wind be always at your back and may you be in heaven a half hour before the devil knows you're dead."

It is a good Irish blessing. But I like a little breeze in my face to remind me that though I fall, I fall into flight with the spirit beneath my wings.

I once said,

"Spirituality is like pornography."

I regretted that one as soon as it was out too, but it did get their attention. It reminded me of my ninth-grade speech class at Kilbourne Junior High in Worthington, Ohio, where I learned about the ho-hum crasher. Now, as "I look back on all the crap I learned in high school,"[92] it appears I learned something after all. A United States Supreme Court Justice (Stewart) once wrote about pornography that, while he could not define it, he knew it when he saw it. *Jacobellis v. State of Ohio,* 378 U.S. 184, 84 S. Ct. 1676 (1964). That is what I meant about fit spirituality. I cannot describe it very well but I often say,

"I know when I am spiritually fit, and you know it when I am not."

I know it because I feel it. I feel its warmth inside. I feel its peace and joy, and when I feel this way, it is hard to hide. Some people say I shine, and if it is so, that is why.

I came to Montana to conquer the world, at least in the sense of bringing about positive change. The line between idealism and delusions of grandeur was fine indeed. Bob Dylan sings in *My Back Pages,*

"I was so much older then, I'm younger than that now."[93]

I must remember that distinction because its truth becomes more apparent as I age. Because it is so, I cannot be sure that I really know much about those things that I formerly espoused with vigor. It is better for me to speak only of my own experience and mindfully keep my thoughts focused on what is in front of me right now.

The world needs youthful idealism, but it also needs worker bees. It is enough for me now to be present in the lives of those around me, not for my sake, but for theirs. I have many living amends to make. Since I am unable to make things right with all the people I have harmed, I must be as unselfish as possible in my relationships today at home, work and in the herds to which I belong. I can lend a hand when asked, listen when needed and be there when I say I will. I can suit up and show up in the lives of the people around me.

"Here I am, Lord."

Now that is a mantra.

I am grateful that in recovery we emphasize progress rather than perfection. None of us can be totally like Francis or Jesus, Gandhi, or Dr. King. That's why we call them God or saint or martyr, or give unto them some such other rarified distinction. There is a God, and I am not it. If Jesus invited me to lunch and told me to invite anyone throughout history, the list would be long now. I see a pattern in the people I am attracted to. They seek peace and justice in service to others. If they change the world, it is simply by example, like Mother Theresa.

There are many women in my life like that now. They are my wise women, although a few others have died. I admire them not just for the calm presence and equilibrium they exhibit, but the manner in which they do it every day. They keep coming back and showing up. If I need them, they are there. And you know what? So am I. I *am* these women.

Now, though I still feel anxious or sad at times, I find myself feeling happy most of the time. I am okay. I have peace, and that with happiness, is like something approaching joy. It is from this place of joy that I respond to the people and things in my life today most of the time. This is the great dividend of transition, transformation really, of body, mind and spirit.

I will buy a grave plot in the cemetery in Silver Star. Not that I am moribund, and even though I do not own the ground upon which I live, I know that Montana is my home. I may yet travel far, but I will always come back here to look up at the blue big sky, to hear the wind in the quakies, to see peaks that scrape the sky. I will watch her wildlife and serve her people. I will breathe deeply of her clear, clean air and know that I will never leave Montana.

ENDNOTES

1   Sue Monk Kidd, *The Dance of the Dissident Daughter, A Woman's Journey from Christian Tradition to the Sacred Feminine*, 1996 Harper Collins, New York, NY 10022.

2   Sue Monk Kidd, *The Dance of the Dissident Daughter, A Woman's Journey from Christian Tradition to the Sacred Feminine*, 1996 Harper Collins, New York, NY 10022.

3   Mary Chapin Carpenter, *The Calling*, 2007, Why Walk Music.

4   Warren Zevon, *Lawyers, Guns, and Money*, 1978 Asylum Records.

5   Sarah McLachlan, *Angel*, 1997, Sony/ATV Songs L.L.C. Tydo Music (BMI).

6   John Denver, *Wild Montana Skies*, 1984, BMG Music.

7   *Brain Gender Identity*, A Presentation by Sidney W. Ecker, M.D., F.A.C.S., Clinical Professor of Urology, Georgetown University Scholl of Medicine, Washington, D.C., 2008.

8   Based on Luke 1:28, 42.

9   Harry Chapin, *Taxi*, 1972, Elektra Records.

10   Emmy Lou Harris, *Deeper Well*, 1995, Hayes Court Music, Irving Music, BMI/Alamo Music Corp.

11   Emmy Lou Harris, *My Baby Needs a Shepard*, 2000, Nonesuch Records, a Warner Music Group Co.

12   Bryan Adams, *(Everything I Do) I Do It For You*, 1991 A&M Records.

13   Billy Joel, *And So It Goes*, 1983, Joelsongs (BMI), 1989, Sony Music Entertainment, Inc.

14   Mary Murphy, *Bootlegging Mothers and Drinking Daughters: Gender and Prohibition in Butte, Montana*, American Quarterly, 46 (June 1994), 174-94, as reprinted in *Montana Legacy*, Fritz, Murphy, Swartout, Jr. (2002) Montana Historical Society Press, Helena, MT 59601.

15   *Id.*

16   James Taylor, *Sweet Baby James*, 1970, Warner Bros. Records.

17   Mary Chapin Carpenter, *The Calling*, 2007, Why Walk Music.

18 *Bunch of Thyme*, Irish Folk Song.

19 Bruce Springsteen, *Jungle Land*, 1975, Columbia Records.

20 Graham Chapman, et al., "The Lumberjack Song," *Monty Python's Flying Circus*, Episode Nine, *The Ant: An Introduction*, 1969, BBC1, performed by Michael Palin.

21 Don Henley, *End Of Innocence*, 1989, Geffen Records.

22 Elton John, *Mona Lisa's and Mad Hatters*, 1972, Uni/MCA.

23 Dan Fogelberg, *Captured Angel*, 1975, produced by Dan Fogelberg on Full Moon/Epic Records.

24 The Goo Goo Dolls, <u>Iris</u>, 1998, Warner Bros. Records, originally released on *The City of Angels* movie soundtrack.

25 Dan Fogelberg, *These Days*, 1975, produced by Dan Fogelberg on Full Moon/Epic Records.

26 Trish Short, *The Chaplet of the Divine Mercy In Song*, (Of St. Faustina) 2002, EADM.

27 Mary Oliver, *The Journey*, from *Dream Work*, 1986, Atlantic Monthly Press, 841 Broadway, New York, NY 10003.

28 Dan Schute, *Here I Am, Lord*, 1981, North American Liturgy Resources/New Dawn Music.

29 Sue Monk Kidd, *The Dance of the Dissident Daughter; A Woman's Journey from Christian Tradition to the Sacred Feminine*, 1996, Harper Collins, New York, NY 10022.

30 The Goo Goo Dolls, *Iris,* 1998, Warner Bros. Records, originally released on *The City of Angels* movie soundtrack.

31 Don Henly, *The Boys of Summer*, 1984, Woody Creek Music (adm. by WB Music Corp.)/Wild Gator Music.

32 Van Morrison, *Tupelo Honey*, 1971, Warner Bros./Polydor.

33 Sue Monk Kidd, *The Dance of the Dissident Daughter; A Woman's Journey from Christian Tradition to the Sacred Feminine*, 1996, Harper Collins, New York, NY 10022.

34 *Id.*

35 The Beatles, *Let It Be*, 1970, Apple Records.

36 Jackson Browne, *Late For the Sky*, 1974, Asylum Records.

37 Jack London, *The Call of the Wild,* Alladdin Paperbacks/Simon & Schuster, 1230 Avenue of the Americas, New York, NY 10020.

38 Emily Dickinson, *Selected Poems*, 1990, Dover Publications, Inc. New York, NY.

39 The Beatles, *Let it Be*, 1970, Apple Records.

40 Dan Fogelberg, <u>Old Tennessee</u>, 1972, Hickory Grove Music.

41 The Beatles, *Let It Be*, 1970, Apple Records.

42 Shankar Vedantam, *The Hidden Brain: How Our Unconscious Mind Elects Presidents, Controls Markets, Wages Wars, and Save Lives*, 2010, Spiegel & Grau of Random House, Inc. New York, NY 10019.

43 Kirby Page, *Living Courageously*, 1936, Farrar & Rinehart, New York, NY (First English translation).

44 Richard B. Roeder, *Crossing the Genderline; Ella Knowles, Montana's First Woman Lawyer*, Montana Magazine of Western History, Summer 1982, vol. 32, Montana Historical Society.

45 *Id.*

46 *Id.*

47 *Id.*

48 *Id.*

49 *Id.*

50 *Id.*

51 *Id.*

52 Mohandas Karamchand Gandhi, 1869-1948, Indian Philosopher and Non-violent Civil Rights Activist, Notes Vol. 13, 1913.

53 Sue Monk Kidd, *The Dance of the Dissident Daughter; A Woman's Journey from Christian Tradition to the Sacred Feminine*, 1996, Harper Collins, New York, NY 10022.

54 Patty Griffin, *Be Careful*, 2002, ATO Records/BMG.

55 Original by the author.

56 The Moody Blues, <u>Knights in white Satin</u>, 1967, Deram Records, UK.

57 *Id.*

58 Wm. Paul Young, *The Shack*, 2007, Windblown Media, 4680 Calle Norte, Newbury Park, CA 91320.

59 Sue Monk Kidd, *The Dance of the Dissident Daughter; A Woman's Journey from Christian Tradition to the Sacred Feminine*, 1996, Harper Collins, New York, NY 10022.

60 Bruce Springsteen, *Human Touch*, 1992, Columbia Records.

61 Bruce Springsteen, *Tougher Than the Rest*, 1987, Columbia Records.

62 The Beatles, *Let It Be*, 1970, Apple Records.

63 Donovan, *Brother Sun and Sister Moon*, 1972 film of the same name; Recorded and released in 2004 by Donovan Discs exclusively on iTunes Music Store.

64 Dan Fogelberg, *There's a Place in the World for a Gambler*, 1974, Hickory Grove Music, produced by Full Moon Productions; Epic, Sony Music Entertainment, Inc.

65 Thomas Merton, *Thoughts In Solitude*, 1958, Farrar, Straus & Cudahy, New York, NY.

66 Sir Walter Scott, *The Lady of the Lake*, 1810.

67 Virginia City Preservation Alliance website, 2009.

68 Three Dog Night, *Pieces of April*, 1972, Dunhill.

69 Louisa May Alcott, *Work*, 1994, Penguin Books, 375 Hudson Street, New York, NY 10014.

70 *Jeremiah Johnson*, 1972, Warner Bros., directed by Sydney Pollack and produced by Joe Wizan.

71 St. Louis Jesuits, *Be Not Afraid,* 1975, North American Liturgy Resources.

72 Arthur Golden, *Memoirs of a Geisha*, 1997, Vintage Books, a Division of Random House, Inc. New York, NY.

73 Mathew 6:26, The Holy Bible, New International Version, 1973, International Bible Society, East Brunswick, NJ 08816.

74 James Taylor, *Down In The Hole*, 1991, Columbia Records.

75 St. Therese of Lisieux, 1873-1897, known as "The Little Flower of Jesus."

76 David Wilcox, *The Hard Part*, 2006, A&M Records.

77 Dan Fogelberg, *There's a Place in the World for a Gambler*, 1974, Hickory Grove Music ASCAP, produced by Full Moon Productions.

78 Desmond and Mpho Tutu, *Made For Goodness, And Why This Makes All the Difference*, 2010, Harper Collins Publishers, 10 East 53rd Street, New York, NY 10022.

79 Harold S. Kushner, *Living a Life That Matters*, 2001, Anchor Books, a Division of Random House, Inc. New York, NY.

80 Original by the author.

81 Andy Pratt, *Avenging Annie*, 1973, Columbia Records.

82 Dr. Martin Luther King, Jr., US civil rights leader and Clergyman (1929 – 1968), Letter from Birmingham Jail, April 16, 1963.

83 Billy Joel, *Angry Young Man*, 1976, Family Productions/Columbia Records.

84   Leslie Feinberg, *Transgender Warriors*, 1996 Beacon Press, 25 Beacon Street, Boston, MA 02108-2892.

85   John Michael Talbot, *The Mystery*, 1980, Sparrow Records, Inc.

86   Emmy Lou Harris, *Deeper Well, supra at* 9.

87   *Legends of the Fall*, 1994, TriStar Pictures.

88   Ann Lamott, *Plan : Further Thoughts on Faith*, 2006, Riverhead Trade, New York, NY.

89   Sue Monk Kidd, *The Dance of the Dissident Daughter; A Woman's Journey from Christian Tradition to the Sacred Feminine*, 1996, Harper Collins, New York, NY 10022.

90   Hermann Hesse, *Siddhartha*, 1951, New directions Publishing Corporation and Bantam Books, 80 Eight Avenue, New York, NY 10011.

91   *Id.*

92   Paul Simon, *Kodachrome*, 1972, Columbia Records.

93   Bob Dylan, *My Back Pages*, 1964, Columbia Records.